Y0-BDI-793

ARCO

Air Conditioning
and Refrigeration
Toolbox Manual

David Tenenbaum

MACMILLAN • USA

This publication is designed to provide accurate and authoritative information in regard to the subject matter covered. It is sold with the understanding that the publisher and author do not render engineering or architectural advice, and no warranties, expressed or implied, are made as to the material contained herein. If expert assistance is required, contact a competent professional person.

Macmillan General Reference
A Prentice Hall Macmillan Company
15 Columbus Circle
New York, NY 10023

An Arco Book

MACMILLAN is a registered trademark of Macmillan, Inc.
ARCO is a registered trademark of Prentice-Hall, Inc.

Library of Congress Cataloging-in-Publication Data

Tenenbaum, David.
    Air conditioning and refrigeration toolbox manual /
David Tenenbaum.
      p.   cm.
    Includes index.
    ISBN 0-13-770264-7
    1. Air conditioning. 2. Refrigeration and refrigerating
machinery.   I. Title.
TH7687.7.T46   1990   90-913
621.56—dc20   CIP

Manufactured in the United States of America

15   14   13   12   11   10   9   8   7   6

What This Book Covers

This manual describes the installation, troubleshooting, and repair of hermetic, semi-hermetic, and open refrigeration systems using the vapor-compression or absorption cycle. The manual is intended to help apprentice and journeyman cooling system technicians do their work safely and more efficiently.

The book covers comfort cooling systems for residences and larger buildings, and refrigeration systems used in commercial and small industrial settings. Installation and repair of domestic refrigerators, freezers, and window air conditioners is not described, although the operating principles and many repair techniques described here do apply to these smaller systems.

A cooling system, no matter what its size or configuration, must comply with certain basic operating conditions:

1. The system must be dry and uncontaminated.

2. The compressor (in a vapor-compression system) or generator (in an absorption system) must remain within safe and efficient temperature, pressure, and electrical conditions.

3. All moving parts that require lubrication must receive enough oil under the proper pressure.

4. No liquid refrigerant can be allowed to reach the compressor through the suction line.

5. The evaporator must receive an adequate supply of liquid refrigerant.

6. Excessive pressure drop must be prevented in the piping.

7. The devices for disposing of unwanted heat must be kept in good working order.

This manual will help you install, diagnose, and service cooling systems in accordance with these basic system requirements. The logical arrangement and index will help you quickly find the information you need. Line drawings, charts, and tables are included for various systems, components, devices, and procedures.

Part A describes tools, materials, and equipment used in the trade, with a focus on choosing the best device for the task and using it safely. Section 1 describes hand tools, Section 2, meters and gauges, Section 3, power tools, Section 4, safety equipment, Section 5, materials and oil, and Section 6, the common refrigerants.

Part B explains the scientific principles of heat, electricity, and magnetism that every cooling system technician must understand. The vapor-compression and absorption cooling cycles are described in detail, using both mechanical and physical principles.

Part C describes the various types of compressors—centrifugal, helical, reciprocating, and rotary—that a service person will encounter.

Part D explains the principles of controls, and describes the operation and servicing of capacity, operating, refrigerant, and safety controls.

Part E describes other essential components—the drives, condensers, evaporators, fans, pumps, and filters—found in most systems.

Part F details the various types of motors that power compressors, fans, and pumps in cooling systems. Suggestions are given for analyzing various forms of motor trouble.

Part G covers the tubing and fittings, and how to cut, braze, solder, and handle these materials.

Part H describes various complete comfort cooling, refrigeration, and defrost systems. Suggestions are given for choosing and installing a system.

Part I contains background material on one of the biggest controversies confronting the refrigeration industry—the discovery that the chlorofluorocarbon refrigerants damage the stratospheric ozone layer. Part I describes how to select and use recovery and recycling apparatus.

Part J has troubleshooting information on compressors, condensers, metering devices, oil control systems, absorption systems, motors, and pumps.

Part K covers the basic procedures of comfort cooling and refrigeration: using the gauge manifold, charging and checking the charge, removing and adding oil, servicing drive systems, and periodic maintenance.

Part L, the appendices, covers mathematics, fundamental formulas, measurement conversions, and rules of thumb. Also included are a list of abbreviations, glossary, and addresses of unions, manufacturers, and trade associations.

I am grateful to Jim McDonald, a veteran steamfitter and instructor of apprentices who contributed immensely to the scope and quality of this book. Simply, this book would not have been written without Jim. John Christenson was a reliable and knowledgeable reviewer of the electrical sections, and Dave Klousie helped clear up some murky spots.

YOUR TOOLS, EQUIPMENT, AND MATERIALS

A good assortment of hand tools, meters, and gauges is needed to install and repair comfort cooling and refrigeration systems. The selection and proper use of these tools is described in Sections 1 through 4. Section 5 describes materials and oils, and Section 6 covers the common refrigerants.

1

Hand Tools

Some of the hand tools used to install and to repair cooling systems can be found in virtually any complete tool kit, while others are unique to the trade. The following items comprise a basic tool kit:

BENDERS

Benders are used to bend tubing without flattening or kinking it, which would reduce its flow capacity or cause leaks. All bends must be done accurately enough that the finished assembly is not under strain. The best tool for a particular bending operation depends on the size of tubing and whether fittings are installed before or after bending.

LEVER

Lever benders can be slipped over the tube and used to produce fast, accurate bends. The bending is accomplished by a lever that is forced against a fixed pin. Some units use gears to create the bending action.

Some lever benders have replaceable parts to accommodate various tubing sizes. Otherwise, a separate tool is needed for each tubing size. The bender may have a scale indicating the amount of stretching that will occur during a bend. A second scale may measure the bend in degrees.

SPRING

Spring benders are coil springs designed to be slipped over (external spring) or into (internal spring) the tubing. Each variety has advantages. An internal bender must be used on a flared tube because the flare would prevent removal of an external spring. An external spring must be used to bend at the middle of a tube because an internal spring could not be extracted from this location. For an especially tight bend, both internal and external bending springs can be used.

A spring bender fits a single size of tubing, so a set of benders is required. Keep internal springs clean, as they can pick up dirt and deposit it in the tubing.

BRAZING AND SOLDERING EQUIPMENT

Brazing and soldering are related processes that must become second nature to a technician. Brazing is performed with a torch burning oxygen and acetylene, while soldering requires an air-acetylene or propane torch.

Use a torch tip big enough to heat the joint quickly, but not so large that it will overheat the base materials. An inadequate tip will take too long to heat the joint and may cause heat damage to adjacent components. The mixing action of a "turbo" torch results in a flame that is hotter than that orifice size would otherwise produce.

The following suggested tip sizes are a good starting point, although you must convert the sizing to the torch manufacturer's scheme:

SUGGESTED OXYACETYLENE TIP SIZES FOR BRAZING

Tubing size	Drill size
¾ inch and smaller (1.90 cm)	54
1 inch to 1½ inch (2.54 to 3.8 cm)	51
2 to 2½ inches (5 to 6.4 cm)	48–44
3 inches (7.6 cm)	44–42
4 inches (10 cm) and up	42 or multiple torch

Torch tanks are usually furnished by the contractor. Green or yellow indicates oxygen; black is usually acetylene.

SAFETY: Because acetylene burns fiercely, oxygen accelerates the combustion of other materials, and a mixture of the gases is explosive, many safety measures must be used with oxyacetylene torches. Tanks must be shipped with the caps screwed over the valve and secured upright. Check tanks, hoses, and fittings for leaks. Do not damage the gauges. Move tanks by rolling on bottom edges. Protect tanks from damage, heat, improper filling, and abuse. Do not oil the regulator.

Always wear the eye protection and gloves while using a torch. Never use flux or brazing material containing cadmium or heat tubing that is under pressure (see Part L, *Safety, Torch*, p. 410 for safety information).

CAPILLARY TUBE CLEANER

A cap tube cleaner creates pressure on the tube to force out wax and debris. The tube is disconnected at both ends and the front end of the cleaner is connected to the tube. By turning the handle, you can create as much as 20,000 psi in the tube. When done, purge the tube with R-11 or the system refrigerant.

FLARING BLOCK

A flaring block is used to produce an accurate flare. First the tube is inserted into the proper opening in the block, then the block is tightened and a jig is placed over the block. The jig holds a die that is forced down into the opening of the tube to create the flare. A special die must be used to create a double flare.

HERMETIC ADJUSTMENT KIT

Many small hermetic systems are not designed with service in mind, primarily because they have no service valves. A hermetic adjustment kit contains a set of valves designed to overcome this difficulty. The kit allows you to install a gauge manifold for system diagnosis or charging with oil or refrigerant. The kit includes adaptors, a line piercing tool, wrenches, a gauge, and other tools.

HOSES

Hoses are used to connect the gauge manifold, service tanks, recycling apparatus, and other equipment to a system for many diagnostic and repair operations. Hoses are made of a neoprene interior and a braided cotton exterior; brass fittings have a neoprene gasket to meet the flare of the connecting valve. Hoses are made in lengths from 3 to 6 feet. The most common use for hoses is to connect the gauge manifold. Gauge manifold hoses have ¼-inch OD flare fittings. Other hoses, generally with ⅜-inch OD flare fittings, may be used separately to quickly drain crankcase oil, hook up a vacuum pump, or pressure test a system with nitrogen.

LINE PIERCING TOOL

This tool installs a tee in a line to allow charging or purging refrigerant in small hermetic systems without service valves. The tool is clamped to the line and the gauge manifold or refrigerant tank is then connected to its valve. Then the valve stem is forced into the line until it pierces through the wall. When the repair is completed, the valve is left in position to plug the line and allow service to be done more easily in the future.

PACKING KEY

A packing key is designed to tighten and loosen internal packing nuts on certain valves. Unlike an external packing nut, which can be turned with a conventional wrench, the slot on an internal nut is found on both sides of the valve stem. A packing key, which is a cylinder-shaped piece of steel with two studs on the bottom, can tighten and loosen this kind of packing nut.

PINCH-OFF TOOL

This tool is used to temporarily close off a process tube after work on a system is completed. Place the tool on the tube, screw it down to pinch the tube, and solder or braze the end of the tube; then remove the pinch-off tool.

PUMP, OIL

Hand or electric oil pumps may be used to force oil into the crankcase while the system is pressurized. This is useful when you want to add oil without tearing apart a system. One hose connects the pump to an oil container, and the second connects the pump to the crankcase oil port.

Never try to pump against a closed valve in the pump discharge, especially with an electrical pump. Be sure to empty one type of oil from the pump before adding a different type. Keep the pump clean, with all openings plugged, when it is not in use. Never allow air to enter the system.

PUMP, VACUUM

Vacuum pumps are used to evacuate air, moisture, and other contaminants from a system before charging or recharging. Once established, the vacuum must be maintained long enough to check the system for leaks before refrigerant is added.

A single-stage pump, capable of pulling a vacuum of 50 microns, is used for a simple evacuation or a triple-evacuation, but a two-stage, or high-vacuum, pump, is needed when the high, or deep, vacuum charging method is used. A very good two-stage pump should be capable of pulling down to 1 micron for use when an extremely low vacuum is required.

Reciprocating vacuum pumps are similar to a reciprocating compressor in design. High-vacuum pumps have one or two rotors linked in series. Each rotor revolves around a shaft and progressively enlarges and shrinks the pumping chamber. Gas is drawn into the chamber by the pressure differential between the chamber and the piping system. As the rotor revolves, the vane forces the gas around and out the exhaust port. The vanes slide inside slots in the rotor as it spins.

As gas is removed from the cooling system pipes and equipment, system pressure drops and the remaining gas expands. Thus the pump draws in progressively less gas for each revolution, so the final stages of an evacuation take longer than the first stages.

Copper tubing or special metal hose should be used for most evacuation work. Charging hoses (used with gauge manifolds) may collapse under the vacuum or release gas under prolonged vacuum. When drawing a deep vacuum, a large line will greatly shorten the pumping time. Changing from a ¼-inch (.635 cm) ID line to a ½-inch (1.27 cm) ID line may speed the pumping up more than switching from a 1 cubic foot per minute (28 liters/minute) pump to a 5 cfm (142 liters/minute) pump.

The oil in a vacuum pump may become contaminated by water and solvents in the system, creating a sludge that will increase pump wear and reduce efficiency. Dirty or watery oil looks white and foamy. Change oil before each pump-down when using either a single-stage or a two-stage pump.

Make sure to release the vacuum before storing the pump; otherwise, the pump cylinder might become filled with oil and resistant to turning.

PLIERS

Pliers are used for general tightening and holding purposes and are especially handy for holding hot pipe and fittings. Arc-joint pliers have opposing jaws which may be adjusted to different sizes. Insulated handles are an excellent safety measure when working near electricity. Do not use plier handles as pry bars.

TUBING CUTTERS

Tubing may be cut with either a tubing cutter (recommended for smaller and softer tubing) or a hacksaw. Some cutters have a device allowing you to slide the cutting wheel to the tube without having to turn the feed screw. During the cut, do not advance the cutting wheel too rapidly, as this will squash the tube instead of cutting it. If cutter parts are worn, the cutter wheel may travel along the tube instead of cutting squarely. A three-wheel cutter is handy for cutting in tight places, as it only requires 120° of rotation. Most tubing cutters have a reamer to clean out burrs when done.

When cutting tubing with a hacksaw, it is best to use a cutting fixture to ensure a straight, square cut. A hacksaw with a wave-set blade with 32 teeth per inch (13 teeth per cm) is recommended.

Take care to prevent chips or filings from entering the tubing. Hold the tube upside down and tap it to remove the chips. If the tube is not movable, insert a coat hanger with a rag plug on the end in the tube before you saw it. When the cut is completed, slowly withdraw the rag to pull out the chips.

VALVE KEY

Because some system valves have no handles, technicians carry a set of valve keys in the toolbox. Also called tee wrenches, valve keys have a square opening on the bottom to accept the valve stem. Common stems sizes are $3/16$, $7/32$, $1/4$, and $\frac{5}{16}$ inch, respectively.

WRENCHES

PIPE

Pipe wrenches are used in a multitude of ways in assembling and disassembling threaded pipe and fittings. The 12-inch to 24-inch wrenches are the most common sizes. A pair of each size is handy. A 36-inch wrench is useful for pipes up to 4 inches in diameter. Aluminum wrenches are helpful due to their light weight.

Keep the jaws sharp and free of rust. Replace jaws when needed. Oil the adjustment threads occasionally. Never put a piece of pipe on the handle for extra leverage.

SOCKET

Socket wrenches are used to tighten plugs and nuts and bolts. Socket sizes from ¼ to 2 inches are ideal. Both ⅜- and ½-inch drive systems should be found in any basic tool kit; a ¾″-inch drive is quite useful for working on large systems. Both 8- and 12-point sockets must be carried to deal with square and hexagonal nuts. Adaptors to drive one size socket from another size wrench are a useful addition. An extension and universal joint will allow you to use a socket set in tight quarters. Never put a piece of pipe on the handle for extra leverage. Make sure the socket does not slip off the bolt when pulling on the wrench. Pulling the wrench is generally safer than pushing.

TORQUE

Torque wrenches are used to ensure that bolts are sufficiently and correctly tightened. Undertightening can result in leakage, while overtightening can cause warping or strip threads. Most torque wrenches are designed for use with socket wrenches. Exert a steady force on the handle to get an accurate reading.

2

Meters and Gauges

CHARGING CYLINDER OR BOARD

A charging cylinder (sometimes called a charging board) is a device for charging refrigerant to a small system. Deluxe charging cylinders have a gauge manifold mounted alongside the cylinder to eliminate the need to hook up a separate set of gauges. Newer charging boards have a digital gauge to measure the flow of refrigerant. Most charging cylinders allow you to install a vapor charge through a top valve, or a liquid charge through the bottom valve.

Some cylinders have a heating element to vaporize the refrigerant and speed up the transfer; other cylinders rely on pressure in the storage cylinder to move the refrigerant. Before using a heating element, make sure the pressure relief valve is operating properly (see Part K, p. 338).

ELECTRIC METERS

Cooling system technicians use a variety of meters to measure current, electromotive force, and resistance in power and control circuits. Although many electric meters measure more than one quantity—frequently resistance and voltage—meters are described individually here in the interests of simplicity.

On many meters, the range of the measurement must be set manually before taking the measurement. If you are unsure about the correct range to use, start with a high range and gradually reduce it until you find the correct one. The range need not be set on auto-ranging meters or most digital meters. However, a manual setting might result in a faster reading than using automatic ranging.

Digital meters have several other advantages over the older, analog types: they are smaller, easier to read, and have no moving parts. Treat all meters with respect: connect them properly, do not drop them, and check their adjustment occasionally. Make sure meter batteries are adequately charged.

AMMETER

An ammeter measures the current flow past a certain point. An ammeter will measure either direct or alternating currents, but generally not both. A conventional ammeter must connected in series with the circuit, so the circuit must be disconnected when hooking up the meter. The more convenient clamp-on type (for AC only) is slipped around the conductor being measured. A current is induced in the meter by the current in the conductor. If the current is too weak to get a good reading, wrap the wire once around one tong and divide the reading by 2.

A device called a current transformer may be used in conjunction with an ammeter to measure large currents. The wire in the circuit to be measured is disconnected, fed through the hole in the current transformer, and reconnected. Then the leads from the current transformer are connected to the ammeter. The current transformer reduces the amperage enough to allow the meter to safely measure it.

CIRCUIT TESTER

Two simple tools can be used to test circuits. A light bulb connected in series with two probes is used to test for the presence of electricity. A continuity tester contains a source of electric power and is used to test if a circuit is complete or not. The continuity tester can use line or battery power. Make sure the circuit being tested is not energized (see Fig. A1).

VOLTMETER

A voltmeter measures the electromotive force (emf) between two points in volts while the circuit is energized. Connect a voltmeter in parallel with the load being checked. A voltmeter can be used for many purposes: to measure input voltage, to determine whether a switch is open or closed, or to find the voltage drop (and hence resistance) across a relay, motor, or other component. Do not use

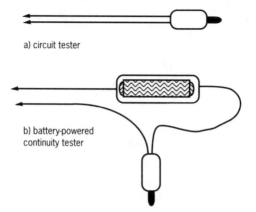

a) circuit tester

b) battery-powered
continuity tester

Fig. A1 Circuit testers

a 120 V voltmeter on a 240 V circuit, as this might burn out the meter (see Fig. A2).

OHMMETER

An ohmmeter measures the resistance between two points in ohms. The meter applies a small current from its battery and measures the drop in voltage caused by the resistance in the circuit. The resistance depends on the conductor composition, and its cross-section, length, and temperature.

Make sure to shut off power before using an ohmmeter. Do not connect an ohmmeter to a circuit which operates at a lower voltage lower than what the ohmmeter creates, or you can damage low-voltage equipment, such as sensors.

A megohmmeter is a kind of ohmmeter used to test the insulation between motor windings and frame. This device applies from 250 to 10,000 volts direct current to the circuit being tested—much higher voltage than standard a ohmmeter. Use a megohmmeter carefully to prevent injury to yourself or damage to equipment.

A megohmmeter can detect motor insulation problems before they grow serious enough to burn out a motor. Motor manufacturers

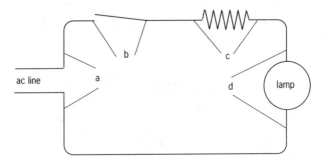

a = line voltage if power is on
b = line voltage if switch is closed, 0 if switch is open
c = voltage drop across resistor
d = voltage drop across lamp. If lamp is shorted d = 0;
    if lamp is broken d = line voltage

Fig. A2 Using a voltmeter

may set standards for the resistance of winding insulation—in general it should test at several million ohms.

Winding tests should be done after a motor has been running for about an hour, as changing temperature may alter the effectiveness of insulation. If you spot a motor with marginal resistance, test it repeatedly with a megohmmeter to see if the trend in resistance is up, down, or stable (see Fig. A3).

VOM OR MULTITESTER

A VOM (volt–ohm–meter) can read both voltage and resistance. A VOM is now incorporated in some clamp-on ammeters, making a very useful tool. The more elaborate models have several scales for greater accuracy. If the meter also includes an ammeter, it is commonly called a multitester.

WATTMETER

A wattmeter measures the power consumed by an electrical device in watts. Connect the meter in series and parallel with the device.

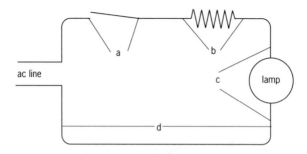

power must be off before testing

a = 0 if switch is closed and in good condition
b = resistance across heating coil
c = resistance across lamp
d = continuity of conductor. Should be 0 if all switches in
line are closed, conductor is in good condition, and no loads
are present.

Fig. A3 Using an ohmmeter

The meter reads the true power consumption by measuring voltage
and current and correcting automatically for the power factor. You
can also find the power draw by measuring with a power factor
meter or calculating the power factor. A clamp-on model is available.

GAUGE MANIFOLD

The gauge manifold is probably the most important single instrument in the air conditioning and refrigeration service business, as
it is used for diagnosing system trouble as well as evacuating,
charging, and adding oil. The manifold has fittings for three hoses,
taps for two gauges, and a valve at each end. One gauge measures
pressure, reading from 0 to 500 lbs. The other, compound gauge
reads pressure from 0 to 250 lbs. and vacuum from 0 to 30 inches.
The pressure gauge is usually on the right tap of the manifold, but
not always (see Fig. A4).

The valve at each end controls whether the end hose is connected
to the center of the manifold or not. Both gauges are always
connected to their respective sides of the system, so high and low
side pressures can be read as long as the manifold is connected.

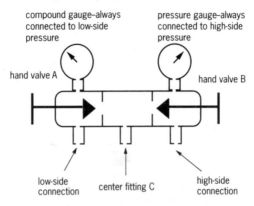

Use of the gauge manifold:
To read pressures only: close A and B
To connect low side to C, open A and close B.
To connect high side to C, close A and open B.
To connect high side to low side, open A and B and cap C.
To connect high side, low side, and C, open A and B.

Fig. A4 Gauge manifold details

The hoses should be colored differently to avoid confusion, although sometimes they are all the same color. Use your own scheme or the following convention in hooking up hoses:

Red: connects the high side to the high-pressure gauge.

Blue: connects the low side to the compound gauge.

White: connects a charging cylinder, oil can, or other service device to the center outlet of the gauge manifold.

HERMETIC ANALYZER

A hermetic analyzer is a electric device used to analyze refrigeration systems and cure some electrical troubles that are found. The device generally contains an ohmmeter, voltmeter, and ammeter, and can be used to check for shorts, grounds, open windings, and continuity. Some hermetic analyzers can also test capacitors and relays. An analyzer has a bank of starting capacitors that can be used to reverse motor rotation and rock a stuck compressor free.

LEAK DETECTORS

Four methods can be used to check that a new or established system is not leaking: the bubble solution, the electronic detector, the halide torch, and refrigerant dye.

BUBBLE SOLUTION

Bubble solution is a primitive method of detecting leaks that should only be used when a better method is not available or cannot be used. A solution of soap and water or a special solution (with longer-lasting bubbles) may be used. In either case, the solution is brushed over the suspect area. Unfortunately, large leaks will blow right through the solution, slow leaks may be difficult to detect, and you may need to use an inspection mirror for hard-to-reach fittings.

There is one situation—testing for leaks near urethane foam—in which the bubble-solution is preferable to the electronic detector or halide torch. Because refrigerants are commonly used to expand foam during manufacture, a halide torch, or an electronic leak detector will read positive when used near foam.

ELECTRONIC

Electronic detectors are the most sensitive type of detector, with some manufacturers claiming their devices will detect leaks as small as $\frac{1}{2}$ oz (14 gram) per year. Most electronic detectors use the dielectric principle, which compares the electrical conduction of surrounding air to the conduction of air near the suspected leak. Both battery-operated and AC-powered electronic detectors are available. The devices generally emit beeps—as the amount of refrigerant in the test sample increases in strength, the beeping speeds up.

Some electronic leak detectors must be adjusted to ambient air before use, while others do this automatically. After adjusting the meter (if necessary) the probe is passed over the suspected area. Molecules of air (and halocarbon refrigerant if present) are drawn into the probe and analyzed. Always place the inlet tube below the suspected leak, because refrigerant is heavier than air. The tip must be moved slowly across the surface—about one inch per second is a good rate. Air movement in the area should be minimized, so be sure fans are shut off. Observe operating temperature restrictions on the device. In atmospheres contaminated with large quantities of refrigerant, the detector may be overwhelmed and will not be very accurate.

HALIDE TORCH

The halide torch works because a green color is produced when refrigerant contacts hot copper. The torch has a hose that is moved in the area of the suspected leak. Air (and refrigerant if present) are drawn through the hose toward a piece of copper which is heated by the torch. A green color indicates the leak. A faint green indicates a small leak, while a green-to-purple indicates a large one.

Keeping a high pressure in the system (about 75 psi or 620 kPa) will simplify use of a halide torch. However, the torch is rather slow and insensitive compared to the electronic detector, and it may be hard to read in bright light. If you have trouble reading the torch in bright light, make a shield from an old tin can and paint the inside black. Cut a viewing slit on the side and you should be able to use a halide torch in the brightest light. Other contaminants may cause a change in flame color. And the torch cannot be used near urethane foam (which likely contains halocarbons) or in areas with flammable vapors or other fire hazards.

REFRIGERANT DYE

Dye added to refrigerant can detect leaks, however, it is best to replace the entire charge with dyed refrigerant, and this raises the prospect of dumping excess halocarbon to the atmosphere. The dye's speed of action depends on how fast oil circulates in the system; you might need to wait as long as 24 hours before getting an indication of a leak. This technique is preferred when the leak detector cannot isolate the leak. However, some compressor manufacturers will not honor a warranty if dye is used.

MANOMETER

A manometer measures the pressure of a fluid. Different manometers must be used to measure air pressure in a duct or vacuum pressure in a system vacuum line. Flexible tubes are a handy feature allowing easy storage of the tool.

A water manometer is used to measure pressure in an air duct, for example to measure static pressure or pressure drop across a filter. Two types of water manometer are available: 1) The U-tube style has a U-shaped tube. One of the tops is connected by a tube to the duct being measured (see Fig. A5). The scale is graduated in fractions of an inch or millimeters. 2) The measuring tube of an

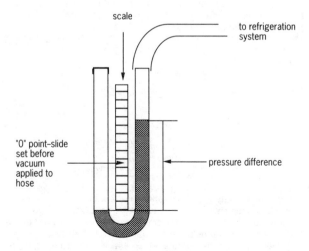

Fig. A5 U-tube manometer

inclined tube manometer slopes upward, allowing accurate pressure measurements in hundredths of an inch.

To measure pressure drop across an air filter, connect a probe to one tube of the manometer, place it in the duct, and open the other end of the manometer to the atmosphere. Then switch the probe to the other side of the filter and read again. Subtract the higher measurement from the lower one to find pressure drop. If the probe tube is long, allow a few minutes for pressure to stabilize before taking the reading.

A dial-type manometer can also be used to measure pressure differential. One of its two probes is inserted in each side of the filter and the differential is read directly from the dial.

A mercury manometer is used to measure system vacuum (this can also be done with an electronic vacuum gauge). The mercury manometer, like the U-tube water manometer, consists of a U-shaped tube equipped with a hose at one end. Between the legs of the manometer is an adjustable scale calibrated in millimeters or centimeters of mercury.

To use a mercury manometer, connect the hose to the system being evacuated. Start the vacuum pump and watch the level of the mercury. When the vacuum stabilizes, slide the zero indicator on the adjustable scale opposite the level of the mercury in one leg of the U-tube, then read the pressure difference from the scale opposite the other leg.

Hints for proper use of manometers:

- *Hold the manometer vertical while in use.*
- *Don't spill the mercury or the water.*
- *Make sure caps are tight during storage.*

SIGHT GLASS, ELECTRONIC

An electronic sight glass uses sonar to detect bubbles in the liquid line refrigerant. The device can be used as a clamp-on sight glass for charging or analyzing a system which has no sight glass or has one in a poor location. The electronic sight glass emits an audible signal when it detects no bubbles, so you need not return to the sight glass while charging or diagnosing the system.

TEMPERATURE-MEASURING DEVICES

Various types of devices are used in the trade to measure the temperature of fluids in the system or the air, product, or water in the cooled space. Thermometers, thermistors, and thermocouples all have their place in the industry. Never allow a measuring device to be exposed to temperatures beyond its measuring range, as this could ruin it.

THERMOMETER

Clip-on and dial-stem thermometers are both popular in cooling system work. Dial-stem thermometers may have a remote-reading bulb. A thermometer used to measure superheat should read rapidly and be capable of making good contact with the suction line or evaporator.

A **recording thermometer** registers temperatures over a 24-hour period. It is used to assess system performance.

A **wet-bulb thermometer** is used to determine the degree of evaporative cooling taking place. In combination with a normal, or "dry-bulb" thermometer, the device can measure relative humidity (see below). The bulb of the thermometer, like a person, is cooled by evaporation of water, so the dryer the environment, the colder the thermometer registers. This allows the thermometer to mimic what a person would feel in the environment.

To use a wet-bulb thermometer, fill the reservoir with water and leave the thermometer for a few minutes in the area to be measured, preferably where it is exposed to rapid air flow. Keep the thermometer away from radiant heat, and take the reading before the bulb dries out.

A **sling psychrometer** combines dry bulb and wet bulb thermometers in a device that can be whirled about on a sling. The movement movement creates enough air flow to ensure an accurate reading on the wet bulb. For best accuracy, use a clean white wick and distilled water on the wet bulb. For locations where the sling would be awkward, an **aspiring thermometer** can be used. This device has a fan to blow air across the wet bulb.

To find relative humidity from a relative humidity table with a sling psychrometer or aspiring thermometer, see Part B: *Measuring Humidity*, p. 80.

THERMISTOR

A thermistor is a semiconductor whose resistance changes in response to changing temperature. Thermistors are used to signal operating and safety controls because they respond quickly to temperature. A second advantage is their ability to send an electric signal that can be interpreted by the device making the operating change in the system.

Thermistors are used to measure temperature in motor windings, conditioned space, and crankcases. Some thermistors change resistance gradually over the entire working range, which is useful in a sensor. Others change resistance rapidly at a specific temperature range, making them useful as thermally operated switches.

THERMOCOUPLE

A thermocouple measures temperature by reading the voltage created when a bimetallic strip is heated. The device can be used as a thermometer or to signal an operating or safety control.

VACUUM GAUGE—ELECTRONIC

This instrument is used to accurately measure high vacuum, for example, when evacuating a system at room temperature before charging. The sensing element is actually a thermocouple that measures the rate of heat transfer. As air is removed from the system, the rate of heat transfer correspondingly decreases, indicating an increasing vacuum.

The gauge is connected to the suction service valve with lines that are as large in diameter and as short in length as possible.

After the vacuum pump is shut off, system pressure will rise for a certain time while the moisture inside evaporates. If the system is tight, the vacuum will stabilize after all moisture is evaporated. If the pressure continues rising, you must repair the leak causing this increase in pressure before charging. Follow the manufacturer's directions for using an electronic vacuum gauge.

3

Power Tools and Equipment

Cooling system technicians use a variety of power tools to speed up the installation and repair of air conditioning and refrigeration systems.

DRILL

Drills are used for many purposes in installation and repair work. Twist drills are measured in fractions of an inch, millimeters, numbers, or letters. Number and letter drills are spaced more closely than fractional drills and are used for drilling when exact sizes are needed, such as before tapping.

Number drills sizes:
No. 1   0.0135 inch . . . No. 80   0.228 inch

Letter drill sizes:
"A"   0.234 inch . . . "Z"   0.413 inch

Drills must be sharp and operated at the correct speed. In general, smaller drills should run faster than large ones. Drills must be carefully chosen for tapping applications. (Consult Table A2.)

SAFETY: Use goggles while drilling. Sharp drills run more smoothly and coolly than dull ones, and are less likely to break. Make sure the object being drilled is secured and apply steady force. Ground the electric drill and do not operate it if the grounding plug has been removed.

TABLE A1
TAPPING DRILL SIZES

Tap	Tap Drill	Tap	Tap Drill
4-36	No. 43	14-20	No. 9
	No. 44		No. 10
	No. 45		No. 11
4-40	3/32	14-24	No. 6
	No. 43		No. 7
	No. 44		No. 8
4-48	No. 41	1/4-20	No. 5
	No. 42		No. 6
5-40	No. 37		13/64
	No. 38		No. 7
	No. 39		No. 8
5-44	No. 36	1/4-28	7/32
	No. 37		No. 3
	No. 38	5/16-18	17/64
6-32	No. 33		G
	No. 34		F
	7/64	5/64-24	J
	No. 36		I
6-40	No. 32	3/8-16	O
	No. 33		5/16
8-32	No. 29	3/8-24	R
8-36	No. 28		Q
	No. 29		3/8
10-24	No. 24	7/16-14	U
	No. 25		
	No. 26	7/16-20	25/64
10-32	No. 19		W
	No. 20	1/2-13	27/64
	No. 21	1/2-20	29/64
	No. 22	9/16-12	31/64
12-24	No. 15	9/16-18	33/64
	No. 16	5/8-11	17/32
	No. 17	5/8-18	37/64
12-28	3/16	3/4-10	21/32
	No. 13	3/4-16	11/16
	No. 14	↗ ↖	
	No. 15	A B	

A—OUTSIDE DIAMETER. B—NUMBER OF THREADS PER INCH.

TABLE A2
NUMBER AND LETTER DRILL SIZES

Drill No.	Drill Size Inches	Drill No.	Drill Size Inches	Drill No.	Drill Size Inches	Drill No.	Drill Size Inches
					Number Drills		
1	0.2280	21	0.1590	41	0.0960	61	0.0390
2	.2210	22	.1570	42	.0935	62	.0380
3	.2130	23	.1540	43	.0890	63	.0370
4	.2090	24	.1520	44	.0860	64	.0360
5	.2055	25	.1495	45	0820	65	.0350
6	.2040	26	.1470	46	.0810	66	.0330
7	.2010	27	.1440	47	.0785	67	.0320
8	.1990	28	.1405	48	.0760	68	.0310
9	.1960	29	.1360	49	.0730	69	.0293
10	.1935	30	.1285	50	.0700	70	.0280
11	.1910	31	.1200	51	.0670	71	.0260
12	.1890	32	.1160	52	.0635	72	.0250
13	.1850	33	.1130	53	.0595	73	.0240
14	.1820	34	.1110	54	.0550	74	.0225
15	.1800	35	.1100	55	.0520	75	.0210
16	.1770	36	.1065	56	.0465	76	.0200
17	.1730	37	.1040	57	.0430	77	.0180
18	.1695	38	.1015	58	.0420	78	.0160
19	.1660	39	.0995	59	.0410	79	.0145
20	.1610	40	.0980	60	.0400	80	.0135

Drill Letter	Diameter In Inches		Drill Letter	Diameter In Inches	
	Lettered Drills				
	Decimal	Fraction		Decimal	Fraction
A	0.234	15/64	N	0.302	
B	.238		O	.316	
C	.242		P	.323	21/64
D	.246		Q	.332	
E	.250	1/4	R	.339	11/32
F	.257		S	.348	
G	.261		T	.358	23/64
H	.266	17/64	U	.368	
I	.272		V	.377	3/8
J	.277		W	.386	
K	.281	9/32	X	.397	
L	.290		Y	.404	13/32
M	.295	19/64	Z	.413	

IMPACT WRENCH

An electric or air-operated impact wrench is used to tighten or loosen nuts and bolts. Use only impact sockets, not standard wrench sockets, on the tool. A ½-inch drive impact wrench is the most useful size.

PIPE MACHINE

A pipe machine is used to cut, ream, and thread steel pipe. Simple machines merely rotate the pipe and allow you to fit the cutter and die to it. More elaborate machines have a reamer, cutter, and adjustable die, all of which can be applied to the pipe with minimal effort. The adjustable die must adjusted to the pipe size manually. Many machines also automatically oil the die while the motor runs.

SAFETY: Keep all clothing clear of rotating parts. Maintain a supply of cutting oil in the reservoir. Oil the die manually if necessary. Always ground the machine.

4

Safety Equipment

Installation and repair of comfort cooling and refrigeration machinery can be hazardous, and several types of safety equipment are necessary.

AIR PACK

An air pack is a small, self-contained breathing apparatus for use in areas that may become contaminated with dangerous gas. These conditions indicate the use of an air pack:

- *Leaking or unstable ammonia systems. Ammonia is toxic and can be lethal.*
- *High concentrations of halocarbon refrigerants, which can displace air and cause death.*
- *Halocarbon refrigerants in the presence of flame, which creates toxic gas.*

The mask covers the head to protect the eyes, nose, and face, and hoses feed air from the tank. A common type of air pack is a mine safety apparatus, which provides "pressure-demand" air supply. A positive pressure equal to about 1 inch of mercury (6.9 kPa above atmospheric pressure) inside the mask prevents toxic gas from entering. An exhaling valve allows easy exhalation. With a 45 cubic-foot (1275-liter) cylinder, the air pack is rated at 30 minutes of breathing time and weighs from 25 (11.3 kg) to 33 lbs. (15 kg), depending on the type of cylinder.

GLOVES

Gloves are a smart precaution, especially when soldering, brazing, grinding, or handling other hot metal. Gloves are also useful when using a hammer and chisel, or working around leaking refrigerants or in particularly cold areas.

GOGGLES

Goggles are a good safety measure when soldering, brazing, grinding, using hammer and chisel, and working with refrigerants. Goggles should always be worn when working with ammonia systems.

5

Materials

INSULATION

Insulation is used to reduce energy loss in refrigerant tubing and cooled spaces. Insulation is rated by the "R-factor," a measure of how well the material resists the passage of heat. The higher the R value, the greater the insulation value. R is the reciprocal of U, the rate of heat transfer in a material:

$$R = \frac{1}{U}$$

R ratings of layers of materials can be added to find the total insulation value.

The two categories of insulation used in cooling systems are cabinet and tubing. Cabinet insulation is the responsibility of the manufacturer.

TUBING

Tubing insulation is used to reduce warming (and consequent energy loss) and sweating (which can damage tubing, fittings, or adjacent areas) of cold refrigerant and water lines. The common insulation materials for this purpose are polyethylene, elastomeric material, and fiberglass. Some materials are designed to be used outdoors, with the proper coating, while others can be used underground. Special shapes of insulation may be available for covering fittings. Consult the manufacturer for detailed instructions on using tubing insulation.

Tubing insulation should be chosen after considering the operating temperature, chemicals in the operating environment, cost, ease of installation, ability to withstand moisture, and ability to conform to the tubing configuration.

Tubing insulation is described by material, ID, and wall thickness. Wall thickness ranges from about ¼ inch (.63 cm) to 1 inch (2.54 cm). Heavier thicknesses are used where the temperature differential between the tubing and the environment is relatively large. Two basic types of tubing insulation are used in the trade: fiberglass and closed-cell foam.

1. Fiberglass is supplied in 3-foot (92-cm) pieces that are split lengthwise and have glue on the joining surfaces. Cover fittings with loose fiberglass, then apply a plastic pre-formed shroud on top. Fiberglass is harder to place over fittings than closed-cell foam. Wear a mask or respirator to prevent irritation from fiberglass fibers.

2. Closed-cell foam is sold in sheets, cylinders, and tape. Sheets are used to insulate flat areas, such as ducts. Cylinders are used for tubing. Some cylinders are sold pre-slit, with adhesive on the slit for sealing after the cylinder is placed on the tubing. Insulation tape is handy for tight areas and for covering fittings. However, you can also miter cylindrical insulation to fit. If the insulation does not cover the entire assembly, use adhesive to seal the gaps between the insulation and the tubing or fitting.

Closed-cell foam absorbs practically no water, and resists solvents and other chemicals and provides some protection against physical damage. In extremely humid areas, a waterproof wrapping may be used to keep the insulation dry. Observe operating temperature range restrictions. Elastomeric material is easy to slip on and can slip over smaller fittings, such as elbows and 45° elbows. For larger fittings, use prefabricated coverings.

CAUTION: Adhesives used with these insulations are toxic and should be used with adequate ventilation. Adhesive vapor is flammable, so keep flame and sparks away. The adhesive may set off an electronic leak dectector, so you should do all leak testing before gluing the joints.

INSTALLING CLOSED-CELL FOAM

Use this procedure to cut and install elastomeric insulation to tubing in a new installation:

1. Cut the material slightly longer than the tubing lengths. Make a square cut to achieve a good seal between adjacent pieces of insulation.
2. Slip the insulation over the length. Glue its lengthwise mating surface.
3. Assemble the tubing.
4. Slide the insulation back from fittings to be brazed or soldered and clamp it out of the way.
5. Make the connections without overheating the insulation.
6. After the connection is cool, remove the clamps and slide the insulation back into position.
7. Apply insulation to the fitting if needed.
8. Use the manufacturer's adhesive to seal all joints between pieces of insulation.

Use this procedure to cut and install elastomeric insulation to tubing in existing systems:

1. Cut the material slightly longer than the tubing lengths, using a square cut to make a good seal between sections.
2. Slit the lengths and slip them over the tubing.
3. Insulate the fittings, using prefabricated pieces if available or by mitering standard pieces.
4. Apply sealant to all joints and slits in the insulation and press together.

OIL

Refrigerant oil is required to prevent metal-to-metal contact in compressor bearings and other surfaces, such as between the piston and cylinder wall. The oil must be capable of withstanding temperatures in the cylinder head and of flowing through the system without congealing in the coldest sections. Although some oil normally flows along with the refrigerant, excess oil in the system can cause many problems, so an oil separator is commonly used to intercept oil in the discharge line and return it to the compressor.

Other design and operating measures may be used to prevent excess oil from traveling through the system or to increase the rate of oil return to the crankcase.

Compressor manufacturers designate the proper oil for their machines, and their suggestions should be followed closely. Under proper conditions of cleanliness and temperature, oil will lubricate for an indefinite period. In large systems, use of a drier element to neutralize acid and annual acidity tests in the oil will help ensure proper lubrication without needless oil changes.

6

Refrigerants

Refrigerants are the fluids that change state and absorb heat in the evaporator and dispose of it in the condenser. Many chemicals have been used as refrigerants over the years. In the vapor-compression cycle, chlorofluorocarbons are widely used, although ammonia is still found in large industrial systems. In the absorption cycle, either water or ammonia is used.

Ideally, all refrigerants should:

1. Work under moderate pressures.

2. Have a high latent heat.

3. Be nontoxic, nonflammable, nonexplosive, noncorrosive, and inexpensive.

4. Be stable under operating conditions.

5. Have low viscosity (to allow rapid heat transfer without high pumping cost).

6. Be easy to detect when leaking.

7. Be stable.

8. Have a low boiling point.

9. Have relatively close condensing and evaporating pressures.

ABSORPTION

The two most common types of absorption systems are described by the combination of refrigerant and absorber they use: 1) Water as the refrigerant and lithium bromide as the absorber; and 2) Ammonia as the refrigerant and water as the absorber.

In addition to the qualities listed above, absorption refrigerants should meet these requirements:

1. Neither the refrigerant nor the absorbent should form a solid phase at operating temperatures, pressures, and chemical conditions.

2. The refrigerant should be more volatile than the absorber at conditions found in the generator.

3. The absorbent should have a strong affinity for the refrigerant.

See below for precautions for ammonia, a common absorption refrigerant.

VAPOR-COMPRESSION

Refrigerants provide heat transfer in the vapor-compression cycle because they are compressed in the compressor, condensed in the condenser and evaporated in the evaporator.

The National Refrigeration Safety Code (NRSC) places refrigerants in three groups:

NRSC REFRIGERANT CLASSIFICATIONS

Group	Fire hazard	Includes
I	Safest	R-11
		R-12
		R-22
		R-500
		R-502
		R-503
		R-744 (carbon dioxide)
II	Toxic and somewhat flammable	R-717 (ammonia)
		R-40 (methyl chloride)
		R-764 (sulfur dioxide)
III	Flammable	R-600 (butane)
		R-170 (ethane)
		R-290 (propane)

R-717 (AMMONIA NH_3)

Ammonia is often used in industrial systems, but because its fumes are hazardous, it is rarely used in small vapor-compression systems (although many absorption systems rely on it). R-717 is lighter than oil and does not present lubrication problems.

Ammonia has a low boiling point and can create below-zero temperatures even when evaporator pressure is above atmospheric pressure. And because it has a high latent heat, a relatively small system is needed. Ammonia attacks copper and bronze, so tubes and fittings are normally iron or steel connected by welding or threaded fittings.

AMMONIA SAFETY: Ammonia is very hazardous to the respiratory system. Levels as low 3 to 5 parts per million (ppm) can be detected by smelling. A respirator is required above 30 ppm. OSHA allows only 5 minutes exposure to levels of 50 ppm. Ammonia is hazardous to life at 5000 ppm.

Wear goggles and stand aside when cracking or opening an ammonia valve, because a quick blast of ammonia could damage your eyes or cause rapid loss of consciousness. Leaks can be detected by smell and located by the stream of smoky fumes that form in the presence of a sulphur candle or sulphur spray vapor. An air pack or a tight mask are excellent safety measures when working around an ammonia system (see Section 4, *Safety Equipment*, p. 25).

HALOCARBONS

Halocarbons (also called chlorofluorocarbons) are compounds designed for the refrigerant industry in 1930 to replace hazardous ammonia as a refrigerant. Halocarbon refrigerants contain atoms of the halogen group (chlorine, fluorine, iodine, and bromine). These compounds are stable, noncorrosive, nonflammable, and possess many other desirable refrigerant properties. Halocarbons can be detected by soap bubbles, and by halide or electronic leak detectors. Halocarbons are heavier than air and will collect in the lowest spot in a room or container.

Unfortunately, the halocarbons have been implicated in destruction of the ozone layer. R-11 and R-12 are some of the worst offenders in this respect (see Part I p. 303).

Halocarbon refrigerants are commonly called by the trade name Freon, but this is a trademark and should not be used in place of halocarbon, chlorofluorocarbon, CFC, or the refrigerant number. Refrigerants may be a pure chemical, such as R-11 in which case they are a ''primary'' refrigerant. Other refrigerants, called azeotropes, are blended at the factory from two or more primary refrigerants, such as R-500. Refrigerants should not be mixed in the field. The chemicals are shipped in cylinders with different colors, but for safety's sake, make sure to read the label.

Older style refrigerant cylinders have a single valve. To obtain a gas charge, the cylinder is left upright; to obtain a liquid charge, the cylinder must be inverted. Newer cylinders have one valve at the top and another at the bottom.

Vapor-compression refrigerants are chosen according to desired evaporator temperature and the kind of machinery. Refrigerants that evaporate at low temperature are used in low-temperature applications; otherwise the compressor would have to create extremely low suction pressures. The system refrigerant must also have enough heat capacity to remove the heat load under the compressor's pumping rate and head pressure.

Refrigerants are described at their pressures at evaporating and condensing temperatures, and by their latent heat capacity (see Table A3).

Refrigerant and performance temperatures

Low-side (evaporating) pressure	at 5°F (−15°C)
High-side (condensing) pressure	at 86°F (30°C)
Latent heat per pound	at 5°F (−15°C)

ADDITIVES

Dehydrating and antifreeze compounds are sometimes added to refrigerant. However, du Pont Corporation recommends against using antifreeze, suggesting that removing the cause of the problem (excess moisture) is preferable to treating the symptom (water freezing in the system). Antifreeze can react with components and contaminate the system. Certain drying agents, such as calcium chloride or calcium oxide, can decompose some refrigerants.

▬▬ HALOCARBON SAFETY

Observe the following minimum safety guidelines when handling halocarbons:

TABLE A3
Refrigerant Specifications and Performance
BASED ON 5°F EVAPORATION AND 86°F CONDENSATION†

No.	Name	Formula	Boiling Point at One Atmosphere °F	Evaporator Pressure PSIG	Condensing Pressure PSIG	Compressor Ratio	Net Refrigerant Effect BTU/LB	Refrigerant Circulated LB/Min	Liquid Circulated Cu. In./Min.	Specific Volume of Suction Gas Cu. Ft./LB	Compressor Displacement CFM	Horsepower Hp	Coefficient of Performance	Temperatures of Compressor Discharge °F
11	Trichloromonofluoromethane	CCL_3F	74.8	24.0*	3.6	6.24	67.3	2.97	56.2	12.27	36.48	0.932	5.06	109
12	Dichlorodifluoromethane	CCL_2F_2	−21.6	11.8	93.3	4.08	50.0	4.00	85.7	1.46	5.83	1.002	4.70	101
22	Monochlorodifluoromethane	$CHCLF_2$	−41.4	28.2	158.2	4.03	70.0	2.86	67.4	1.24	3.55	1.011	4.66	128
113	Trichlorotrifluoroethane	CCL_2FCCL_2F	117.6	27.9*	13.9*	8.02	53.7	3.73	66.5	27.39	102.03	0.973	4.84	86
114	Dichlorotetrafluoroethane	$CCLF_2CCLF_2$	38.4	16.1*	21.6	5.42	43.1	4.64	89.2	4.34	20.14	1.049	4.49	86
500	Azeotrope of r-12 and	CCL_2F_2/CH_3CHF_2	−28.0	16.4	113.4	4.12	61.1	3.27	79.3	1.52	4.97	1.012	4.66	105
502	Azeotrope of r-115 and R-22	$CCLF_2CF_3CHCLF_2$	−50.1	36.0	175.1	3.75	45.7	4.38	99.4	0.825	3.61	1.079	4.37	99
717	Ammonia	NH_3	−28.0	19.6	154.5	4.94	474.4	0.422	19.6	8.15	3.44	0.989	4.76	210

† SATURATED SUCTION VAPOR EXCEPT FOR R-113 AND R-114. IN THESE CASES ENOUGH SUCTION SUPERHEAT WAS ASSUMED TO GIVE A SATURATED DISCHARGE VAPOR

* INCHES OF MERCURY VACUUM

COURTESY OF MUELLER BRASS

1. Ventilate the room if you suspect a leak.
2. Keep the system at or below its design operating pressure.
3. Do not mix refrigerants.
4. Do not allow flames near a system suspected of leaking—this can create toxic gas.
5. Wear goggles and gloves, especially when charging or discharging a system.
6. Do not fill a service cylinder more than 80 percent full with refrigerant, as the fluid needs room to expand if temperature increases. A full cylinder is a bomb waiting to explode.
7. Store cylinders in a cool place.
8. Do not refill disposable cylinders.
9. Do not fill cylinders with anything except what is marked on the label.
10. Do not sniff refrigerants—some can kill you.
11. Do not depend on your nose to detect a leak—use an approved method.
12. Liquid refrigerant can quickly freeze the skin. Wash it off immediately with water and treat frostbite if needed.

THEORY OF HEAT
AND ENERGY

The principal function of a refrigeration system is to transfer heat from one place (the cooled space) to the surroundings. Cooling systems must comply with the laws of physics, especially laws governing the interaction of various forms of energy, the transfer of heat, and the effects of temperature and pressure on fluids. Other theoretical topics of importance include the two measuring systems, electricity and magnetism, the vapor-compression and absorption cooling cycles, corrosion, and psychrometrics—the study of the relationship between temperature and humidity and human comfort. Understanding these principles will help technicians diagnose and repair faulty systems faster.

Energy is the ability to do work, thus energy and work are measured in the same units. These units are the foot-pound in the English system and the joule in the SI (International, or metric) system.

PRINCIPLES OF ENERGY

To understand what is going on inside a refrigeration system, you must understand these important principles of energy:

1. Energy is always "conserved," meaning it always goes somewhere, it is not created or destroyed (except in a nuclear reaction). A refrigerator can move heat from one place to another, but cannot destroy it.

2. Energy may be present as heat energy, potential energy, or kinetic energy:

   a. *Potential energy* is energy that is available but not doing work. Potential energy is present in batteries that are not giving out electricity, water that is stored behind a dam, an object that is raised above a surface, and in a magnetic or electric field.

b. *Kinetic energy* is energy that is doing work. Kinetic energy is present in batteries which are converting chemical energy to electrical energy, water flowing through turbines to create mechanical energy, and a falling object. Kinetic and potential energy can take the form of electromagnetic, chemical, or mechanical energy, and these forms can be converted into each other.

c. *Heat* is the form of energy that results from the vibration of the molecules of a substance. The faster the vibration, the greater the intensity of heat—the greater the temperature. Heat energy is present in a flame, the element of an electric stove, and some forms of radiation. Temperature measures the intensity of heat energy, but temperature and heat are different quantities. The total amount of heat energy in a material is a function of its temperature, mass, and specific heat capacity. The heat content of a fluid, called its "enthalpy," reflects its chemical nature, its pressure, and its temperature.

3. Substances expand as they warm because the molecules begin moving more rapidly and bounce off each other more energetically. This expansion causes the decrease in density that accompanies warming.

4. Heat flows from warmer bodies to cooler ones, never in the reverse direction. Cold, which results when heat is absent or removed from a material, does not flow.

5. The various forms of energy can be converted. Batteries convert chemical energy to electrical energy, which can then be converted to heat, mechanical, or electromagnetic energy. Gasoline engines convert chemical energy to heat energy and then to mechanical energy. Automobile brakes then convert the mechanical energy back to heat energy. Electric motors convert electromagnetic energy to kinetic energy which can be used to move refrigerant, air, water, or any number of other substances.

6. Liquids absorb heat (the latent heat of vaporization) in the process of changing to a gas. Gases give off heat (the latent heat of condensation) when changing to a liquid. For a given fluid, these quantities are equal—the same quantity of heat required to boil one pound of water must be removed to condense it.

7. Temperature will remain constant during a change of state

between gas and liquid if pressure also remains constant. In other words, water at atmospheric pressure will remain at 212°F (100°C) until it has all boiled. Then the temperature of the steam will begin to rise as long as heat is added.

HEAT ENERGY

Heat is the form of energy that most concerns air conditioning and refrigeration technicians. When a substance is warmed, it absorbs heat. The rate of temperature rise depends on the mass of the substance, its specific heat capacity, and the amount of heat added.

In the American system, heat is measured in British thermal units, or Btus. One Btu will raise the temperature of one pound of water by 1°F. In the SI system, heat is measured in joules, although in refrigeration, the kilojoule (1,000 joules) is more practical. 4.187 kilojoules (kJ) will warm 1 kilogram of water 1°C. Calories are another SI unit of heat. One calorie (cal) will warm one gram of water 1°C. 1 cal = 4.187 J. The larger kcal (1,000 calories) is often used instead. 1 kcal = 4.187 kJ.

To find the heat required in conventional units to raise the temperature of a certain amount of water without changing its state, multiply mass in pounds or kilograms by the temperature change (also called delta T). The specific heat capacity of water equals 1:

$$\text{Mass} * \text{temperature change} * \text{specific heat capacity} = \text{heat added or lost}$$

To heat 250 lb. of water 42°F:
$$250 * 42 * 1 = 10500 \text{ Btu}$$
To heat 20 kg of water 12°C:
$$20 * 12 * 1 = 240 \text{ kcal}$$

To find kilojoules, multiply by 4.187:

$$240 * 4.187 = 1004.88 \text{ kJ}$$

When 1 pound of water is cooled 1°F, one Btu is released. The calculation is no different than the one above for warming, except that heat is removed instead of added.

TEMPERATURE VERSUS HEAT

Temperature is a measure of how warm a substance is. In scientific terms, temperature measures the intensity of motion of the molecules, not the amount of heat a mass contains. The amount of heat energy present in a substance depends on its temperature, its mass, and its specific heat. One ton of water at 100°F has 2000 times as much heat energy as one pound of water at 100°F, even though they have the same temperature.

As temperature falls, molecular motion decreases. At absolute zero, all motion apparently would cease. Because the properties of fluids are related to their absolute temperature (temperature above absolute zero), some refrigeration calculations require the use of the Rankine or Kelvin scales, which start at absolute zero. Doubling the temperature of a confined gas will double its pressure.

TEMPERATURE SCALES

In United States units, the Fahrenheit scale is the common temperature scale, but a variation called the Rankine scale starts at absolute zero. Units in each scale have the same size, so converting is just a matter of adding or subtracting 460°.

In SI units, the Celsius scale starts at 0°, the freezing point of water. The Kelvin scale begins at absolute zero; its units are of the same magnitude as Celsius units. Units may be converted by adding or subtracting 273°.

See Table B1 for comparisons of the four temperature scales.

EQUIVALENTS:

Rankine to Fahrenheit:	$R - 460$	$= F$
Fahrenheit to Rankine:	$F + 460$	$= R$
Celsius to Kelvin:	$C + 273$	$= K$
Kelvin to Celsius:	$K - 273$	$= C$
Celsius to Fahrenheit:	$(9/5C) + 32$	$= F$
Fahrenheit to Celsius:	$5/9(F-32)$	$= C$

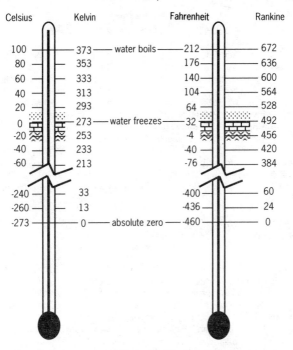

TABLE B1 4 TEMPERATURE SCALES

SENSIBLE VERSUS LATENT HEAT

Heat is either sensible or latent. Sensible heat, the familiar type, can be felt with the hand or measured with a thermometer. Latent heat cannot be measured by a thermometer. Latent heat is the amount of heat required to change the state of a substance, for example from a solid to a liquid, without changing its temperature.

The amount of the latent heat of vaporization is important in determining whether a substance will make a good refrigerant. The higher the latent heat, the greater amount of cooling that each pound of refrigerant flowing through the system will supply, all other things being equal.

Each substance has two latent heats, and each of these can be named in two ways, depending on whether the temperature is rising or falling:

Change of state	Temperature rising	Temperature falling
Solid—liquid	Heat of melting =	Heat of fusion
Liquid—gas	Heat of vaporization =	Heat of condensation

Note that latent heat is reversible: just as many Btus are required to boil a pound of water as to condense a pound of steam.

Some materials can go directly from solid to gas state, without passing through the liquid phase. Solid carbon dioxide, or dry ice, undergoes this so-called "sublimation." The latent heat of sublimation equals the sum of the latent heat of vaporization and the latent heat of fusion.

Refrigeration technicians need not worry about the latent heats of fusion or melting, because systems should not be operated at conditions that will cause refrigerant to freeze. However, the heat of freezing for water is important when calculating refrigeration loads or when using ice as a cooling agent.

FOUR STATES OF MATTER

Matter can take four states (also called phases): solid, liquid, gas, and plasma. The state of matter is determined by a substance's inherent properties, and the temperature and pressure at which it exists:

1. A solid retains its own shape without needing a container because its temperature is so low that the molecules remain fixed in position. This is reflected in the solid's shape and hardness. Ice is the solid form of water.

2. A liquid takes the shape of its container and yet is tightly bonded together. The molecules move within the container by the force of convection, with the warmer ones rising and the lighter ones falling. Water is the liquid form of water. A liquid is a fluid—a substance that takes the shape of its container.

3. A gas is the second form of fluid. It also takes the shape of its container, but unlike a liquid it expands to fill its entire container because the molecules are too energetic to stick to each other. Gases, like liquids, are subject to convection currents. The term "vapor" is often used in the trade to refer to a gas. Steam is the gaseous form of water.

4. A plasma is an electrically charged phase that is found in the sun, electric arcs, and fluorescent lamps. In general, plasmas are present only at very high temperatures, and they play no part in cooling systems.

HEATING ICE INTO STEAM— ENERGY REQUIRED

When a substance changes phase, it gains or loses latent heat. The amount of heat gain or loss depends on the material and whether it is changing from a gas to a liquid or from a liquid to a solid. Water requires 144 Btu per pound (335 kJ/kg) to melt from solid to liquid (the latent heat of fusion). Water requires 970 Btu per pound (2,257 kJ/kg) to change from liquid to vapor (the latent heat of vaporization).

To put these concepts into use, suppose you must heat one pound of water from 0°F to 300°F. As you raise the water to thawing, 32°F, each Btu will raise the temperature one degree. Because each Btu raises the temperature, this is sensible heat. When the ice reaches 32°, the temperature stops rising while 144

Btus of "latent" heat is added. Then the ice melts, and the water continues warming at 1° per Btu until it reaches 212°. To vaporize the water, the latent heat of vaporization—970 Btus—must be added. Finally, 88 Btus more is needed to raise the temperature to 300°F:

Temperature range	Btus required	Type of heat
0°F to 32°F	32	Sensible
32°F to 32°F—ice to water	144	Latent heat of melting
32°F to 212°F	180	Sensible
212°F to 212°F—water to steam	970	Latent heat of vaporization
212°F steam to 300°F steam	88	Sensible
Total heat 0°F to 300°F	1414 Btus	

As you can see, more heat is needed to vaporize the water into steam than for the other steps combined. The boiling requires 69 percent of the total energy used in this warming process. This is why cooling systems that depend on the latent heat of vaporization can be so effective at moving heat.

Although you cannot detect temperature change during the latent heating stages of this process, the water is still gaining total heat energy. The rate of molecular vibration is increasing, so the molecules become more likely to break the bonds restraining them. When enough heat is added, this vibration becomes so violent that a solid becomes a liquid, or a liquid becomes a gas.

Another way of looking at latent heat is to consider the vapor pressure at the boundary between a liquid and a gas. Each liquid has a characteristic vapor pressure that varies according to temperature and results from the motion of the liquid molecules. The warmer the liquid, the faster the molecules move and the greater the vapor pressure. While you add latent heat, the temperature does not change but vapor pressure increases until it equals the pressure of the gas in the container. Finally the molecules become energetic enough to break the bonds holding them as a liquid and to overcome the pressure from the gas above, and the liquid molecules become gas molecules. Then the liquid starts boiling.

However, even below boiling temperature, some of the liquid molecules have enough energy to vaporize. Evaporation takes energetic molecules out of the liquid, so the remaining liquid is cooled.

Latent heat is a vital concept for understanding what happens in the condenser (where the hot, high-pressure refrigerant transfers its heat of condensation to the surroundings) and the evaporator (where the liquid refrigerant boils and absorbs the latent heat of vaporization from the surroundings). The latent heat of vaporization moves from the cooled area through the fins and tubes of the evaporator. As the cooled space transfers this heat into the refrigerant, its temperature drops. Note that the refrigerant remains at a steady temperature while it changes state. Only when the change of state is complete does the refrigerant gain sensible heat again.

SATURATION TEMPERATURE-PRESSURE

At certain ranges of pressure and temperature (called saturation temperature-pressure) both liquid and gaseous forms of a fluid can coexist in a container. This saturation temperature-pressure is the condition inside most parts of evaporators and condensers when cooling systems are operating.

As pressure increases, the saturation temperature rises; as pressure falls, saturation temperature also falls. Saturation temperature for water at sea level pressure is 212°F (100°C). At higher altitudes, where atmospheric pressure is lower, the saturation temperature is also lower.

Refrigeration engineers sometimes speak of a refrigerant's "pressure-temperature" to refer to saturation conditions. In other words, if you know the pressure of a saturated fluid, you can find its temperature by looking at a chart of the material's properties.

SUBCOOLING AND SUPERHEATING

Subcooling and superheating are two basic concepts for refrigeration systems. Both conditions represent a change in temperature, with pressure remaining constant, from saturation pressure-temperature. While a fluid at saturation temperature-pressure will boil as it gains heat and condense as it loses heat, a subcooled liquid cannot boil immediately and a superheated gas cannot immediately condense.

1. As a fluid that has just totally condensed starts to lose sensible heat, it forms a subcooled liquid. A subcooled liquid is entirely liquid because it is below the saturation temperature for its pressure, and it must gain sensible heat (its temperature must rise) and/or have its pressure reduced before it can begin to absorb latent heat and undergo boiling. Liquid water at sea level pressure is subcooled when it is below 212°F (100°C).

2. When enough heat has been added to entirely boil a liquid, it will form a gas at saturation conditions. As the gas gains sensible heat, its temperature will rise and it will become superheated. A superheated vapor is entirely vapor because it is above saturation temperature for its pressure. This vapor must be cooled and/or subjected to greater pressure before it can condense. Vapor water (steam) at sea level is superheated when above 212°F.

The importance of subcooling and superheating is that they provide insurance against unwanted conditions inside a refrigeration system. In the liquid line, liquid refrigerant should be subcooled, so it can remain liquid until it passes through the metering device. Otherwise, it can flash to a gas after a slight pressure drop, as in a filter-drier.

Superheating is desirable in an evaporator because 1) it ensures against floodbacks because the liquid phase cannot exist in superheated conditions, and 2) it ensures all the cooling power of the refrigerant is used because superheating must follow complete evaporation. However, excessive superheat 1) wastes evaporator room, because the area of superheating is warmer than the area of boiling so the rate of heat transfer is less, and 2) reduces cooling of a hermetic compressor because the suction gas will be too hot and not dense enough.

The superheat adjustment of an expansion valve is usually set at the factory to about 8° to 10°F. The most common reason to adjust this setting is a previous maladjustment (see p. 124, *Thermostatic expansion valve* for more on measuring and adjusting superheat).

HEAT TRANSFER

Heat transfer occurs because heat energy tends to flow from a warmer object to a cooler one. Heat can move by three methods:

1. *Radiation* is the travel of electromagnetic energy through space or a conductor. All warm bodies radiate to some extent, depending on their temperature, surface, and composition. The sun's heat reaches Earth by radiation. Fireplaces do most of their warming by radiation. Electromagnetic radiation is the form of energy found in electric motors and electric and electronic circuits.

2. *Convection* is a movement that takes place in fluids because cool fluids are denser than warm ones. Convection causes cool fluids to move down and displace warm ones. This principle is used in forced-air distribution systems, which use a fan (to increase the air's kinetic energy) and convection to move air around a building.

3. Conduction is a transfer of heat that takes place when bodies at different temperatures touch each other. Evaporator tubes use conduction to transfer heat from the cooled space to the refrigerant. The degree of heat transfer depends on the temperature difference, the extent of contact between the bodies, and the properties of the two materials.

Often, several means of heat transfer operate in unison. A pot on an electric stove absorbs radiated, convected, and conducted heat from the burner. A welder working in a closed room may be warmed by convection and radiation.

Some materials, such as copper and aluminum, have a high rate of heat conduction. Insulators have a very low rate. In vapor-compression refrigeration systems, most heat transfer takes place in the condenser and evaporator, so these components are designed to conduct a great deal of heat. The material chosen for these heat exchangers must have good conduction and the design must ensure a temperature difference between the elements. All other things being equal, the greater the difference in temperature, the faster heat will flow.

The following factors tend to increase the rate of transfer between fluids separated by a metal wall, as in an evaporator or condenser:

- *Thin walls*
- *Walls made of heat-conductive material, such as copper or aluminum*
- *Rough or dull wall surfaces*
- *High fluid velocity*
- *Large temperature difference between the fluid and the surroundings*
- *Large amount of surface area (small diameter, long tubes have greater wall area per volume than short, large-diameter tubes.)*

Good heat transfer is also necessary in other parts of cooling systems, such as compressor heads, sensing bulbs, and heat exchangers.

SPECIFIC HEAT CAPACITY

Specific heat capacity measures the ability of a material to absorb heat. In the conventional units, specific heat capacity is defined as the amount of heat that must be added or removed to change the temperature of one pound of a substance by 1°F. The quantity is measured in Btus per pound. In the SI system, specific heat capacity is the amount of heat added or removed to change the temperature of one kilogram by 1°C. Specific heat capacity in SI is measured in kilojoules per kilogram kelvin (kJ/kg∗K).

Specific heat capacity is used to calculate how much heat must be added or removed from a certain amount of a substance:

$$\text{Btu} = \text{mass in lb.} * \text{Specific heat capacity} * \text{temperature change in °F}$$

In SI units,

$$\text{kJ} = \text{mass in kilograms} * \text{specific heat capacity} * \text{temperature change in kelvins (K°)}$$

Equivalents:

$$1 \text{ kJ/kg∗K°} = 0.2388 \text{ Btu/lb °F}$$
$$1 \text{ Btu/lb °F} = 4.187 \text{ kJ/kg∗K°}$$

TONS OF REFRIGERATION

Cooling systems are rated by comparing them to the cooling effect of ice. A refrigeration machine rated at one ton cools as much in 24 hours as one ton of ice would by melting in the same period. One ton of ice at 32°F melting to water at 32°F (with no gain of sensible heat) absorbs 288,000 Btus of the latent heat of fusion:

$$2000 \text{ lb} * 144 \text{ Btu/lb} = 288,000 \text{ Btus.}$$

Thus, a one-ton refrigerator can remove 288,000 Btus per day from a cabinet. This translates to 12,000 Btu/hour (288,000/24).

The SI system has no equivalent to the ton rating. However, one ton of refrigeration equals about 303,845 kJ, or 12,660 kJ/hour (303,845 /24). This equals 3.52 kW.

FLUID FLOW

A fluid flows from one point to another due to a difference in pressure caused by different density (convection), a pump or the relative heights of the containers. In mechanical systems, a compressor pumps refrigerant through the piping. This flow may be resisted by 1) gravity (if the fluid must flow upward), 2) viscosity (the fluid's resistance to flow), and 3) friction caused by pipes and fittings. In a closed loop, gravity can be ignored because the falling fluid counterbalances the rising fluid.

Pressure drop in a system is an important consideration in design for several reasons. The tubes must be large enough to conduct the fluid with little drop in pressure, because this drop reduces system efficiency. However, oversize tubes have relatively little surface area, which reduces heat transfer. In addition, the reduced fluid velocity will impair oil return to the compressor. Thus the proper size of piping reflects a compromise between minimum pressure drop and maximum heat transfer and oil return.

The type of fluid flow affects the efficiency of the evaporator. Smooth-flowing fluids can develop an insulating film which inhibits transfer of heat from the evaporator wall to the refrigerant. Turbulent, quick-flowing, or rapid-boiling fluids all promote a quick transfer of heat into the refrigerant.

PRESSURE

Pressure is force applied per unit of area. In United States units, pressure is measured in pounds per square inch (psi). In SI units, it is measured in pascals (Pa), a force of one newton per square meter. Kilopascals (kPa) are often used because one pascal is a small amount of pressure. 6.895 kPa = 1 psia.

Although scientists say there is no such thing as suction, it nevertheless appears to pull something toward it when actually greater pressure somewhere else is pushing it. The trade uses terms like "suction line" and "pulls down" in reference to specific components and actions. These terms will be used here for convenience, while recognizing that suction is merely the absence of pressure, much like cold is the absence of heat.

Atmospheric pressure at sea level is 14.7 lb/in², or 101.3 kPa. In a perfect vacuum, pressure equals zero. In the United States system, vacuum is usually measured in inches of mercury vacuum instead of psi. A perfect vacuum measures 29.92 inches of mercury, and atmospheric pressure measures 0 inches of mercury. In the SI system, pressure measurements start at zero (there is no gauge pressure) and vacuum is measured in microns of mercury. One micron equals one-millionth of a meter.

Pressure affects the boiling point of liquids, because a liquid's vapor pressure must equal ambient pressure before it can boil. At atmospheric pressure water boils at 212°F, but at 10,000 feet of altitude, the reduced pressure lowers the boiling point to about 193°F. Increasing pressure raises the boiling point, so water in a vessel under 100 psi boils at about 338°F. This explains why pressure cookers cook food faster and hotter than boiling water.

GAUGE AND ABSOLUTE PRESSURE

A service technician using the American system of measuring must distinguish between gauge pressure (pounds per square inch gauge, or psig) and absolute pressure, (pounds per square inch absolute, or psia). Absolute pressure is the sum of atmospheric pressure and

TABLE B2

Vacuum Pressure Scales			
Inches of Hg	mm of Hg	psia	Ft. of Water
30		15	
(29.92)	760	(14.7)	33.40
29		14.5	
28	711	14	32.2
27		13.5	
26	660	13	29.9
25		12.5	
24	610	12	27.6
23		11.5	
22	559	11	25.3
21		10.5	
20	508	10	23.0
19		9.5	
18	457	9	20.7
17		8.5	
16	408	8	18.4
15		7.5	
14	356	7	16.1
13		6.5	
12	305	6	13.8
11		5.5	
10	254	5	11.5
9		4.5	
8	203	4	9.2
7		3.5	
6	152	3	6.9
5		2.5	
4	102	2	4.6
3		1.5	
2	51	1	2.3
1		0.5	
0	0	0	0

CHART CONVERTS INCHES OF MERCURY (IN. HG) INTO POUNDS PER SQUARE INCH ABSOLUTE (PSIA).

gauge pressure. Most gauges read 0 at atmospheric pressure, although the actual pressure is 14.7 lb/in². Many calculations require absolute pressure instead of gauge pressure. Thus a gauge pressure of 5 lb/in² equals an absolute pressure of 19.7 lb/in². Psi usually indicates gauge pressure, but the use of psia and psig instead of the ambiguous psi prevents confusion.

In the SI system, pressure starts with 0 (a complete vacuum) and there is no gauge pressure.

GAS LAWS

Several laws describe the behavior of gases held in containers. The combined laws of Boyle and Charles describes the relationships of pressure, volume, and temperature:

$$PV/T = pv/t$$

The left side of the equation lists characteristics of the gas before a change is made, and the right side lists them afterward:

> P and p = absolute pressure in lb/in³ or kPa
> V and v = volume in in³ or m³
> T and t = temperature in Rankine or Kelvin

In a chamber with a constant volume, $P/T = p/t$. Thus, doubling the pressure will double the temperature.

This equation explains that, in the cylinder of a compressor, increasing pressure and decreasing volume both cause a rise in temperature. In an evaporator, pressure decreases and volume remains constant, so the temperature must fall.

Another way of looking at the relation between temperature and pressure is to remember the law of conservation of energy: energy cannot be created or destroyed except in nuclear reactions. Work done by the compressor increases the vibration of the gas molecules and raises their temperature. This added heat is pumped into the condenser, where it leaves the warm gas and enters the cooler condenser walls. As the heat departs, the motion of the molecules slows and the gas condenses. In the evaporator, the refrigerant's pressure is reduced to the saturation point, and the liquid starts to boil as it gains heat energy from the surroundings.

PERFECT GAS EQUATION

A more complete version of the behavior of gases is contained in the "perfect gas equation," $PV = MRT$. This law also takes into account the mass of gas present and a mathematical factor (called a gas constant) unique to each gas.

> P = pressure in lb/in³ or kPa
> V = volume in in³ or m³
> M = mass in lb. or kg
> R = gas constant
> T = temperature in Rankine or Kelvin

The gas law can be used to predict one attribute of a gas if the other four are known. Thus, given the mass, identity (so you can find the gas constant), temperature, and volume of a gas, you could easily calculate its pressure.

DALTON'S LAW

Dalton's law of partial pressures explains the behavior of several gases in a mixture. The law states that the total pressure of gases confined together equals the sum of the individual gas pressures. Further, each gas behaves as if it occupies the space alone. These principles are crucial to the absorption cycle refrigerator using hydrogen, ammonia, and water.

ENTHALPY

Enthalpy is the amount of heat energy in a particular substance. Enthalpy is a function of the mass, temperature, pressure, and identity of a substance. Enthalpy is calculated by figuring out how much heat must be added or subtracted to bring the substance to reference conditions (for water: 32°F or 0°C; for refrigerant: −40°F or −40°C). The calculation must take into account both latent and sensible heat.

> H = enthalpy, M = mass, TD = temperature difference
> H = M * TD * specific heat (for changes in temperature that do
> not cause a change of state)

A related quantity is called specific enthalpy, or enthalpy per pound or kilogram of the substance.

The enthalpy of a refrigerant rises in the compressor (where both pressure and temperature increase) and the evaporator (as it takes up heat from the cooled area). Enthalpy falls in the condenser (as it gives off heat to the condensing medium) (see Tables B4 and B5, pages 74 and 75).

ELECTROMAGNETIC ENERGY

Electricity and magnetism are two related forces that play vital roles in refrigeration and air-conditioning work. Electricity usually provides the power to run compressors and fans and to operate control circuitry. Magnetic attraction and repulsion is used in motors, solenoids, and relays.

Magnetism and electricity are forms of radiation in the "electromagnetic spectrum," the entire range of radiation which includes visible light, Xrays, and radio waves. The intimate relationship between electricity and magnetism can be seen in two phenomenon:

- *A current passing through a conductor creates a magnetic field.*
- *A current is induced in a conductor that moves through a magnetic field.*

These two principles are fundamental to the operation of electric motors, controls, generators, and many other devices.

MAGNETISM

Magnetism is a field of force around a magnet that attracts certain substances toward the magnet. Each magnet has two poles—north and south—and a magnetic field that connects the poles. When the fields of two magnets overlap, unlike poles attract each other and like poles repel each other. Attraction and repulsion are used in compasses and motors, among many applications.

A magnet will induce magnetism in "magnetic" materials within its field. A permanent magnet is made of materials that become magnetized by exposure to a magnetic field and retain the magnetism. These materials include hardened steel, certain ceramics, and an aluminum–nickel–cobalt alloy called alnico. Permanent magnets will remain magnetic indefinitely and are used in servo motors and to produce a snap action in some electrical contacts. Temporary magnets also have a role in electric devices. For example, soft iron is used as a core in electromagnets due to its ability to become temporarily magnetized.

Electromagnetism results when a current passes through a conductor. To intensify the field, most electromagnets are formed by wrapping a coil of wire around a core of a magnetic material. Electromagnets are used in motors and solenoids.

If a conductor is moved in a magnetic field, an electric current will be produced. This principle of "induction" is used in generators, motors, clamp-on ammeters, and many other devices.

ELECTRICITY

Electricity is one of the most versatile forms of energy, as it is able to produce kinetic energy and heat energy. Electricity can only flow through a complete circuit, from a power source, through a resistance, and back to the power source.

Electric circuits are described by three basic units: current (measured in amperes), electromotive force (emf or potential, measured in volts), and resistance (measured in ohms). In simple terms, the current is the volume of electricity; the electromotive force propels the current; and the resistance opposes the current. These three qualities are often compared to the flow of water. Voltage corresponds to the water pressure, amperage corresponds to the quantity of water moving, and resistance corresponds to the resistance of the piping and gravity to the water flow.

These three quantities are related according to Ohm's law, which uses these terms:

electromotive force (E)—measured in volts

current (I)—measured in amps

resistance (R)—measured in ohms

Ohm's law simply states that current is equal to electromotive force divided by resistance: $I = E/R$. Knowing two of these values, you can find the third: $E = IR$; $R = E/I$

In the more familiar amps, volts, and ohms, Ohm's law states:

$$amps = volts/ohms \qquad volts = amps * ohms$$
$$ohms = volts/amps$$

UNITS

Many units are used to measure and describe electricity:

Coulomb is the unit of electron flow. One coulomb is a flow of 6.24×10^{18} (6,240,000,000,000,000,000) electrons past a certain point on a conductor each second. One coulomb of flow per second produces one ampere of current, but coulombs measure electrons while amps measure current.

Ampere (amp, or A) is the unit of current. One ampere of electricity is one coulomb flowing past a point in a circuit each second. Amperage is measured with an ammeter. One milliamp equals 0.001 amp. Conductors are rated by their ability to carry a certain number of amperes.

Volt (V) is the unit of electrical "pressure." One volt will push one ampere of current through a resistance of one ohm. Voltage is measured with a voltmeter.

Volt-ampere (VA) is the unit of ac power. It is found by multiplying volts times amperes (V $*$ A = VA). Volt-amperes may be different from watts, which is the product of volts, amperes, and power factor. However, volt-amperes equal watts when the power factor is 1.

Ohm (Ω) is the unit of resistance. One ohm of resistance will allow one volt of pressure to push one ampere of current through a conductor.

Farad (F) is the measure of capacitance. One farad of capacitance is the ability to store one coulomb on the capacitor plates having a potential of one volt between them. This is a large amount of electricity, so the unit microfarad (.000,001 farad, μF) is commonly used. The total capacitance of capacitors connected in parallel can be found by adding the ratings of each capacitor. To find the capacitance of capacitors in series, calculate as follows:

$$1/F(total) = 1/C_1 + 1/C_2 + 1/C_3 \text{ etc,}$$

Watt (W) is the unit of power—the rate at which electricity can do work. (V $*$ A $*$ power factor = W). One kilowatt (kW) equals 1,000 watts. One kilowatt hour (kWh) is the equivalent of 1kW working for one hour. Watts are measured with a wattmeter or calculated if voltage, amperage, and power factor are known. In direct current circuits, amps times volts equals watts. In AC circuits, wattage may be less than V * A because alternating current is a wave phenomenon (see *Power factor*, p. 60).

Horsepower (hp) is another unit of power. One horsepower (hp) equals 746 watts.

FUNDAMENTAL ELECTRICAL CONCEPTS AND COMPONENTS

Capacitance is a form of electricity storage that is measured in farads. Capacitors are devices that store electricity as free electrons and release them on demand; they are used to start electric motors and to increase the power factor.

WARNING: Capacitors can store large amounts of electricity even after the current is turned off. Capacitors must be discharged before they are touched or carried. Contact the terminals with a steel tool with an insulated handle, or better, with a 100,000-ohm resistor.

A **solenoid** is a magnetic actuator that can be used to close a valve or a switch. The device works because an electromagnet tends to pull a magnetic core to the center of the coil when current flows. By attaching a switch, valve, or lever to the iron core, a solenoid can convert electrical energy to control something in a system (see Fig. B1).

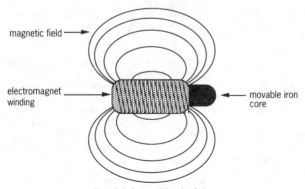

magnetic field

electromagnet winding

movable iron core

Fig. B1 Solenoid principles

A **thermocouple** is an electric device used to measure temperature. The thermocouple works because an electromotive potential develops if two metals are joined and the connection is heated. This voltage can be measured and converted into temperature on a scale. A thermocouple may be capable of reading extremely high temperatures.

A **thermistor** is a semiconductor capable of sensing temperature because its resistance falls as temperature rises and vice versa. The signal can be read by an electronic control that responds to changing temperature in the system.

Direct current (DC) is a form of electricity produced by batteries. The current flows in one direction and does not have a wave form. Direct current is difficult to transmit and is inconvenient for other reasons, so its use is very limited, although it is used extensively in semiconductors.

Alternating current (AC) is the common form of electricity that is generated and distributed through power lines. For each wave of AC, the current and voltage start at zero, rise to a peak, fall to zero, and rise to another peak, then fall to zero again. Two peaks and two zeros comprise one complete cycle of single-phase current or voltage. Thus, 60-hz (cycle per second) AC rises and falls 120 times per second.

The peak voltage of a 120-V circuit is actually 170 volts, but the system is said to have 120 volts because the wave only carries peak voltage for a portion of each wave form. The term "root mean squared," or RMS, is used to describe the actual voltage of an AC circuit.

If the voltage and current waves rise and fall in unison, AC will carry its maximum theoretical power, because power is volts times amps. However, often the waves are not simultaneous, and the circuit is said to have a power factor less than one.

Phase is the number of waves of AC that coexist in a circuit. The current shown in Fig. B2 is single-phase current (designated 1φ). Although single-phase current is commonly found in household use, multiple-phase current is available in commercial and industrial installations. Many power supplies deliver three-phase current (designated 3φ), in which three waves of AC are superimposed. The advantage is that when the voltage and current for one wave reach zero, the other two waves are carrying power. Unlike single-phase current, the current is always delivering power

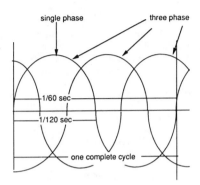

Fig. B2 AC waves

to the motor. Because three-phase motors are usually more efficient than single-phase motors, they are common for applications above ½ hp. Single-phase motors are most common in sizes less than one hp and must be used if three-phase AC is unavailable.

Cycle per second (hz, or hertz) is the number of complete oscillations of AC current per second. AC is usually delivered at 60 cycles per second, properly called 60 hertz and abbreviated 60 hz.

Grounding is the connection to a "ground" wire for safety. In 110-V circuits, the ground wire allows safe return of the current if the neutral wire fails. In a second form of grounding, called "frame grounding," each component with a conducting frame or exterior is grounded to prevent metal parts from becoming "hot" when insulation fails. The standard wire color for ground is green or green with yellow stripe. Never use wire with these colors for any other purpose.

Never cut off the grounding lug of a three-wire plug. Have a qualified electrician adapt the outlet to accept such a plug instead. If it is necessary to remove the ground wire on any fixture, control, or device during servicing, be sure to replace it before restoring the current.

For portable tools, the best protection against shock, especially when working outdoors or in damp locations, is to use an extension cord protected by a ground fault circuit interrupter (GFCI). This device will detect if a current as low as 5 milliamperes leaks from a circuit (indicating a fault in the insulation) and immediately shut off the current. "Double-insulated" electric tools have a secondary layer of insulation and do not need a GFCI to protect the operator (see *Safety, electricity*, p. 404).

Inductance is the creation of current in a conductor that is moving in relation to a nearby magnetic field. The "induced" current is proportional to the strength of the field, the rate of motion, and the size and shape of the conductor. Inductance is used in many electrical machines, including transformers, motors, and generators. Because of the wave nature of AC, the field of an AC electromagnet is constantly rising and falling, and a current can be induced in a conductor even if neither the magnet nor the conductor is moving.

Power factor (PF) is the actual power available in an AC circuit. PF demonstrates that AC is a wave phenomenon and that the peaks of voltage and current do not always occur at the same time. If they occur at different times, they are said to be "out of phase." This reduces the power in a circuit by a percentage called the "power factor." Power factor can never exceed 1.

The out-of-phase condition is generally caused by inductive loads, such as transformers and electric motors, and by capacitive loads such as capacitors. Heating and other resistive loads do not affect power factor very much. Lowering the power factor reduces the efficiency and power of an electric motor. However, many motors rely on an out-of-phase condition to create starting torque.

Many utilities require that customers set up their circuits so that a power factor of at least 0.85 is achieved. This can be done by measuring wattage and experimenting with capacitors across a motor terminal.

Power factor can be read directly with a power factor meter or calculated with a voltmeter, ammeter, and wattmeter:

$$\text{Power factor (PF)} = W/(A * V)$$

LINE VOLTAGE

Line voltage is the voltage supplied to a motor or device. It is often higher than the control circuit voltage. Motors are designed to operate on a specific line voltage. A voltage 5 percent below or 10 percent above the rating is acceptable, but variation should not exceed these values. If motor troubles are occurring, one of the first diagnostic steps is to measure the voltage with a voltmeter and compare it to the rating on the motor nameplate.

Transformers are devices that change the voltage of the current passing through them. The "primary" coil in a transformer is connected to the input, and the "secondary" coil is connected to the load. Transformers work because the primary coil induces a current in the secondary coil. The ratio of the number of windings in the two coils determines the voltage of the secondary current. A "step-up" transformer increases the output voltage, while a "step-down" transformer decreases it. An autotransformer has a single coil instead of the usual two coils.

A **correction line voltage transformer** may be installed in the line to get the correct value—from 208 to 240 volts, or from 120 to 240 volts.

Rectifiers are devices used to change AC to DC. They are called diodes in electronics and are used to create the DC needed by most electronic devices.

THREE-PHASE CURRENT

Three-phase current is preferrable to single-phase current in large motors due to its efficiency and its greater starting capacity. Several methods are used to deliver three-phase power, depending on the transformer design and the equipment needs.

CIRCUITS

A circuit is a complete path allowing electrons to travel from a source of electricity, through a load (also called a resistance), and back to the source. A circuit must have some resistance. Looking at Ohm's law ($I = E/R$), current equals voltage divided by resistance. A circuit with no resistance has a resistance of 0, so the current is theoretically infinity—a rather dangerous amount. A large current causes the conductor to heat up until (usually) the fuse or circuit breaker blows; otherwise a fire or other damage is likely.

In a "closed" circuit, current can flow all the way around. In an "open" circuit, no current flows because something is disconnected or a switch is open. In a "grounded circuit," a conductor is touching ground and the component will not function. A "short circuit" has no resistance and will overheat and trip a protective device. Insulation failure generally causes a grounded circuit, but it can look like a short circuit in terms of overheating and tripping the circuit protector.

The two basic types of circuit designs are series and parallel. Current in a series circuit passes through each component in turn. The resistance is the sum of the resistance of each component. Voltage is the sum of the voltage drop across each load. The current is equal throughout the circuit, but the voltage drops as the current proceeds.

In a parallel circuit, the current can flow through multiple conductors in its round trip from supply through load and back to supply. Voltage is constant in each branch circuit. Total current equals the sum of the current in each branch of the parallel section of the circuit.

Many circuits combine series and parallel wiring and are thus called series-parallel circuits (see Fig. 3).

READING DRAWINGS

Electrical diagrams are the road maps to electrical circuits. Drawings describe what controls and switches are in a system, how they are linked together, and (sometimes) where the components are located. Service people must read electrical diagrams for trouble-shooting or to help an electrician install a sysytem. (Electricians may not know enough about cooling equipment to do the wiring properly.)

Diagrams rely on a uniform series of symbols that are shown in Table B3. Symbols unique to a particular manufacturer are usually defined in a block on the diagram.

Refer to electrical diagrams when attempting to diagnose any suspected electrical problem.

Read a diagram by starting at the power supply and working toward the suspect component. Note which terminals the current should pass through and which switches and contacts control the current. Test the current at these locations to see whether it is being switched off improperly.

Three types of drawings may be used to describe electrical circuits in a cooling system. Some diagrams are really a combination of diagram types or divide the whole into sections that are easier to read. Some manufacturers supply multiple types of diagrams to simplify matters.

1. A connection diagram shows the components in their relative positions. Terminals are numbered, but wires are not shown. Terminals with the same number are connected by a wire. This method is often used for control panels in large systems. It is easy to read because there is no need to trace through a maze of wires. You can tell at a glance whether relays are open or closed. This diagram may be combined with a schematic diagram.

2. A schematic diagram shows symbols for the various components,

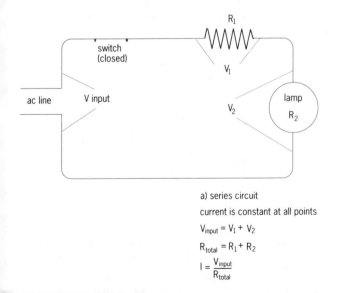

a) series circuit

current is constant at all points

$V_{input} = V_1 + V_2$

$R_{total} = R_1 + R_2$

$I = \dfrac{V_{input}}{R_{total}}$

Fig. B3 Circuit types

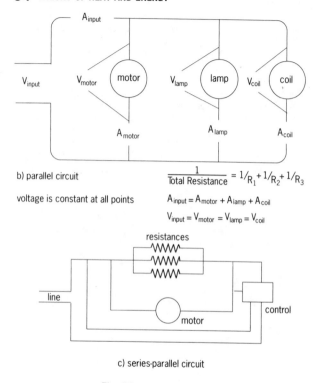

b) parallel circuit

$$\frac{1}{\text{Total Resistance}} = 1/R_1 + 1/R_2 + 1/R_3$$

voltage is constant at all points

$$A_{input} = A_{motor} + A_{lamp} + A_{coil}$$

$$V_{input} = V_{motor} = V_{lamp} = V_{coil}$$

c) series-parallel circuit

Fig. B3 Circuit types (cont.)

and links them with lines indicating wires. The diagram can be laid out vertically or horizontally. Power wiring is usually shown heavier than other wiring; power supply is usually located at the top or left side. Wire colors and terminal colors may be noted to help trace the connections. Schematics are mostly used to diagram control systems.

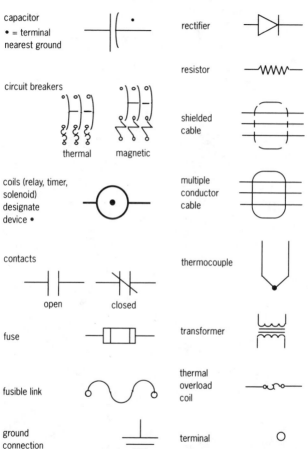

capacitor
• = terminal
nearest ground

rectifier

resistor

circuit breakers

thermal   magnetic

shielded
cable

coils (relay, timer,
solenoid)
designate
device •

multiple
conductor
cable

contacts

open   closed

thermocouple

fuse

transformer

fusible link

thermal
overload
coil

ground
connection

terminal

TABLE B3 ELECTRICAL SYMBOLS

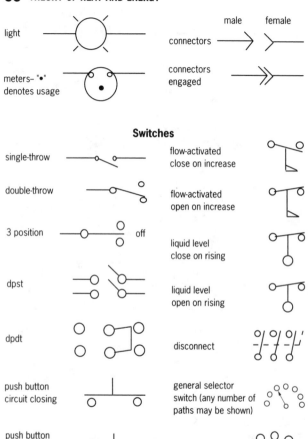

TABLE B3 (cont.) ELECTRICAL SYMBOLS

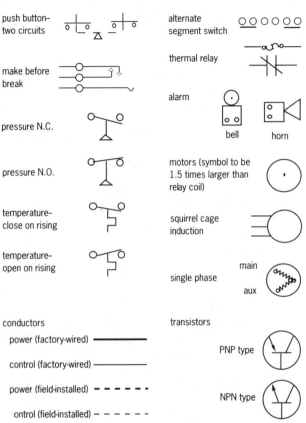

push button–
two circuits

alternate
segment switch

thermal relay

make before
break

alarm

pressure N.C.

bell   horn

pressure N.O.

motors (symbol to be
1.5 times larger than
relay coil)

temperature–
close on rising

squirrel cage
induction

temperature–
open on rising

single phase

main

aux

conductors

power (factory-wired)

control (factory-wired)

power (field-installed)

control (field-installed)

transistors

PNP type

NPN type

ELECTRICAL SYMBOLS RECOMMENDED BY THE R.S.E.S. EDUCATIONAL ASSISTANCE COMMITTEE.

TABLE B3 (cont.) ELECTRICAL SYMBOLS

A schematic diagram follows these conventions:

- *Switches and relays are shown in the deenergized position.*
- *A switch is always located between motor windings and L1 (the hot wire) in single-phase motors.*
- *Lower-voltage circuits are shown toward the bottom of the diagram.*

The ladder (or vertical) type of schematic use the same conventions as the standard schematic. The supply wiring is located at the left and right sides and the "rungs" are individual circuit branches connecting them. Power wires to the motors are not usually shown. Lines are numbered because switches in one line may affect actions in another line. The contacts controlled by an electromagnetic relay are usually listed alongside it.

3. A line diagram shows each component as a unit. All switches that are physically located on the component are placed together. Connecting wires run from hot to ground through each component, so you can find problems with components by locating and testing switches and controls that affect their operation. The diagram shows both control circuits and the line voltagé circuits. Power wiring is shown heavier than other wiring. This can get pretty confusing and cluttered but it does show the action of the contacts.

ELECTRICAL CODES

The National Electric Code has been developed to standardize safe practices in electrical construction and installation. Many localities add regulations to the National Code. The National Code permits cooling system technicians to make Class 2 connections. Class 2 circuits are used in relays, control, signals, and communications.

Class 2 is defined as up to approximately 100 volt-amperes:

Less than 15 V	up to 5 A
15 to 30 V	up to 3 A
30 to 60 V	up to 1.5 A
Above 60 V	less than 1 A

ACIDITY

Solutions have a quality called acidity or alkalinity. Acids are liquids with an excess of hydrogen ions, while bases are liquids with the ability to take up extra hydrogen ions. Thus, acids and bases neutralize each other.

Acidity and alkalinity are measured on the pH scale. pH 7 is neutral; numbers higher are basic and lower are acidic. Because each unit below 7 indicates a tenfold increase in acidity, pH 5 is 100 times as acidic as pH 7. pH 3 is 100 times more acidic than pH 5.

MEASURING SYSTEMS

Two types of measuring units may be used to engineer and repair air-conditioning and refrigeration equipment. The English, or United States system, uses the familiar feet and inches, pounds, and degrees Fahrenheit. The SI (International) system of units uses either centimeter-gram-second (cgs), or meter-kilogram-second. For a multitude of reasons, the SI system is accepted among scientists and practically every nation in the world, with the exception of the United States. One good reason to use the SI system is the ease of converting from one unit to another. One meter is 1000 millimeters. One cubic centimeter of water weighs almost exactly one gram. One watt equals one joule per second. These conventions simplify calculations in the SI system.

In the United States system, energy is measured in foot/pounds (ft. lbs.). One ft. lb. is a force of one pound operating through a distance of one foot. In the SI system, work is measured in joules, a force of one newton operating through one meter. One joule = 1 newton/meter (1 Nm). Electrical quantities are always listed in SI system values (amperes, volts, and ohms). Other measurements, such as noise, time, and rotation, are made in the same units in both systems.

Quantities are listed in this manual in both SI and United States systems unless the conversion is unnecessary or irrelevant. Conversions to the SI system are rounded off to a reasonable degree of accuracy (see Table L1, p. 381 for energy conversions and equivalents).

COOLING CYCLES

A refrigeration system is basically a device to transfer heat from one place to another. A modern comfort cooling and refrigeration system generally uses either the vapor-compression or the absorption cycle to transfer heat from where it is unwanted to where it is acceptable. Within each of these cycles, a great variety of systems can be developed to achieve specific operational and economic objectives. The compressor, controls, and components can be altered to allow cold-weather operation, defrosting, capacity control, or the use of multiple evaporators.

The elements of the system are described in *Compressors, Motors,* and *Components.* The objective here is to describe the two basic systems in terms of energy and basic design.

ABSORPTION CYCLE

In the absorption cycle, heat energy moves the refrigerating fluid and energizes the heat transfer. This contrasts to the mechanical energy used in the vapor-compression cycle. The basic cycle involves the repeated absorption, separation, condensation, evaporation, and reabsorption of the refrigerant. Instead of using a compressor to compress gaseous refrigerant, the system uses an absorbing fluid (the absorbent) to absorb it. Heat added in the generator raises the solution temperature and drives the refrigerant gas from the absorbent (because cool liquids can dissolve more gas than warm liquids). The gas then condenses and is evaporated in an evaporator, much as in the vapor-compression cycle.

Absorption machines have several advantages. They are simple, requiring neither metering devices nor moving parts (although thermostats, fans, pumps and other components are often used). They require relatively little maintenance. Because some absorption systems require no electricity, they can be used in remote locations and in campers. Because steam is an inexpensive means of supplying heat to the generator, absorption systems are also used in industrial refrigeration and in chilling applications in buildings, such as hospitals or laboratories, which have a year-round supply of steam.

VAPOR-COMPRESSION CYCLE

Most refrigeration units move heat with the use of the vapor-compression cycle (also called mechanical refrigeration cycle). In this cycle, a refrigerant in the vapor phase is compressed to a hot, high-pressure gas, cooled and condensed to a liquid, evaporated to a cold gas, and compressed again.

Vapor-compression cycle systems have a high-pressure side and a low-pressure side. The high side starts at the compressor outlet and ends at the metering device. In this side, the refrigerant exists as first a hot, high-pressure vapor and then as a warm, high-pressure liquid. The low side starts at the metering device and ends at the compressor outlet. Pressure on each side of the system remains relatively constant: pressure drops at the metering device and increases at the compressor.

ENERGY IN THE VAPOR-COMPRESSION CYCLE

Electrical energy in the vapor-compression cycle is converted to magnetic and then mechanical energy in the motor. This mechanical energy moves the compressor, which compresses the gas and adds heat energy to the refrigerant.

Because the cycle is continuous, it can be said to begin at any point (see Fig. B4). High-pressure liquid refrigerant is held in the receiver (A) at roughly ambient temperature. The liquid line (B) conveys refrigerant to the metering device (C), which allows the liquid refrigerant to enter the evaporator (D) at reduced pressure. This reduction in pressure causes the refrigerant to boil to form a cold vapor. The latent heat which creates the boiling is extracted from the cooled space outside the evaporator. The evaporator is linked by the suction line (E) to the compressor (F), which pulls refrigerant from the evaporator into the compressor. The compressor compresses the gas, adding energy and raising the temperature. Hot gas leaves the compressor through the discharge line (G) and enters the condenser (H), where the latent heat of vaporization is lost to the surrounding air or water. The refrigerant condenses and

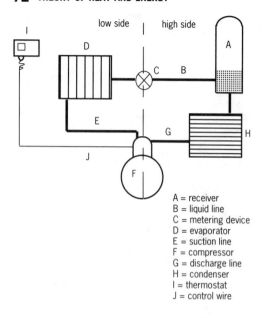

Fig. B4 Stages of the vapor-compression refrigeration cycle

the liquid passes through another liquid line to the receiver (A), to complete the cycle. The system is commonly controlled by a thermostat (I) which measures temperature in the cooled space and signals the motor to operate as needed through the control wire (J).

The refrigerant remains in a saturated condition at every point in the evaporator where both liquid and vapor refrigerant are present. Thus the inside of the evaporator has a characteristic pressure-temperature of saturation and the temperature does not rise while the refrigerant absorbs the heat of vaporization. This allows the evaporator to cool the load evenly, with the rate of heat transfer from the evaporator being determined largely by surface area, temperature difference, and refrigerant flow rate.

THE PRESSURE-HEAT DIAGRAM

Engineers use a diagram called a pressure-heat (also called a pressure-enthalpy) diagram to describe the interactions of heat, pressure, temperature, heat content, and cooling capacity of a vapor-compression system. This diagram charts pressure along the vertical axis and enthalpy (the heat content of the refrigerant compared to a reference value) along the horizontal axis.

Table B4 is a pressure-heat diagram showing energy flow and changes of state in the vapor-compression cycle.

The curve for the refrigerant crosses several important lines and areas in the pressure-heat diagram:

In the *all-liquid area*, all refrigerant is a subcooled liquid.

In the *all-vapor area*, all refrigerant is a superheated gas.

In the *liquid-vapor area* (also called saturated vapor area), refrigerant is a saturated mix of liquid and vapor. This condition is found in both the condenser and the evaporator.

The *saturated liquid line* separates the liquid-vapor area from the all-liquid area. Refrigerant along this line is not subcooled, but it becomes subcooled is it enters the all-liquid area.

The *saturated vapor line* separates the liquid-vapor area from the all-vapor area. Superheating begins as soon as the gas moves past this line into the all-vapor area.

The *line of constant quality* is a line along which the refrigerant has constant proportions of gas and liquid.

The *line of constant heat* (enthalpy) is a vertical line along which refrigerant has equal total heat content.

The *line of constant temperature* marks locations along which the refrigerant has constant temperature. The line is vertical in the all-liquid area, horizontal in the saturated vapor area, and nearly vertical in the all-vapor area.

The *line of constant pressure* is a horizontal line describing locations with constant pressure.

The pressure-heat relationships of the refrigerant are mapped along the polygon ADEFG. The actions of a vapor-compression cycle can be understood by referring to Table B5.

A The hot vapor has been compressed in the compressor and is at

TABLE B4 UNDERSTANDING THE PRESSURE-HEAT DIAGRAM

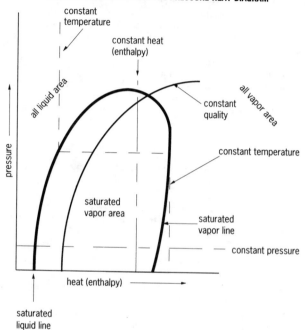

its maximum pressure, temperature, and enthalpy. Without losing pressure, the vapor enters the condenser

B and begins to lose the latent heat of condensation, as shown by the leftward movement (loss of enthalpy) across the diagram. The condenser pressure remains constant while the refrigerant loses heat. At

C the refrigerant is totally condensed and at the saturated liquid line. The condenser continues drawing heat from the refrigerant,

TABLE B5 PRESSURE-HEAT DIAGRAM

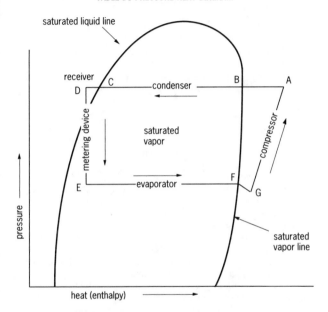

which finally becomes a subcooled liquid and begins to lose sensible heat. Now the liquid refrigerant enters the liquid line. Temperature and pressure remain constant in the liquid line until

D the metering device. Now the pressure falls suddenly along line DE as the refrigerant recrosses the saturated liquid line and enters the evaporator at

E The pressure is low and the liquid refrigerant begins to vaporize. After evaporator pressure stabilizes at E, the refrigerant gains heat and boils until

F when it is entirely vaporized. Now the refrigerant is entirely vapor. This vapor begins to superheat in the suction line until it reaches the compressor

G The compressor squeezes the refrigerant, raising pressure, temperature, and enthalpy, and the cycle repeats as the refrigerant reaches A.

HEAT PUMP

A heat pump is a combined refrigerating and heating system which can use refrigeration techniques to produce either cooling or heating. A heat pump has two reversible heat exchangers, one inside the cooled space, the other outside it. These heat exchangers accept the role of condenser or evaporator according to whether the system is heating or cooling. This allows the heat pump to transfer heat to or from the conditioned space, depending on the control and valve settings. Heat pumps usually employ the vapor-compression cycle, although some use the absorption cycle.

The key feature of a heat pump is a four-way valve which directs the discharge gas from the compressor to the proper heat exchanger (see Part G, *Four-way Valve*, p. 238). (Because the roles of the evaporator and the condenser are reversed in winter and summer, it is clearest to call these components heat exchangers when discussing heat pumps.) The outdoor heat exchanger serves as a condenser during the cooling cycle (as it would in an air conditioning unit) and as an evaporator during the heating cycle.

Two metering devices are required for a heat pump, a thermostatic expansion valve supplied for each heat exchanger. A bypass allows refrigerant to bypass the TXV when it is exiting the heat exchanger at its normal entry point. Notice that refrigerant always flows in the usual direction through the compressor, but that it can change direction in the rest of the system, depending on whether heating or cooling is required. In summer, heat pumps can dispose of condenser heat to the air, water, or to underground piping.

During the heating cycle, the heat pump operates as follows: The compressor pumps hot, high-pressure gas to the condenser, which is in the conditioned space. During the process of condensation, the refrigerant gives off the latent heat of condensation to the room. The high-pressure liquid flows to the outdoor heat exchanger, which now serves as evaporator. As long as the saturation temperature in the evaporator is below the ambient temperature, the refrigerant will pick up the latent heat of vaporization from the outside and vaporize. This gas returns to the compressor, where it is compressed and pumped to the condenser.

During the cooling cycle, the four-way valve directs hot, high-pressure gas to the outdoor heat exchanger, and the system functions as a normal air conditioning system.

A heat pump can only heat effectively if the minimum outdoor temperature does not run much below freezing, and it will be most efficient if the heating load is approximately the same as the cooling load. Some systems have supplemental electric heaters in the inside heat exchanger for use when the outside temperature is so low that the heat pump cannot extract enough heat from the surroundings.

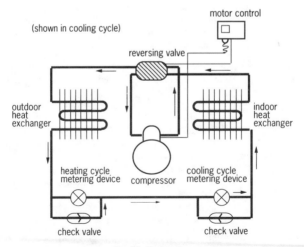

Fig. B5 Heat pump

Corrosion

Corrosion is the degradation of metal by oxidation. Corrosion not only weakens metal but also decreases its ability to conduct electricity and heat and impairs appearance. Unchecked corrosion can cause total failure, but even moderate amounts can cause great damage. Corrosion losses are estimated to cost the United States economy more than $15 billion annually.

Corrosion affects the air conditioning and refrigeration trade in two important ways. It can damage all manner of connections between wires, terminals, and contacts on motor starters and other relays. In tubing and evaporators, corrosion can impair transmission of heat and reduce strength, and eventually lead to leaks and failure.

The rate of corrosion depends on the metal, the electrical and chemical environment, and the effectiveness of any coatings used. Corrosion is greatly accelerated by the presence of acids, bases, water, and salts. Certain metals are extremely prone to corrosion, notably iron and steel, which suffer a special form of corrosion called rust. Some metals, such as copper and aluminum, corrode on the surface but are immediately protected because the oxide adheres to the base metal and hinders further corrosion. Under some circumstances, such as in acidic conditions, this "self-protection" is ineffective and the metal will corrode all the way through. Rapid fluid flow also reduces the effectiveness of self-protective coatings.

Three general types of corrosion can cause problems:

- *General attack is a uniform attack to an entire surface.*
- *Pitting (localized attack) can perforate metal very quickly and is considered the most dangerous form of corrosion.*
- *Galvanic corrosion occurs between certain metals when they touch each other. Galvanic corrosion results from an electrical process and it can very effectively degrade metal. Ferrous metals in contact with nonferrous metals, such as galvanic pipe connected to copper fittings, are subject to galvanic corrosion.*

These combinations of metals (among others) are subject to galvanic corrosion: steel and brass; aluminum or zinc and brass.

Many measures can be taken to reduce corrosion:

- *Prevent contact between galvanic metals.*
- *Minimize system acidity.*
- *Add anti-corrosion solutions to closed-circuit cooling water systems. These solutions are classified as anodic and cathodic, depending on what part of the corrosive cell they coat. General corrosion inhibitors reduce corrosion in both parts of the corrosive cell.*
- *Use effective coatings and make sure they are not damaged.*
- *Install dielectric unions when joining dissimilar metals.*
- *Do not allow condensation to drip onto surfaces where it can cause corrosion.*
- *Establish electrical currents that counteract the electrochemical processes that greatly accelerate corrosion.*

PSYCHROMETRICS

Psychrometrics is the study of the relationship between humidity and air. The topic is important to cooling system technicians because of the intimate relationship between humidity and comfort. Because evaporation from the skin is a major source of cooling, temperatures that are comfortable when humidity is low can be unbearable when humidity is high. Humidity is nearly as important as temperature when analyzing complaints about human comfort.

Although psychrometrics properly is limited to humidity and air, the study of comfort is not complete without considering the third important factor determining our ability to dispose of heat: air flow. Air flow can increase the amount of evaporation (aside from its benefit in providing fresh air and removing odors).

Relative humidity is a percentage reflecting the degree of water vapor that is held in air compared to what it could hold at its temperature.

$$\text{Relative humidity} = \frac{\text{absolute humidity}}{\text{maximum possible humidity}}$$

Absolute humidity is the number of grains or pounds of moisture per pound of air. (One pound equals 7,000 grains.) This value does not change as a given volume of air warms or cools, unless condensation takes place. Relative humidity, however, does change as a volume of air warms or cools. As air warms, it gains ability to hold moisture, and relative humidity falls even if absolute humidity remains the same. (This is why houses can be so dry in winter—the cold air that is heated has little moisture, and when it warms, its relative humidity plummets.)

As air cools, it loses the ability to hold moisture. When the temperature falls far enough, it reaches the dew point, the temperature at which relative humidity reaches 100 percent. Further cooling will produce condensation on the walls of the container or rain. This reduction in air's ability to hold moisture accounts for condensation that builds up on evaporators. While this condensation can cause frost problems, in some cases it is beneficial. For example, condensation lowers the absolute (and relative) humidity in a comfort cooling system, greatly increasing comfort in humid weather.

Psychrometrics is also important in commercial cooling applications. Each stored food product has an ideal temperature and humidity that the cooling system should attain.

MEASURING HUMIDITY

Humidity can be measured in a number of ways. Direct-reading instruments are available, but for much less money, you can buy a sling psychrometer or aspiring thermometer, which will enable you to measure wet-bulb and dry-bulb temperatures (see Part A, *Temperature Measuring Devices*, p. 19). These readings can be converted into relative humidity with a relative humidity table as follows:

1. Swing the sling psychrometer around (or run the aspiring thermometer) until both thermometers reach stable readings.

2. Note both wet- and dry-bulb readings.

3. Subtract the dry-bulb reading from the wet-bulb reading to find the wet-bulb depression.

4. Find the dry-bulb reading on the left column and the wet-bulb depression on the top row.

5. Read down from the top and across from the left, and read relative humidity at the intersection (see Table B6).

TABLE B6
RELATIVE HUMIDITY
Wet Bulb Depression

Dry Bulb Degrees F	1	2	3	4	5	6	7	8	9	10	12	14	16	18	20
30	89	78	67	56	46	36	26	16	6						
32	89	79	69	59	49	39	30	20	11	2					
34	90	81	71	62	52	43	34	25	16	8					
36	91	82	73	64	55	46	38	29	21	13					
38	91	83	75	66	58	50	42	33	25	17	2				
40	92	83	75	68	60	52	45	37	29	22	7				
42	92	85	77	69	62	55	47	40	33	26	12	2			
44	93	85	78	71	63	56	49	43	36	30	16	7			
46	93	86	79	72	65	58	52	45	39	32	20	11			
48	93	86	79	73	66	60	54	47	41	35	23	15			
50	93	87	80	74	67	61	55	49	43	38	27	20	5		
55	94	88	82	76	70	65	59	54	49	43	34	26	14	5	
60	94	89	83	78	73	68	63	58	53	48	40	32	21	13	5
65	95	90	85	80	75	70	66	61	56	52	44	37	27	20	12
70	95	90	86	81	77	72	68	64	59	55	48	42	33	25	19
72	95	91	86	82	77	73	69	65	61	57	49	43	34	28	21
74	95	91	86	82	78	74	69	65	61	58	50	45	36	29	23
76	96	91	87	82	78	74	70	66	63	59	51	46	38	31	25
78	96	91	87	83	79	75	71	67	63	60	53	47	39	33	27
80	96	91	87	83	79	75	72	68	64	61	54	49	41	35	29
85	96	92	88	84	81	76	73	70	66	62	56	49	44	38	33
90	96	92	89	85	81	78	74	71	68	65	58	52	47	41	36
95	96	93	89	85	82	79	75	72	69	66	61	55	50	43	38
100	96	93	89	86	83	80	77	73	70	68	62	56	51	46	41

For example, if the wet-bulb reading is 74°F (23.3°C) and the dry-bulb reading is 70°F (21°C), the wet-bulb depression is 4°F (2.2°C) and the relative humidity is 81 percent.

A psychrometric chart is a graph showing the relationship of many physical variables in a volume of air. A complete psychrometric chart will have this information: absolute humidity, temperature (dry bulb and wet bulb), dew point, vapor pressure, total heat (enthalpy), and relative humidity. If you know any two of these quantities about a volume of air, you can find any other factor from the chart. The chart is often used to convert readings from a sling psychrometer into relative humidity.

To read relative humidity with a psychrometric chart, follow steps 1 and 2 above and then:

TABLE B7 PSYCHROMETRIC CHART

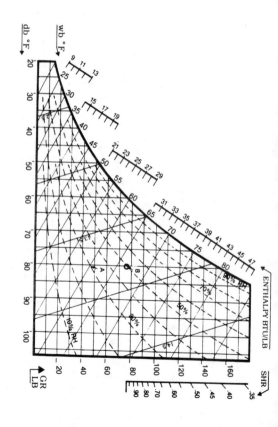

Dotted lines indicate relative humidity in percent. Dry bulb (db) temperature is shown at bottom. Wet bulb (wb) temperature is on uppermost curve. Right side gives grams/lb. (GR/LB). Point A indicates relative humidity of 30 percent. Note reading of '35 cu. ft. near center. This is volume of 1 lb. of air at dry bulb temperature and grains/lb. given at crossing points. See Fig. 18-34. Also note 'SHR' scale, each line of which angles away from central comfort zone point B. SHR means Sensible Heat Ratio.

(Reprinted from AIR CONDITIONING CONTRACTORS OF AMERICA'S (ACCA) Basic Installation Manual by permission of ACCA)

3. Find the dry-bulb temperature on the bottom scale, marked db °F.

4. Find the wet-bulb temperature on the curving scale on the top, marked wb °F.

5. Follow the line sloping toward the lower right from the wet-bulb scale.

6. Read the relative humidity at the intersection of this line with the line curving toward the upper right (this line is marked %) (see Table B7).

EXAMPLE: If the dry-bulb temperature is 80°F (26.7°C) and the wet-bulb temperature is 60°F (15.6°C), the relative humidity is 30 percent.

COMPRESSORS

Modern vapor-compression systems for comfort cooling and refrigeration use one of four types of compressors: reciprocating, rotary, helical (screw-type), and centrifugal.

In some systems, the compressor is driven by an external motor (called open-drive or open system). These systems are easier to service but the seal on the crankshaft bearing can be a big source of leaks. Open system drives commonly use V belts or flexible couplings to transmit power from the motor to the compressor.

The second major category is the hermetic system, in which the motor is placed inside a housing with the compressor. In hermetic systems, the motor is cooled by refrigerant vapor rather than outside air, the crankcase serves as the intake manifold, and intake valves need not be directly connected to the suction line. Hermetic systems have fewer leak problems than open systems because they have no crankcase seal. However, hermetics are more difficult to service, although some components subject to failure are usually placed outside the housing. These components are connected to the compressor and motor by leakproof devices. Motors in hermetic systems must not emit arcs (so they cannot use brushes) as they would pollute the refrigerant and oil, and cause a burnout.

Hermetic systems are classified as 1) full hermetic or 2) serviceable hermetic (semi-hermetic). Many smaller hermetics, especially those used for domestic refrigerators, have welded housings that are not serviceable. If the motor or compressor fails, the entire unit must be replaced.

Semi-hermetic systems are commonly used in large reciprocating and centrifugal compressors. The housing in a semi-hermetic system is bolted and gasketed together and may be dismantled for major service operations.

COOLING

Compressors build up considerable heat in the course of compressing refrigerant vapor. Most of this heat travels with the high-pressure vapor to the condenser, but the compressor head must also dispose of unwanted heat to remain within safe operating temperatures. This is normally accomplished with either fins or water passages.

In hermetic and semi-hermetic systems, the suction line feeds a stream of cool refrigerant to the cylinder heads. Thus, the temperature and pressure of the suction gas are critical to maintaining proper compressor temperature. Suction gas entering the compressor should not be above 65°F (18°C) on a low-temperature installation, or 90°F (32°C) on a high-temperature system. A hotter gas is less dense and will pick up less heat in the compressor because there is less of a temperature differential between the motor and the suction gas. The low-pressure cutout protects the motor from inadequate suction line pressure.

Air-cooled open compressors may be cooled by placing them directly in the blast of the condenser fan. An alternative is to dedicate a fan to compressor cooling (see Table H1, p. 282). Water-cooled compressors have a jacket allowing water to circulate through the head. Heat picked up by this water is dumped to water or air in the condenser.

CENTRIFUGAL

Centrifugal compressors use impellers which spin and fling the refrigerant away from the center, using the force called centrifugal force (sometimes incorrectly called centripetal force). Centrifugal force is the principle that allows you to swing a bucket overhead without spilling the water in it. Because each impeller adds relatively little pressure, several impellers are often ganged together to create the necessary high-side pressure.

Centrifugal compressors are used in large systems, often in semi-hermetic or open configurations. The compressor may operate in a system with positive pressure or vacuum in a suction line, depending on the refrigerant used and evaporator temperature desired. A large centrifugal system may be shipped ready-charged with refrigerant and oil.

The centrifugal compressor has no connecting rods, pistons, and valves, so the shaft bearings are the only points subject to wear. The compressor head, or pressure, is a function of gas density, impeller diameter and design, and impeller speed. Centrifugal compressors rotate very rapidly:

Low speed	3600 rpm
Medium speed	9,000 rpm
High-speed	above 9,000 rpm

Power is supplied by an electric motor or steam turbine. Vapor enters the intake on the impeller near the shaft and is taken up in the impeller blades. As the impeller accelerates the gas, the kinetic energy in the impeller is converted to the kinetic energy of fast-moving gas. As the gas meets the housing, or volute, it is compressed, and the kinetic energy is converted to the potential energy of compressed gas. The velocity of the gas leaving the impeller is extremely high.

Capacity may be controlled by vanes in the inlet that regulate the supply and direction of refrigerant vapor. Large compressors, with over three stages, may omit the inlet vanes.

Floodback on a centrifugal compressor is dangerous due to the high speed of the impellers. To prevent floodback, make sure the refrigerant charge is not excessive and that the superheat is adequate.

Many centrifugal compressors have a purge device built in to allow the disposal of unwanted air from the system. The purge unit is a compressor and condenser that draws vapor from the top of the system condenser and compresses and condenses it. Because only refrigerant will condense at the pressure created by the purge system, the air that collects on top can be purged manually through a valve. Liquid refrigerant flows through a float-operated valve in the purge unit condenser back to the main system.

If a filter-drier is installed in a centrifugal system, it can be placed in a bypass around the float valve. Placing the filter-drier in the main output would impair the compressor operation too much. Even though the bypass only takes a portion of the flow, it will eventually remove enough moisture to control system acidity.

HELICAL (SCREW)

Screw-type compressors are generally used in systems with capacity of at least 20 tons. These compressors use a pair of helical screws, or rotors, which rotate together inside a chamber and force refrigerant toward one end of the chamber. As the gas is forced forward, it is compressed into the shrinking gaps between the screws, creating the compression action. No valves are needed at the intake and exhaust ports. Because the rotors spin continuously, there is less vibration than with a reciprocating compressor. Helical compressors are used in open or hermetic systems.

The rotors are termed "male" for the drive rotor, and "female" for the driven rotor. The male, with more lobes, spins more rapidly than the female. Capacity control is accomplished by a slide valve which opens in the compression chamber and allows vapor to exit without being compressed. Some units are able to operate efficiently at only 10 percent of rated capacity (see Fig. C1).

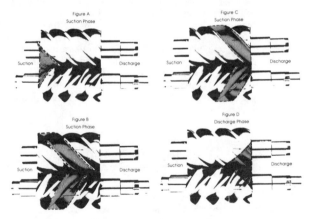

Courtesy of Dunham-Bush

Fig. C1   Screw compressor

RECIPROCATING

Reciprocating compressors use a piston sliding inside a cylinder to compress refrigerant in a structure that resembles an internal combustion engine. On the intake stroke, the piston draws refrigerant through the open intake valve (see Fig. C2, p. 90). When the piston reaches the bottom of the stroke ("bottom dead center"), the intake valve closes and the piston begins rising and compressing the refrigerant vapor. The vapor exits when the discharge valve opens as the piston nears the top of the stroke ("top dead center"). The hot, compressed vapor passes toward the condenser.

At the top of the stroke, the piston must come very close to the cylinder head. The smaller the clearance space, the greater the pressure that the piston stroke will create. This clearance may range between .010 and .020 inches (.254 mm to .508 mm).

Small systems use a single piston, while larger systems use several. The crankcase must be designed to dispose of the heat of compression. Compressor crankcases are made of cast iron and have fins for air cooling or a water jacket, which operates much like an auto engine's cooling system. In semi-hermetic and hermetic systems, cooling is handled by refrigerant from the suction line.

Pistons in large reciprocating compressors have separate oil and compression rings. Oil rings, lower on the piston, are used to reduce the amount of oil entering the cylinder from the crankcase. In small systems, oil rings may be omitted and oil grooves used instead to control oil flow. Compression rings are used to make a tight seal against the cylinder walls, ensuring that each stroke pumps as much refrigerant as possible.

CRANKSHAFT AND CONNECTING RODS

In a reciprocating compressor, the crankshaft converts rotary motion from the motor to reciprocating motion for the pistons. Crankshafts rotate within main bearings which must firmly support the crankshaft and resist end loads placed on the shaft by the motor and connecting rods. The exact amount of end play should be specified in manufacturer's literature.

Several types of linkages may be used to connect the connecting rod to the crankshaft:

1. A conventional connecting rod, the most common linkage on commercial systems, is clamped to the throw.

2. The eccentric crankshaft has an off-center, circular boss on the

crankshaft to create the up-and-down motion. This system eliminates the need for caps or bolts on the connecting rod. Instead, the one-piece rod end is fitted to the crankshaft before final assembly.

3. The Scotch yoke uses no connecting rod. Instead, the lower portion of the piston contains a groove which accepts the throw of the crankshaft. The groove permits the crank throw to travel laterally and to drive the piston only up and down. Both the Scotch yoke and the eccentric are found primarily on domestic and automobile systems.

CRANKSHAFT SEAL

In open-drive systems, the seal between the crankshaft and the crankcase is a common source of problems. The seal is subjected to a great deal of pressure variation and must operate whether the crankshaft is rotating or stationary. Clearances must be accurate (to .000001 inch or .0000254 mm) between the rotating and stationary surfaces, and lubrication must fill that tiny gap. The seal is commonly made of hardened steel and bronze, ceramic, or carbon. The absence of the crankshaft seal is a major advantage of the hermetic design.

The rotary-type seal is a simple, common seal that rotates on the shaft in operation. A spring, in combination with internal pressure, forces the seal face against a stationary seal face.

The major source of problems with crankshaft seals is leakage due to misalignment. Take care when aligning the motor to the compressor so the seal will not be stressed during operation.

In most cases, the seal is lubricated by the oil pump. Make sure the compressor is operated occasionally during long shutdowns to keep the seal lubricated. A slight leakage after startup, during which a dry seal is lubricated with oil, may be normal.

A leaking seal can be detected with a leak detector. To inspect a leaking seal:

1. Pump down the system into the high side (receiver or condenser).
2. Remove the coupling at the shaft end.

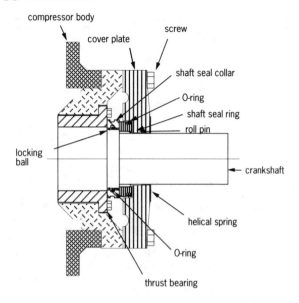

Fig. C2 Crankshaft seal

3. Remove the seal cover and any rings holding the rotating seal in place.
4. Clean the ring surfaces with a very soft cloth.
5. Inspect the sealing surfaces and replace the entire seal if any scoring, scratching or grooving is visible.
6. Reassemble the system.
7. Check the alignment of the seal.
8. Evacuate the system and open necessary valves to restore the system to operating conditions.

(See Procedures, *Evacuating an open compressor*, p. 362.)

HEADS AND VALVE PLATES

Cylinder heads are generally made of cast iron and must be designed to hold the gaskets that hold the valve plate in position against the block. Cylinder heads must have passages to admit suction gas into the cylinder. The head is generally affixed to the block with cap screws.

Intake valves are designed to admit refrigerant during the intake stroke and close during the compression stroke. Discharge valves are closed during the intake stroke and opened at the end of the compression stroke. The valve plate is the assembly holding both valves tightly in place.

Valves are usually made of spring steel and designed to make a tight seal until the pumping action of the piston opens them. The mating surfaces of valves must be perfectly flat, and defects as small as .001 in. (.0254 mm) can cause unacceptable leaks. In service, the valve must open about .010 in. (.254 mm). Larger openings will cause valve noise, while smaller openings will prevent enough refrigerant from entering and exiting the cylinder.

Operating temperature has great effects on valve durability. Intake valves operate in a relatively cool environment and have constant lubrication from oil vapors. Discharge valves probably are the hottest component in a refrigeration system, operating as much as 50°F to 100°F hotter than the discharge line, so they are more commonly a source of trouble than intake valves. Discharge valves must be fitted with special care. Heavy molecules of oil tend to accumulate on them, causing carbon buildup and interfering with performance. Discharge valves and oil will be damaged by temperatures hotter than about 325°F to 350°F (163 to 177°C). In general, keep the discharge line temperature below about 225°F to 250°F (107 to 121°C).

Discharge valves may have a relief spring to enable them to open abnormally wide if slugs of liquid refrigerant or oil enter the compressor from the suction line.

MEASURING COMPRESSOR OUTPUT

Two important statistics that describe the action of a reciprocating compressor are volumetric efficiency and pumping ratio. For information on clearance space, piston displacement, and compression ratio, see Part L, *Glossary*, p. 410.

The following abbreviations commonly apply to compressor formulas:

$$\pi = 3.14$$
$$D = \text{diameter of cylinder in inches}$$
$$r = \text{radius of cylinder in inches} = D/2$$
$$L = \text{length of stroke in inches}$$
$$\text{RPM} = \text{revolutions per minute}$$
$$N = \text{number of cylinders}$$
$$\text{cfm} = \text{cubic feet per minute}$$
$$h = \text{height from piston to cylinder head at top dead center}$$

1. *Volumetric efficiency* is the actual amount of refrigerant gas pumped compared to the compressor's theoretical maximum, which is the piston displacement.

$$\text{Volumetric efficiency} = \frac{\text{quantity of refrigerant pumped}}{\text{piston displacement}}$$

High volumetric efficiency is needed for system efficiency. These factors can reduce volumetric efficiency:

- *High head pressure.*
- *Low low-side pressure (this makes it more difficult for the compressor to draw in vapor during the intake stroke).*
- *Large clearance space.*
- *Valves which stick, fail to open fully, or are undersize.*
- *Restrictions in intake or discharge lines.*

2. *Pumping ratio* (sometimes called compression ratio) equals absolute high-side pressure divided by absolute low-side pressure. An excessive pumping ratio will cause unacceptably high discharge temperature, causing degradation of oil, refrigerant, and

equipment and reducing compressor efficiency. In addition, constant pressure on the piston starves the piston pin of lubricant and causes abnormal wear.

$$\text{Pumping ratio} = \frac{\text{absolute high-side pressure}}{\text{absolute low-side pressure}}$$

To understand how a high pumping ratio can reduce efficiency, think about what takes place inside the cylinder of a reciprocating compressor. When the piston reaches top dead center, all the gas is at roughly equal compression. Most of the gas exits the discharge port, but some remains in the cylinder. This gas prevents suction gas from entering the cylinder until the piston drops enough for the pressure in the cylinder to fall to suction pressure. Only when the suction gas starts to fill the cylinder does the compressor have new gas to compress.

For proper operation, keep the pumping ratio to a maximum of about 10:1. Higher pressures cause heat and carbonization of oil in the discharge gas. The pumping ratio may be lowered by raising the suction pressure, which increases compressor cooling (in hermetics), raises efficiency, and reduces deterioration of oil, refrigerant, and equipment.

When calculating pumping ratio, make sure to convert gauge pressure to absolute pressure. For a system with a discharge pressure of 150 psig and a suction pressure of 5 psig, the calculation would be as follows:

$$\frac{150 + 15}{30 + 15} = \frac{165}{45} = 3.7$$

Because vacuum is measured by inches of mercury, calculating compression ratio is somewhat complicated when suction pressure is below atmospheric pressure. Convert a mercury vacuum reading to pounds absolute pressure with this formula:

$$\text{Absolute suction pressure} = \frac{30 - \text{vacuum in inches Hg}}{2}$$

The actual output of a reciprocating compressor depends on many factors. These factors play a role in determining the actual output of a reciprocating compressor:

- *Type of refrigerant.*

- *Compression ratio.*
- *Volumetric efficiency.*
- *Cooling system efficiency and suction line pressure. Cooler suction gas is denser, so more can be drawn into the cylinder.*
- *Cylinder cooling—Good cooling increases volumetric efficiency.*
- *Compressor speed—At high speed, valve inertia can reduce gas flow.*
- *Valve type and size—Large valves with good seals will increase output.*
- *Friction of refrigerant vapor—An elaborate evaporator impedes flow and reduces refrigerant supply to the cylinder.*
- *Mechanical condition of equipment—Good seals, piston rings, bearings and valves increase output.*
- *Lubrication—Proper amounts, type, and distribution of oil decreases friction and promote a seal between the piston and cylinder.*

CHECKING HEAD VALVES

Use this procedure to check the operation of head valves in a reciprocating compressor (see Fig. C3).

1. Install the gauge manifold with both gauges closed.

2. Frontseat the suction service valve C. Crack the discharge service valve just off the backseat to get a gauge reading.

3. Allow the compressor to run down to 10 lb. psig (172 kPa) on the suction side (you might need to hold in the low-pressure cutout by sticking a screwdriver under the lever in the switch).

4. Stop the compressor when it reaches about 10-lb. pressure. If the compressor cannot pull down to 10 lb., the suction valves are probably bad, or a head gasket is blown between the suction and discharge sides of the system.

5. If the compressor can pull down, watch for a rapid rise in suction pressure after shutdown. If this occurs, the discharge valve is leaking back and you must pull off the heads and investigate. Before doing so, discharge any excess pressure to an empty drum or recovery apparatus.

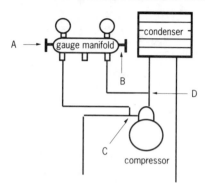

A: low-side manifold valve (closed)
B: high-side manifold valve (closed)
C: suction service valve (frontseated)
D: discharge service valve (backseated)

Fig.C3 Checking
compressor valves

RECIPROCATING
COMPRESSOR TROUBLES

If a compressor fails, you should inspect it to determine the cause
of the problem. Use the following chart to analyze the failure.
Many problems in reciprocating compressors result from problems
elsewhere in the system, and replacing a compressor may not solve
the problem, but only lead to further expense when the real
problem destroys another compressor. For example, compressor
overheating may be due to excess superheating in the suction line,
failed motor safeties, or problems in the lubrication system (see
Part J, *Troubleshooting*, p. 312).

TABLE C1
Identifying Compressor Failures

Most compressors fail due to system malfunctions which must be corrected to prevent repeat failures. After a compressor fails, field examination of the failed compressor often will reveal symptoms of system problems. Corrections will help eliminate future failures.

LIQUID SLUGGING

Broken reeds, rods, or crankshaft
Loose or broken discharge bolts
Blown gaskets

Slugging is a result of trying to compress liquid in the cylinders. Liquid may be either refrigerant or oil or more likely a combination of both. Slugging is primarily the result of off cycle refrigerant migration on refrigerant cooled compressors and floodback on air cooled compressors.

Correction: (1) **Maintain proper compressor and evaporator superheat.**
      (2) **Prevent uncontrolled liquid return (particularly oil) with accumulators.**
      (3) **Locate compressors in warm ambient or install pump down cycle.**
      (4) **Correct abnormal low load conditions.**

LIQUID WASHOUT

Worn rods and bearings
Worn pistons and cylinders on lower end
Worn crankshaft and oil pump
Scored cover bearing and crankshaft

This is a result of refrigerant washing oil off wearing surfaces. Off cycle migration of saturated refrigerant into crankcase. Compressor starts up resulting in a mass of foam which when pumped washes bearing surfaces clear of oil film necessary for proper lubrication. Severe migration results in slugging.

Correction: (1) **Locate compressor in warm ambient or install pump down cycle.**
      (2) **Check crankcase heater operation.**

LIQUID DILUTION

Rotor drag/shorted stator
Worn bearings
Scored and/or broken rods
Scored crankshaft
Worn oil pump

This is a result of liquid refrigerant returning to compressor during running cycle. Oil becomes diluted and lubrication for oil pump and end bearing may be adequate, but

TABLE C1

Identifying Compressor Failures

as it progresses down the crankshaft insufficient oil to lubricate the rods and main bearings will occur. This may allow the rotor to drag on the stator and short out the stator.

Correction: (1) Maintain proper compressor and evaporator superheat.
(2) Prevent uncontrolled liquid return with accumulator if necessary.
(3) Correct abnormal low load conditions.
(4) Check defrost cycle.
(5) Check for oversized TXV.

HIGH DISCHARGE TEMPERATURE

Discolored valve plate
(Cannot rub off)
Overheated or burned valve reeds
Worn rings and pistons
Worn cylinders
Scored rods, bearing, and crank-shaft
Spot burn in stator

This is a result of temperatures in the compressor head and cylinders becoming so hot that the oil loses its ability to lubricate.

Correction: (1) High compression ratio: check for low suction and high discharge pressures. Low load and evaporator problems.
(2) Check low pressure control setting.
(3) Check for dirty condenser, inoperative condenser fan and ambient temperature.
(4) Check air flow across compressor.

LACK OF OIL

Scored bearings
Broken rods
Scored crankshaft
Low oil in crankcase

This is a result of lack of enough oil in crankcase to properly lubri-cate the running gear.

Correction: (1) Check oil failure switch operation.
(2) Check pipe sizing and also for oil traps.
(3) Check for inadequate defrost.
(4) Correct abnormal low load conditions.
(5) Eliminate short cycling.

Rotary

Rotary compressors use one or more blades to create the compressing action inside a cylinder. Unlike the reciprocating compressor, no piston is used. There are two basic types—the rotating vane and the stationary blade.

In both types, the blade must be able to slip within its housing to accommodate the motion of the impeller, which rotates off center within the cylinder. Inlet ports are much larger than discharge ports because the discharge gas is much denser than the inlet gas. There is no need for intake and discharge valves, eliminating a major source of trouble. However, check valves are desirable in the suction line to prevent oil and high-pressure vapor from entering the evaporator when the compressor is not operating (see Fig. C4).

Tolerances are so tight in rotary compressors that gaskets are not needed.

ROTATING BLADE (VANE)

In a rotating vane design, a shaft rotates inside a cylinder, but the center axes of the cylinder and the shaft are not identical. The rotating shaft has several grooves that accept the sliding vanes. As the shaft spins, these vanes are forced against the cylinder by centrifugal force. As gas enters the compressor from the suction line, it is swept around by the vanes. Because the rotor is not centered in the cylinder, the space holding the gas decreases as the vanes force the gas around the cylinder. The result is compression. When the gas reaches minimum volume and maximum compression, it is forced out the discharge port. The clearance volume of this system is very low and the compression efficiency very high.

Rotating vane compressors are commonly used for the first stage of a cascade system. These units may have between two and eight blades; larger systems have more blades. The edge of the blade where it meets the cylinder must be smooth and accurately ground or leakage and excess wear will result. The blade must fit precisely into the slots in the rotor.

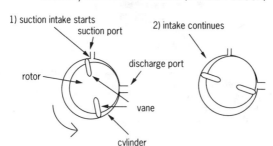

3) discharge

Fig. C4 Rotary compressor

STATIONARY BLADE (DIVIDER BLOCK)

In the stationary blade system, a sliding blade in the cylinder housing separates the low-pressure vapor from the high-pressure vapor. The impeller rotates on an eccentric on the compressor shaft and draws vapor from the suction line and squeezes it toward the discharge port. Pushed by a spring, the blade retracts and protrudes to seal between the impeller and the cylinder.

PART D
CONTROLS

Air-conditioning and refrigeration systems are dependent on several types of controls. In some cases, controls can serve multiple functions, or several types of controls can be housed in a single component. Modern solid-state control systems typically affect a great number of variables from a single unit.

These types of controls are described in this part:

1. Capacity controls determine how much refrigerant each revolution of the compressor actually pumps to the condenser.

2. Operating controls regulate the supply of electricity to the compressor motor.

3. Refrigerant controls, also called metering devices, regulate the flow of refrigerant in the system.

4. Safety controls prevent the system from operating during conditions that might injure people, equipment, or facilities.

Other components that help to control system operation, such as two-temperature valves and pressure limiters, are described in Part G.

Controls may cause almost any sort of problem in a cooling system. However, due to the complicated nature of modern controls, troubleshooting them may be difficult. If a control is suspected, you can try to bypass it and watch what happens. If the problem is corrected, you probably have isolated the difficulty. Another simple troubleshooting technique is to replace the control with one known to be good.

If you are working on an electronic control, use care, as they can burn out quickly. Refer to manufacturer's literature when troubleshooting electronic controls.

Principles of Controls

The goals of a control system are to:

1. Regulate the establishment of design conditions with minimum deviation.
2. Restore conditions quickly when they deviate from design settings.
3. Ensure safe operation for building occupants, products, and mechanical equipment.
4. Assure economical operation.

A closed-loop control system is one in which the controller makes a change in a variable which the control actually senses. Closed-loop systems are found in the majority of air conditioning and refrigeration systems. These elements are needed for a closed-loop control system:

1. A process needing control, such as a comfort cooling system or a walk-in cooler.
2. An element capable of sensing a disturbance in the controlled variable, such as the bimetallic strip in a thermostat.
3. A controller that receives a signal from the sensor and causes some action (such as sending a signal) if the set point is exceeded.
4. A final control element that acts in response to the signal received from the controller (the compressor motor relay).

These are some important means of detecting disturbance—the first step in establishing control:

Liquid level	Float
	Static pressure element
Pressure	Diaphragm
	Bellows
	Pressure bell
	Piezoelectric crystal
Temperature	Bimetallic strip or coil
	Rod-and-tube element
	Sealed bellows
	Remote bulb
	Thermistor
	Resistance bulb
	Thermocouple

In recent years, a spate of integrated electronic controls have entered the market. These controls have many advantages in terms of reliability and flexibility, but they can be difficult and confusing to service. It is recommended that the technician become familiar with the most common electronic controls first, and increase knowledge as the opportunities arise. Troubleshooting guides available from manufacturers are a good place to learn the operation of integrated controls. Manufacturers of integrated controls often have their own technicians who are expert in that particular brand.

TERMINOLOGY

A proper discussion of controls depends on the ability to talk about them precisely. This terminology will help you describe problems to control specialists and read manufacturer's literature:

Actuator. A device that converts a signal into a movement that in turn changes the controlled variable. EXAMPLE: a solenoid valve regulating liquid refrigerant flow to an evaporator.

Close-on rise. A control device which makes contact as temperature or pressure rises. EXAMPLE: close-on rise thermostats are commonly used to regulate refrigeration systems.

Closed-loop system. A group of components with feedback. The system is called a closed loop because the action of the final control element changes conditions which its sensor later detects. EXAMPLE: practically all cooling systems have closed-loop control systems.

Control agent. The thing which is manipulated to achieve desired conditions. EXAMPLE: the cold air in a forced-air cooling system.

Control fixture. The fixture containing the control device. EXAMPLE: the cabinet containing the thermostat.

Controlled device. The device which responds to a signal from the controller. EXAMPLE: a compressor motor.

Controlled variable. The condition which is regulated by the control system. EXAMPLE: temperature in most air conditioning and refrigeration systems.

Deviation. The difference between the value of the controlled variable at any time and the set point of the control for that variable.

Differential (two-stage control). The gap between the cut-in and cutout settings.

Direct-acting. A control whose output changes in the same direction as the controlled variable. (See Reverse-acting.)

Hunting (also called **surging** or **cycling).** A tendency of a feedback mechanism to continually overcorrect itself by adjusting too far in one direction and then too far in the opposite direction. In refrigeration systems, hunting commonly refers to metering devices which open too much and compensate by closing too much.

Limit control. A device designed to prevent unsafe conditions in the controlled variable. EXAMPLE: A high pressure cut-out prevents excessive pressure in the discharge line.

Normally closed (NC). A device that closes when the control signal is removed.

Normally open (NO). A device that remains open when the control signal is removed.

On-off control. A switch with only two positions, on and off.

Open on rise. A control device, such as a heating system thermostat, which breaks contact as temperature or pressure rises.

Reverse-acting. A control whose output changes in the opposite direction from the controlled variable.

Sequencing control. A device which energizes several stages of a cooling system according to need. EXAMPLE: a control that signals several compressors to operate in response to load conditions.

Set point. The point at which a controller will act to make a change in the controlled variable.

Slave fixture. A fixture whose condition (usually temperature) is dependent on measurements taken in another fixture; does not contain a device to measure pressure or temperature.

Supply pressure. The pressure of the compressed air in a pneumatic control system. Usually 15 or 20 psi.

System feedback. The return of information about the controlled variable to the controller. Essential for a closed-loop system.

Transducer. A device that changes one form of energy, such as heat, to another, such as kinetic energy. EXAMPLE: the bimetallic strip of a thermostat.

ELEMENTARY CONTROL SYSTEMS

These modes of control may be used in control systems:

An *on–off* (two-position) is the simplest type of control device. The device can only be on or off; it has no intermediate positions. On–off control is suited to simple heating and some cooling systems.

A *multi-position* (multi-stage or sequencing) control can actuate several on–off devices. EXAMPLE: a control used to bring additional compressors on line to meet increasing demand.

Floating control. The final control may take any position between full on and full off. The controller may rest in "neutral" and send no signal to the final control element.

A *modulating*, or proportioning, or throttling, control is similar to a floating control, except it has no neutral zone, so a signal is always sent to the final control element. For example, a thermostatic expansion valve varies the opening into the evaporator in response to evaporator conditions.

A *step controller* can operate several circuits. The controller may have an electronic or mechanical timer, which has a shaft with cams that trip switches to control the various functions.

The final control element generally depends on one or more of these sources of power to make necessary changes in the system:

Electricity. A low-voltage or line-voltage circuit delivers power to a control device. EXAMPLE: a solenoid valve.

Manual. Certain devices depend on a human operator. EXAMPLE: manual-resetting valves and switches.

Oil pressure. Oil pressure developed by the compressor oil pump is directed to devices. EXAMPLE: a cylinder unloader.

Pneumatic (air). An air circuit delivers air pressure to the control element at either 15 psi or 20 psi (207 kPa or 241 kPa). The air presses on a piston to move the final control element. EXAMPLE: a pneumatic valve.

System pressure. The device receives pressure from the system to actuate it. EXAMPLE: the pilot valve on the four-way valve used in heat pump systems. The pilot valve directs refrigerant pressure to the proper spot on the slide that controls flow through the four-way valve. The refrigerant pressure moves the slide, not the signal reaching the valve from the sensor.

SENSING ELEMENTS

A variety of sensing elements have been developed for controls. Electromechanical temperature sensors include:

A *bimetallic element* is a sandwich of two types of metal with different coefficients of expansion. The element bends as temperature changes. Generally the element has a spiral or curved shape, to save space and increase accuracy.

The *rod-and-tube* is a variation of the bimetallic element. A rod of a low-expansion material is housed in a tube of high-expansion material. The components are bonded at one end, and the relative movement of the tube compared to the rod at the other end provides the signal.

A *sealed bellows* is filled with a gas or liquid charge and sealed. As the device warms or cools, the bellows expands or contracts, indicating a change in temperature.

A *remote bulb* works like a sealed bellows: the fluid expands or contracts in response to changing temperature. The bulb is connected by a capillary tube to a bellows or diaphragm, which registers the change in temperature and affects the final control element.

A *fast response element* is a variation on the remote bulb in which a coil of capillary tube replaces the bulb. With its higher ratio of surface to volume, the device registers temperature changes faster than a remote bulb.

An *averaging element* is a variation on the fast response element. In this case the capillary tube is wrapped around a duct to take an average temperature reading.

A *thermistor* is an electronic device whose resistance depends of temperature. The specifics of operation can be matched rather closely to the application.

A *resistance bulb* is a coil of wire around a bobbin. Resistance increases along with temperature, unlike the thermistor.

A *thermocouple* registers the change in voltage created at the junction of two metals as the temperature changes.

SWITCH TYPES
AND ELECTRICAL MECHANISMS

Several mechanisms can be used to control the electrical signal from the controller to the actuator or controlled element. Several of these devices are relays, or power-operated switches. Relays are widely used because they avert the need to run heavy cables between the control device and the motor. Relays save time, space, money, and hazard.

Switches must be able to rapidly connect and disconnect. This reduces arcing, the flow of electricity across the narrow gap that forms as the contacts open and close. Arcing causes heat and corrosion, which increases resistance between the contacts. This increased resistance can lead to switch or equipment failure.

SWITCH TYPES

Switches are classified by number of poles and number of throws. A pole is a single current path through the switch. A throw is a position in which the switch can complete a circuit. Thus a single-pole, double-throw switch has a single power input which can be connected to either of two output conductors. A switch is said to be "made" when closed and "open" when not closed. A single-break switch opens and closes only one conductor of the circuit, while a double-break switch opens both conductors in a circuit (see Fig. D1).

SNAP-ACTING SWITCH

This type of switch uses a sprung piece of metal that is moved by a plunger in response to a signal from the sensing element. The metal contacts move rapidly apart, minimizing arcing. Either spst or spdt switches are possible. The switch need not be installed level, and it can be actuated by just a slight movement of the plunger. Vibration is not a problem. However, you cannot see the degree of contact in the switch. This switch, unlike a mercury switch, cannot be fully sealed against dust (see Fig. D2).

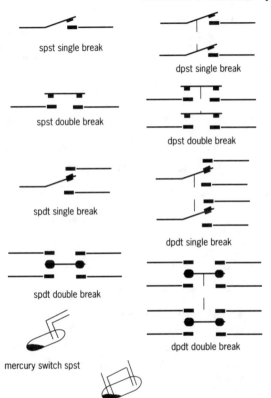

spst single break

dpst single break

spst double break

dpst double break

spdt single break

dpdt single break

spdt double break

dpdt double break

mercury switch spst

mercury switch spdt

Fig: D1 Switch diagrams

MERCURY SWITCH

The mercury switch is one of the simplest types and is found in many thermostats. A bulb holding mercury and contacts is attached to a rocking plate that is actuated by the sensing mechanism. When the tube is tilted toward the contacts, the mercury rapidly flows into the gap between them and closes the circuit. Mercury switches are simple, with sealed construction and visible action. However, they must be levelled carefully and are unsuitable in locations with much vibration or where temperature reach $-38.87°C$, mercury's freezing point. Either spst or spdt mercury switches are made to switch currents ranging from 0.1 A to 10 A.

MERCURY PLUNGER RELAY

This switch is capable of handling currents as large as 60 A. Like the mercury switch, the closing is made by mercury. However, the mercury is displaced by the action of a plunger, not by the tilting of a glass bulb. When the coil surrounding the relay is deenergized, the plunger, containing a small pool of mercury and one contact, floats in the large pool of mercury. When the coil is energized, the plunger is pulled into the large pool, displacing mercury and forcing the two pools into contact with each other. Since each pool is already touching one contact, the switch is closed, and it remains closed as long as current flows to the coil.

ELECTROMAGNETIC RELAY

This is another form of electrically operated switch. Like the mercury plunger, it can be used to switch heavy currents, but it can also be used for more complex switching applications, such as energizing several loads from a single current source or signaling several control circuits to operate in sequence.

A rocking armature holding the contacts is regulated by springs and controlled by an electromagnet. Unlike the solenoid switch, the armature is not inside the magnet but adjacent to it. Each circuit is provided with a pair of contacts, one fixed and the other attached to the armature. When the magnet is deenergized, the spring moves the contacts to the normal position. When the magnet is energized, its force overpowers the spring and the contacts move to the opposite position. The switches can be normally open or normally closed. The relay can contain almost any combination of poles and throws (see Fig. D2).

POTENTIOMETER

A potentiometer is used in proportioning controls to send a signal of varying voltage to another device. The remote device is designed to act in proportion to the voltage of the signal, so it is called a modulating control. The coil of a potentiometer has fine wire with a potential across it. A lever called a wiper slides across the coil and completes the circuit to any point on the coil. As the wiper moves, the resistance varies between its terminal and either coil terminal, so the output voltage depends on the position of the wiper on the coil (see Fig. D2).

ELECTRONIC CONTROLS

An electronic controller is a device that compares the signal from a sensor to a reference value (the set point) and gives an output called an error signal. The error signal is amplified and connected to. the final control element. The degree of amplification is called "gain."

Electromechanical relays, with their superior ability to handle large current, are often used to switch the output current, even in systems using electronic controls.

The most common type of electronic controller is a form of the resistance bridge called the Wheatstone bridge. A bridge compares the sensor signal to the set point and amplifies the resulting error signal enough to make a useful output signal. The variable resistor of a Wheatstone bridge is replaced by the thermistor or other electronic sensor. With suitable modifications, this device can be adapted to all modes of control, including two-position and proportional.

PNEUMATIC CONTROLS

Pneumatic controls generally employ the same combination of sensing element and relay as electromechanical and electronic controls. The air supply—at 15 or 20 psi (207 to 241 kPa)—provides volume to fill the control and associated piping, and pressure to move the final control element in the desired direction.

Two circuits—the pilot and the amplifier—are found in a pneu-

a) snap-acting switch spdt

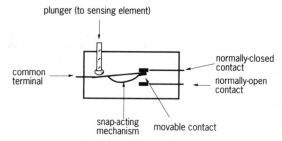

b) electromagnetic relay spdt

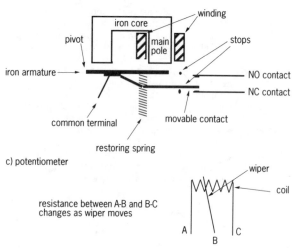

c) potentiometer

resistance between A-B and B-C
changes as wiper moves

Fig. D2 Relays and potentiometer

matic control. The pilot circuit takes the signal from the sensor and actuates a device which regulates the amplifier circuit. The amplifier circuit handles a large enough volume of air to accomplish the desired movement of the final control device. The output signal can be on–off or proportional. The engineer or system manufacturer will supply a pneumatic control diagram.

Capacity controls

Capacity controls are designed to allow a system to meet varying cooling needs. The obvious example is the office building system, which must cool night and day. During the day, the heat load is the sum of loads from equipment, appliances, lighting, solar energy, and human occupants. During the night, some loads are eliminated and others drastically reduced, yet the system must be able to meet the remaining demand.

However, operating at such small minimum load can cause serious problems. Low-suction pressure can cause frosting of dry evaporators and freezing of water chillers. The reduction in suction gas density can overheat a hermetic compressor or impair oil return, causing loss of compressor lubrication and oil logging in the evaporator. For these reasons, capacity controls are commonly found in larger systems instead of just on–off motor controls.

MOTOR—ON-OFF

On–off operation is an acceptable means of controlling capacity in small systems but in large systems it will lead to short cycling under light loads. In some systems, technicians attempt to prevent short-cycling by lowering the cutout pressure, thus lengthening the on-cycle. However, this will not prevent problems due to operating at extremely low suction pressure. Therefore, several more sophisticated capacity controls have been developed: the multistage compressor, the variable speed motor, the hot gas bypass, and various unloader devices.

MULTISTAGE COMPRESSOR

In this system, a number of conventional compressors are linked in parallel. As the load increases, more compressors are brought on line; as the load reduces, compressors are taken off line. Each compressor feeds refrigerant into a header that supplies the condenser. The system has a built-in backup so if one compressor fails, others are available to handle the load. The electric power requirement is proportional to the load.

VARIABLE OR MULTI-SPEED MOTOR

Variable speed motors are sometimes used for capacity control, mostly in larger installations running centrifugal and reciprocating compressors. These motors are expensive and usually require three-phase power. An alternative is the two-speed motor, which may be controlled by a two-stage thermostat that senses the demand and drives the motor at the appropriate speed.

HOT GAS BYPASS

A hot gas bypass directs hot refrigerant gas from the high side to the low side, bypassing the condenser. The bypass reduces cooling capacity because the gas bypasses the condenser and has no chance to dispose of heat. In fact, instead of using compressor energy to cool the conditioned space, a hot gas bypass uses it to increase the heat load, allowing a compressor to operate down to zero load.

When low-side pressure drops below the setting, a modulating discharge bypass valve opens, allowing gas to exit the discharge line toward the low side. The valve closes when low-side pressure exceeds the setting. The valve may be directly operated or pilot operated.

Limit the length of the bypass to 35 feet (10.7 m), and insulate it or there is a danger of refrigerant condensing or oil gathering in it. An oil return, as shown in Fig. D3, may be used to promote oil return in long or cold bypass lines.

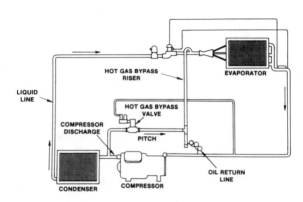

Fig. D3 Hot gas bypass capacity control

The routing of the bypass line varies with the system. The hot gas can be directed to 1) the line between the metering device and the evaporator, 2) the suction line near the compressor, or 3) the chiller inlet.

1. A bypass to the evaporator inlet may be used to vaporize any liquid refrigerant in the evaporator. In addition to controlling capacity, this setup prevents oil logging in the evaporator. The system may be used to modulate capacity down to zero on systems using cylinder unloaders for initial stages of capacity control. This bypass setup does not impair motor cooling because the TXV still regulates superheat. Oil return is assisted by the increased volume of gas in the evaporator. This method is the simplest and least expensive bypass system (see Fig. D3). The line between the suction line and the bypass valve is a pilot line to detect low pressure, indicating low demand. When pressure

drops below the setpoint, the bypass opens to allow hot vapor to enter the evaporator. The valve keeps suction pressure high enough to defeat the pressure control that would shut down the compressor.

2. A bypass to the suction line may be installed in a multiple-evaporator system, or in a system with a remote evaporator. There is danger of overheating the motor in this setup, so a desuperheating valve is needed at the inlet into the suction line, and a mixing chamber is desired.

3. A bypass to the chiller inlet may be used to provide a hot gas cooling load equal to the compressor's minimum capacity with all unloaders operating. Suction pressure and suction temperature are maintained by the hot gas down to a condition of zero actual load.

UNLOADER

Several types of unloaders are used to allow systems to operate more efficiently at low demands. These devices will allow, for example, a six-cylinder compressor to simulate the efficiency of a smaller device. They also reduce high-side pressure to allow the motor and compressor to start easily. The action of an unloader may be powered by electricity or oil pressure. An unloader is able to gradually reduce output down to near zero demand.

1. The unloader holds the suction valves open to cause some cylinders on a multi-cylinder compressor to pump vapor into the suction line instead of the discharge line.

2. A second type of unloader returns refrigerant from the discharge side to the suction side without giving it a chance to lose any heat. These devices are becoming rarer because they tend to heat the compressor. Two varieties are found:

   a. A three-way bypass valve in the compressor head directs gas into the discharge line during normal operation. During low demand, it bypasses the gas back to the suction side.

   b. An external bypass routes refrigerant through a pipe back to the suction inlet. A solenoid valve controlled by a timer (for start-up unloading) or a pressure switch (for capacity control) determines whether vapor goes to the condenser or directly to the suction side.

Operating Controls

Operating controls are responsible for ensuring that an air-conditioning or refrigeration system fulfills its obligations to deliver the right amount of cooling while using the least amount of energy. Many control systems are integrated with other systems, such as a combined heating-cooling thermostat, or a "smart-building" control which governs the operation of fire detection and security devices in addition to heating and cooling equipment.

THERMOSTAT

A thermostat is a control that stops and starts components depending on the temperature at the sensor location in the cooled area or on the evaporator tubing.

Different types of thermostats are used for heating and cooling systems. A heating thermostat turns the system on when the temperature drops below the set point (close on drop); a cooling system thermostat turns on a system when the set temperature is exceeded (close on rise). In practice, both functions often are housed in a single device. (A duct thermostat, or "duct stat" is used to measure temperature in an air duct.)

In addition to turning on a compressor, a cooling system thermostat may operate louvers, pumps, power circuits, or a humidifier.

Solid-state thermostats are now in use, as are devices that have different set points at different times of day. Thermostats operate from 24-, 120-, or 240-volts current. Low-voltage thermostats are desirable because high voltage running through a device can throw the reading off by warming the whole unit ("thermostat droop"). Low voltage wires are also easier, cheaper, and safer to run through a building. Current from a low-voltage thermostat is used to power a relay, motor starter, or contactor, which supplies line current to the compressor motor.

A mercury switch is often used as a quiet switch inside the thermostat.

Systems controlled by a thermostat are subject to overshooting the set point after shutoff. This is because the heating or cooling system is still adding or subtracting heat from the room. Thus, if a cooling system thermostat is set to shut off at 72°F, the room may cool down to 70° due to residual cooling in the duct. In a heating thermostat, this phenomenon can be reduced by an "anticipator," a resistor inside the thermostat that adds a little heat to allow the thermostat to shut off prematurely and allow residual heat to raise room temperature to the desired level. An anticipator may also be used to turn on a cooling cycle slightly early to prevent a room from becoming uncomfortably hot. In buildings with pneumatic control systems, large refrigeration systems may use pneumatic-operated relays and valves. In this setup, a thermostat controls a variable air pressure supply to the control device. When temperature and air pressure exceed the set point, the air closes or opens a pressure-electric ("PE") switch. The electric circuit then powers a solenoid valve in the system or a relay that supplies power to a motor.

To test and calibrate a thermostat, read the ambient air temperature with a thermometer. Adjust the thermostat to make or break at that temperature. You may be able to see when the mercury bulb flips over. As an alternative, use a VOM or continuity meter to detect the instant of contact. If the thermostat does not make or break at that point, try to adjust the temperature setting, depending on the design of the device. The thermostat will also have some sort of delay arrangement to prevent short-cycling.

Programmable thermostats are electronic controls which can vary the temperature according to the time of day and the day of the week, several devices, or allow manual override of the setting if desired. Digital displays are becoming more common, and a battery backup may be provided to retain the device's memory in case of power loss.

Thermostats can use most of the techniques listed under Sensing Devices, to sense heat. The bimetallic strip is a common sensing element for small air conditioning systems.

CHECKING OPERATION

First check the continuity between the thermostat and the motor control. Then make sure all other system components are working properly by bypassing or testing with a VOM. You can bypass a mechanical thermostat and see if the compressor will start, or wire a thermostat that you know is good in the circuit. If the problem remains, look further. If not, leave the good thermostat in place.

Integrated controls and electronic thermostats present a special challenge. This equipment is sensitive and must be tested carefully. Most equipment manufacturer offer troubleshooting charts, which is the best way to deal with these devices.

LOCATING THERMOSTAT SENSING BULB

The sensing element can measure the temperature of the product, of the evaporator or evaporator return air, or of the conditioned space. The major requirement is that the sensing bulb directly contact the area to be controlled.

1. A product temperature sensor is used when the system is cooling a liquid, such as milk or ice cream. The sensor may be inserted into a well surrounded by product and insulated from ambient air. A capillary tube may be wrapped around the drum holding the product.

2. A sensing element may be clamped to evaporator tubing, placed in a well contacting the tubing, wound around the tubing, or affixed to a plate evaporator.

3. A *space sensor* in a cooler should be placed away from doors in a place with good air circulation. Return air sensors should be located in the return air stream to the evaporator, but they should not contact the evaporator.

A comfort cooling thermostat should be placed where it can accurately measure conditions in the cooled rooms. The thermostat should be about 5 feet (1.5 m) above the floor on an inside wall and away from drafts. Do not locate the thermostat near ducts, radiant heating devices, or concealed sources of heat or cold in the wall.

PRESSURE MOTOR CONTROL

In this system, a control operates the compressor motor by measuring pressure in the evaporator or suction line. Pressure motor controls work because pressure is a good representation of evaporator temperature. When evaporator pressure exceeds the control's set point (indicating a warm evaporator), the bellows expands to trip a switch and signal the motor to operate.

Like the thermostat, the method of adjusting a pressure control can vary. Some devices have separate adjustment screws for cut-in and cut-out, while others have range and cutout adjustments.

Pressure motor controls that have been removed from the system may be adjusted with a vacuum pump and a compound gauge.

The pressure motor control, sometimes called a low-pressure cut-out (LPCO), can also serve as a safety control to shut off current to the motor when suction line pressure drops too low. (See *Low-pressure cut-out*, p. 155.)

RANGE AND DIFFERENTIAL

Range is defined as the cut-in and cut-out points of an operating control. Differential is defined as the temperature difference between the cut-in and cut-out points. For example, in a comfort cooling system set to cut-in at 70°F and cut-out at 74°F, the range would be 70° to 74°F, while the differential would equal: 4°F (74° − 70°). In the SI system, the concept is similar: With a cut-in at 21°C and a cut-out of 23°C, the differential would equal 2°C.

Range and differential are vital to understanding the working of operating controls. This is because attempting to maintain exact temperature (inadequate differential) in the cooled space could result in unacceptably short cycling. Thus most cooling equipment is designed to operate within a range of operating temperature and pressures.

With the on–off system, the compressor rests whenever the cooled area is between the chosen minimum temperature and the chosen maximum temperature (between the cut-out setting and the cut-in setting).

Adjusting the range will alter both cut-in and cut-out temperatures, but will not affect the differential. The higher the range, the lower the load on the system. Markings on the adjusting screw may indicate which direction to turn to increase or decrease the range.

Adjusting the differential will change either the cut-in or the cut-out point, but not both. Increasing the differential will extend the on-cycle and off-cycle. Because altering the differential will change the cut-in or the cut-out temperature, it will change the range as well.

FINDING CUT-IN AND CUT-OUT POINTS

Use the following procedure to set a thermostat cut-in and cut-out for a reach-in refrigerator for a product that requires an average temperature of 41°F:

Maximum permissible temperature:	45°F	7.2°C
Minimum permissible temperature:	37°F	2.8°C
Evaporator temperature differential:	15°F	4.4°C

Follow these steps:

1. Set the cut-in at the maximum permissible product temperature (45°F).

2. Find the control differential:

Maximum permissible temperature	45°F	7.2°C
− Minimum permissible temperature	− 37°F	− 2.8°C
	8°F	4.4°C
+ Evaporator temperature differential	+ 15°F	8.33°C
= Control temperature differential	23°F	12.73°C

3. Subtract the control temperature differential from the cut-in temperature to find the cut-out setting.

Cut-in temperature	45°F	7.22°C
− Control temperature differential	− 23°F	− 12.78°C
Cut-out setting	22°F	− 5.55°C

4. If you are setting a pressure control, convert the cut-in and cut-out temperatures to pressure and adjust accordingly.

Thermostats which read evaporator temperature generally have a relatively wide differential because evaporators warm up faster than a cooled space or product during the off-cycle.

CHECKING OPERATING CONTROLS

The following four controls may affect motor performance: pressure motor control, thermostat, high-side cut-out, and oil pressure safety. When diagnosing a balky system, you must make sure these controls are not improperly interfering with the motor. (If the controls are shutting the system down for a good reason, you must turn your attention to fixing that problem first.)

Problems with operating controls can stem from leaking lines, broken bellows or springs, corroded points, maladjustment, or units that are out of level. Replace cracked mercury switches and corroded points (you can temporarily dress points with sandpaper, but never with emery cloth).

If an inspection does not reveal a problem, test a temperature-sensitive operating control by running the system and observing the control's operation, or by replacing the suspect control with one known to be good.

To check pressure controls, install the gauge manifold and use the compressor to run the system until you see the motor cut in and cut out. Compare these values with normal system values. An alternative is to test cut-in and cut-out with gauges and a hand vacuum and pressure pump. For information on testing a low-pressure cut-out, see *Testing Safety Controls*, p. 152.

Refrigerant Control (Metering Device)

A refrigerant control, also called a metering device, is a mechanism that feeds liquid refrigerant into the evaporator at the desired rate and for the desired period of time. By reducing evaporator pressure, the metering device separates the high-pressure side of the system from the low-pressure side. The common metering devices include three types of valve (automatic expansion, thermostatic expansion, and thermal-electric expansion), two types of float (high-side and low-side), and the capillary tube.

All metering devices except the high-side float and the capillary tube use feedback about conditions in the evaporator and/or suction line to regulate the flow of refrigerant. The high-side float controls the level of refrigerant in the receiver. The capillary tube merely presents a fixed restriction to the flow of refrigerant—its action is determined by its ID and length.

The following chart compares some major features of the refrigerant controls:

Metering device	Evaporator	Evaporator type	Motor control
Thermostatic expansion valve	Single or multiple	Dry	Temperature
Automatic expansion valve	Single	Dry	Temperature
Thermal-electric valve	Single	Dry	Temperature or pressure
Low-side float	Multiple	Flooded	Temperature or pressure
High-side float	Single	Flooded	Temperature or pressure
Capillary tube	Single	Dry	Temperature

Refrigerant controls are not equipped to deal with flash gas, the premature vaporization of liquid refrigerant before it passes through the metering device. Flash gas intereferes with correct refrigerant metering and system capacity. Flash gas can be prevented by using a heat exchanger to reduce the temperature of liquid refrigerant, and by minimizing restrictions in the liquid line.

AUTOMATIC EXPANSION VALVE (AXV OR AEV)

The automatic expansion valve, also called the pressure controlled expansion valve, meters refrigerant on the basis of low-side pressure. The goal is to maintain constant pressure in the evaporator while the compressor is running. Because the evaporator never fills with liquid refrigerant, systems using AXVs are considered dry. AXVs are used with a temperature-sensitive motor control, and were commonly used on brine or alcohol-ballasted coils with a relatively constant load. AXVs may read evaporator pressure with either a bellows or a diaphragm.

Three fluid pressures and two spring pressures are responsible for actuating the AXV. Referring to Fig. D4, notice that pressure from the control spring and the evaporator tend to close the valve while atmospheric pressure, liquid line pressure, and the adjusting spring tend to open it. By changing the adjusting spring pressure, the valve can be adjusted to achieve the right evaporator pressure.

The AXV works in conjunction with the motor control to regulate evaporator pressure. As the valve meters refrigerant into the

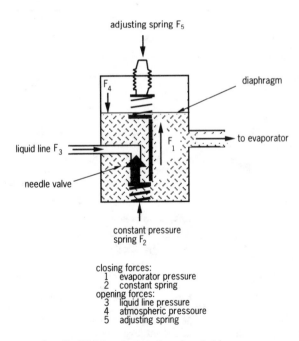

closing forces:
    1   evaporator pressure
    2   constant spring
opening forces:
    3   liquid line pressure
    4   atmospheric pressoure
    5   adjusting spring

Fig. D4 Automatic expansion valve principles

evaporator, suction pressure rises and the valve begins to close enough to regulate suction pressure to the set point. When the motor control sensing bulb detects that the suction line or cooled space is sufficiently cold, it signals the thermostat to shut off the motor. The compressor stops and raises the suction pressure, causing the AXV to close.

AXV capacity should match the load and the system. An undersized valve will starve the evaporator and reduce capacity. An oversized valve will permit excess refrigerant into the evaporator and possibly cause sweating or frosting on the suction line.

Some automatic expansion valves have a small groove in the seat to allow system pressures to balance during the off cycle. The groove is too small to impair the valve seal while the compressor runs, but large enough to allow the evaporator to fill with liquid refrigerant after the compressor shuts down. Balancing the load allows the motor to start more easily. If the AXV has such a seat, an accumulator should be located at the evaporator outlet to prevent floodbacks to the compressor.

INSTALLING AND SERVICING

The AXV is usually used in small equipment, such as domestic comfort cooling, vending machines, and air dryers. The liquid line is usually small enough to use a threaded fitting, although it may have a soldered fitting. Follow these steps to mount and adjust an AXV:

1. Mount the valve at the evaporator inlet.

2. Attach the gauge manifold.

3. Charge the unit with the proper amount of refrigerant (charge level is critical with the AXV).

4. Start the unit and allow it to operate for a few minutes to settle down.

5. Find the desired evaporator operating temperature. Convert this temperature to pressure for the system refrigerant.

6. Move the adjusting screw in or out until the suction gauge shows the desired suction pressure. Some valves have a pressure setting stamped near the adjusting screw. Move the pointer to the proper setting and check the actual pressure with the gauge manifold.

7. Watch the system run through a few cycles, making sure it maintains the desired pressure without hunting.

THERMOSTATIC EXPANSION VALVE (TXV OR TEV)

The thermostatic expansion valve is a very common and effective means of controlling the flow of refrigerant. Like the AXV, it detects evaporator pressure. But unlike the AXV, the TXV detects temperature (and sometimes pressure as well) at the evaporator outlet. The TXV does not sense atmospheric pressure.

In operation, the opening pressure from the sensing bulb and liquid line counteract the sum of the evaporator pressure on the valve diaphragm and pressure from the adjustment spring.

Referring to Fig. D5, notice that the sensing bulb is connected to the diaphragm by a tube. Pressure from the bulb is transmitted through the tube to press the diaphragm and needle down, forcing the valve open and allowing refrigerant into the evaporator. This takes place when the evaporator is warm and the compressor is running. However, the action of the sensing bulb is resisted by the pressure of refrigerant in the evaporator and the adjusting spring.

TXVs intended for large systems use flat seats rather than needle valves. For extremely large units, the valve may serve as a pilot for a second, larger valve that actually meters the refrigerant.

SUPERHEAT

A superheated gas is above saturation temperature for its pressure. In terms of thermostatic expansion valves, superheat is the number of degrees the refrigerant warms up between the saturation conditions in the body of the evaporator and the evaporator outlet. The sensing bulb detects this outlet temperature and allows the valve to maintain constant superheat. A superheat setting of about 10°F (5.6°C) is commonly used. The superheat setting may also be called the "superheat of the bulb over the evaporator."

Adequate superheating of the suction gas is desirable to:

1. Keep the point of complete boiling away from the evaporator outlet to prevent liquid refrigerant from damaging the compressor and;

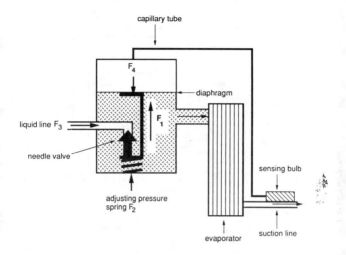

Fig. D5 Thermostatic expansion valve
internally equalized

2. Evaporate all liquid refrigerant for the sake of efficiency.

   Excess superheat may cause:

1. Overheating of a hermetic compressor, which must depend on
   suction gas for cooling and;

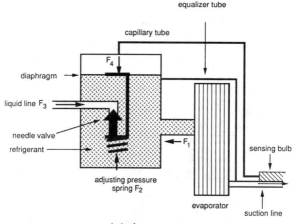

equalizer tube

capillary tube

F_4

diaphragm

liquid line F_3

needle valve

refrigerant

adjusting pressure
spring F_2

F_1

sensing bulb

evaporator

suction line

<u>closing forces:</u>
1   equalizer or evaporator pressure
2   adjusting spring

<u>opening forces:</u>
3   increasing liquid line pressure
4   increasing sensing bulb pressure

Fig. D5 (con't) Thermostatic expansion valve
externally equalized

2. Loss of capacity because the region between the point of complete
    boiling and the evaporator outlet is warmer than saturation
    temperature.

Poor superheat adjustment may 1) tend to flood or starve the
evaporator and 2) lead to short cycling, which reduces efficiency,
stresses system components and may allow liquid slugs to reach
the compressor.

TXV OPERATION

To understand the operation of a TXV more fully, let's watch one
through a complete on–off–on compressor cycle:

Courtesy of Sporlan Valve Co.

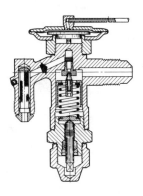

Fig. D6 TXV cutaway view

1. The compressor is running and the TXV is feeding refrigerant into the evaporator. As the evaporator fills with refrigerant, the pressure on the valve diaphragm rises and tends to close the valve. Meanwhile, the sensing bulb is cooling down, reducing the pressure forcing the valve open.

2. The valve closes, and the remaining liquid refrigerant continues vaporizing in the evaporator as it absorbs heat from the load. As the evaporator outlet and the sensing bulb warm, the pressure in the capillary tube from the sensing bulb increases, counteracting the combined spring and evaporator pressure that tends to close the valve. This signal from the sensing bulb forces the valve to open and feed more refrigerant into the evaporator.

3. This cycle maintains the superheat setting and continues as long as the compressor is running. When the temperature or pressure control shuts the motor down, the pressure in the evaporator rises and the valve closes.

4. When the compressor starts in response to warming of the cooled space, the evaporator pressure drops. The TXV opens in response to the combination of decreased evaporator pressure and warming of the sensing bulb.

5. As the evaporator fills, its pressure tends to close the valve, and the cycle continues.

SENSING BULB

Four types of charges are used in TXVs: liquid charged and cross-charged, and gas charged and cross-charged. A "charged" bulb contains the refrigerant in the system, while a "cross-charged" bulb contains a different refrigerant. "Cross-charge" refers to the fact that the pressure-temperature curve of the system refrigerant crosses the curve of the sensor fluid.

Gas-charged sensors tend to respond faster to changes than liquid-charged sensors, but this increases their tendency to hunt. Either type of gas charge is commonly found in TXVs, especially in comfort cooling systems.

Manufacturers of TXVs have charts which match sensor fluid with evaporator temperature and refrigerant for particular applications. The following are some characteristics of TXV charges:

1. A liquid-charged element contains the system refrigerant under enough pressure to ensure that some remains in the liquid phase. This charge is common in air-conditioner controls. The sensor exerts a force on the valve equal to the saturation pressure of the refrigerant at the sensing bulb. Because the charge is the system refrigerant, this sensor can be used at a wide range of temperature and pressures. However, some evaporator flooding is possible as the compressor pulls down the system. This sensor is designed for evaporator temperatures ranging from -20 to $40°F$ (-28.9 to $4.4°C$).

2. A liquid cross-charged element reduces hunting because suction pressure does not rise and fall as rapidly as bulb temperature. This charge is designed for an evaporator temperature ranging from -40 to $40°F$ (-40 to $4.4°C$).

3. A gas-charged sensing element is not designed to respond to an increase in sensor pressure. However, when the sensor gets cold, the gas in its bulb condenses, reducing the pressure and opening

the valve. This charge is designed for evaporator temperatures ranging from 30 to 60°F (−1.1 to 15.6°C).

4. A gas cross-charged sensing element can be adapted to virtually any system operating at a wide range of temperatures. At operating temperatures, all the gas remains as a vapor.

A second type of gas cross-charged sensing element uses a combination of a noncondensing gas and a substance which can adsorb this gas. (Adsorption is the ability of a gas to stick to the surface of a solid substance without undergoing a chemical change.) At low temperatures, more gas is adsorbed and the gas pressure falls. At high temperatures, the gas pressure rises because it is no longer adsorbed. This rising and falling pressure controls the needle valve as with the other sensor systems.

EXTERNAL EQUALIZER

An external equalizer is a small tube connecting the TXV body to the suction line near the sensing bulb. The equalizer allows the valve to read pressure directly from the sensing bulb location rather than the evaporator inlet. This system allows precise superheat adjustments, especially in large evaporators (pressure drop above 4 psi (28 kPa)) or systems with refrigerant distributors.

A valve with no external equalizer is said to have an "internal equalizer" because it detects evaporator pressure internally. Internally equalized valves are used on small systems which have little pressure drop in the evaporator. An equalizer will not cause a problem in a system with little pressure drop because it will still read correct evaporator pressure.

Note that in Fig. D7, the evaporator inlet pressure is 33 psi while its outlet pressure is 27 psi. The closing spring pressure is 7 lb.

With the equalizer, the closing spring pressure (7 lb.) and the evaporator outlet pressure (27 lb. through the equalizer) combine to balance out the sensing bulb pressure of 34 lb., creating a superheat of 9°F.

Without the equalizer, the closing spring pressure (7 lb.) and evaporator inlet pressure (33 lb.) combine to a closing pressure of 40 lbs. This would starve the evaporator and a much higher superheat would be needed before the sensing bulb created 40-lbs. pressure to open the valve. Such an increase in superheat would also lead to compressor overheating.

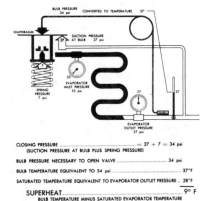

CLOSING PRESSURE .... = 27 + 7 = 34 psi
(SUCTION PRESSURE AT BULB PLUS SPRING PRESSURE)

BULB PRESSURE NECESSARY TO OPEN VALVE .... 34 psi

BULB TEMPERATURE EQUIVALENT TO 34 psi .... 37°F

SATURATED TEMPERATURE EQUIVALENT TO EVAPORATOR OUTLET PRESSURE .. 28°F

SUPERHEAT.. 9° F
BULB TEMPERATURE MINUS SATURATED EVAPORATOR TEMPERATURE

Fig. D7 Function of an equalizer

To prevent oil from clogging the equalizer tube, the equalizer should be connected to the top of a horizontal suction line. If a control valve (such as an evaporator pressure regulator) is installed in the suction line, the equalizer should be between that valve and the evaporator, not between the valve and the compressor (as this would read the results of the pressure regulator instead of evaporator pressure). If a TXV has an equalizer fitting, it must be connected to the suction line—otherwise the valve will not operate properly. The equalizer line must never be capped or kinked.

PRESSURE DROP

A TXV will only operate properly if it receives a supply of liquid refrigerant under sufficient pressure. Excessive pressure loss can cause flash gas and interfere with TXV operation and system efficiency. These types of pressure loss must be totaled before a TXV can be selected or its troubles diagnosed:

Static loss results if liquid refrigerant must be lifted to a metering device above the compressor. Static loss is shown on Table D1a.

Friction loss is due to elbows, tubing and components such as evaporator, condenser, valves. Loss due to one of these restrictions (a refrigerant distributor) is shown in Table D1b. Friction loss can be calculated with information from valve and component manufacturers.

TABLE D1a
Liquid Line Pressure Loss

	Vertical Lift—Feet				
	20	40	60	80	100
Refrigerant	Static Pressure Loss—psi				
12	11	22	33	44	55
22	10	20	30	40	50
500	10	19	29	39	49
502	10	21	31	41	52
717 (Ammonia)	5	10	15	20	25

TABLE D1b
Liquid Line Pressure Loss

Refrigerant	Average Pressure Drop Across Distributor
12	25 psi
22	35 psi
500	25 psi
502	35 psi
717 (Ammonia)	40 psi

COURTESY OF SPORLAN VALVE CO.

SELECTING A TXV

The TXV must be chosen on the basis of capacity, system refrigerant, and sensing element charge. Manufacturers use a color-coding system to match valves to refrigerant. For example, yellow is often used to signify valves designed for R-12. Numbers or letters are used to identify the charge in the sensing element.

The capacity of the TXV must be chosen carefully. An oversized valve will cause erratic performance while an undersized one will starve the evaporator. The rated capacity of a valve is not a good indicator of its actual performance in an application.

TXVs are specified by the system engineer. Replacement valves should generally be exact duplicates of the old valve. When replacing a valve which cannot be identified, or which you suspect is incorrectly sized, the best procedure is to size the valve with a manufacturer's "Extended Capacity Chart." You must know these values when using such a chart:

- *System load in Btu/hour or tons (this may be less than the compressor's rated capacity).*

- *Temperature of liquid entering the valve (use a strap-on thermometer). Nominal valve ratings assume that the entering liquid temperature will be 100°F. The extended capacity chart compensates for other entering temperatures.*

- *Saturation temperature in the evaporator.*

- *Actual, measured pressure drop across the valve (see Pressure Drop, above). Subtract outlet pressure from inlet pressure. Do not subtract suction pressure from head pressure.*

An extended capacity chart may show that a valve has more or less capacity than its nominal capacity. Use of a capacity chart is important because a valve nominally rated at 2 tons may be big enough for a 3-ton system. In that situation, a valve with a nominal rating of 3 tons would be too large, and might flood the evaporator or cause erratic operation. To find the proper valve for a 2-ton system under these conditions, you would return to the extended capacity chart and start with a smaller valve.

INSTALLING A TXV

Follow these guidelines when installing a TXV:

- *Install the TXV as close to the evaporator as possible in a location that can be serviced.*

- *Some valves must be insulated after installation.*

- *Some valves should not be located in the coil area. Place these valves in a warmer location.*

- *Install the valve body in the correct orientation.*

- *No restrictions should be allowed between the TXV and the evaporator. The only exception is the refrigerant distributor (see Part E, Distributor, Refrigerant, p. 167).*

- *Gas-charged TXVs must be installed in a location warmer than the sensing bulb. Do not allow the gas-charged tubing to touch a cold surface other than the suction line as this will reduce accuracy by causing vapor to condense in the tubing.*

- *Water can condense and accumulate inside the flare nut connecting the TXV to the liquid line. This water can freeze and collapse the line, so special flare nuts should be used (see Part G, Tubing, p. 215).*

INSTALLING THE SENSOR BULB

TXV performance depends on proper installation of the sensing bulb. Clamp the bulb to a clean, horizontal section of the suction line near the evaporator outlet. On small lines, the temperature will be the same at the top and bottom of the line, so you can clamp it to the top. On lines larger than ⅞-inch OD, the bulb should be clamped at the 4 o'clock position to get an average reading of suction line temperature. If the bulb is clamped below this position, it might respond to oil or liquid refrigerant temperature instead of refrigerant vapor temperature (see Fig. D8.)

Make sure not to choose a location where liquid can be trapped, as this liquid can vaporize and throw off the bulb reading. Steel pipe may need to be coated with aluminum paint before the bulb is clamped. Protect the bulb from any airstream using a nonabsorbent insulator. In applications where the bulb is submerged in water or brine, insulate the bulb with a pitch having a low melting point. If multiple TXVs are used on several evaporators, make sure each remote bulb measures superheat on the proper evaporator.

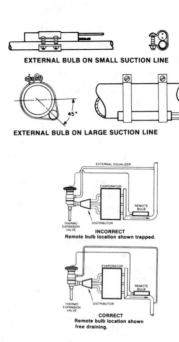

EXTERNAL BULB ON SMALL SUCTION LINE

EXTERNAL BULB ON LARGE SUCTION LINE

Courtesy of Alco Controls

Fig. D8 TXV sensor bulb location

MEASURING SUPERHEAT

You must determine the current superheat setting when analyzing TXV operation and before adjusting the superheat. The correct setting should be listed in literature that comes with the valve. For an older valve, the usual practice is to set the superheat between 11 and 15°F. (6 and 8.3°C).

Then use this procedure to measure superheat:

1. Find the evaporator pressure. Install a compound gauge in the suction service valve (or install the gauge manifold).

   If no service valve is available, use one of the following alternatives:

   a. Place a tee or tap in the TXV equalizer line and attach the gauge to it.

   b. Braze a Shraeder valve in the suction line near the evaporator outlet.

   c. If there is little pressure drop in the evaporator, you can subtract the inlet temperature from the outlet temperature and use this as the actual superheat. This method is accurate only if the pressure drop is small, but it will always underestimate the actual superheat.

   d. Use suction pressure (taken at the compressor) as the evaporator saturation pressure. Pressure drop in the suction line causes this technique to exaggerate the actual superheat.

   Errors resulting from techniques c and d will tend to be smaller in packaged and small systems than in large, built-up systems. For this example, assume that evaporator pressure is found to be 35 psig (344.7 kPa).

2. Tape the sensing element of a refrigeration pocket thermometer or the thermocouple of a potentiometer to the suction line near the sensing bulb. Insulate this connection against ambient temperature. Write down your reading. For this example, use 50°F (10°C).

3. Convert the suction line pressure to temperature with a pressure–temperature chart. Assume the system has R-12. Go to the chart, look under the proper refrigerant and note that a saturation temperature of 35 psig equals 38°F (3.33°C). Subtract 38° from 50° to find the present system superheat: 12°F (10°C − 3.33°C = 6.67°C).

Refrigerant R-12		
Outlet temperature =	50°F	10°C
Evaporator pressure is 35 psig =	38°F	3.33°C
Superheat =	12°	6.67°C

ADJUSTING SUPERHEAT

If a TXV is properly installed and in good working condition, you raise or lower its superheat setting by manipulating the adjusting screw to change the pressure on the adjusting spring. Adjustments are usually needed after someone else has maladjusted the valve.

Proper adjustment requires small (approximately one-quarter turn) adjustments and plenty of patience. Assume the superheat is 15°F (8.33°C) and you want it to be 10°F (5.56°C). The manufacturer's installation slip should indicate the effect of one turn of the screw on the superheat. If the slip is missing, turn the screw towards decrease one-quarter turn and wait at least 15 minutes for the system to stabilize. Working more rapidly will probably cost you more time in the long run. Remember that these adjustments will change evaporator temperature, but its pressure will remain constant. Take the suction line temperature again and convert to pressure and use the above formula to calculate the superheat. Make further adjustments if needed after the system stabilizes. When the outlet temperature remains at 10° above TXV temperature (or whatever your target is) the superheat is correct.

The greatest stability is achieved when the temperature of the suction line remains as steady as possible while the system cycles on and off. This point is called the Minimum Stable Signal point, or MSS.

REPAIRING EXPANSION VALVES

Both automatic and thermostatic expansion valves are subject to similar problems. The following material applies in general to both types, but remember that equalizers and sensing bulbs are only found on TXVs, so any mention of these elements refers to a TXV.

Expansion valves are subject to several problems:

- *Inaccurate superheat adjustment.*
- *Lost charge in the sensing bulb.*
- *Poorly placed equalizer line (for example, in a liquid trap).*
- *Sticking due to dirt, moisture, or sludge.*
- *Dirty liquid screen.*
- *Flash gas in the liquid line due to pressure drop.*
- *Undercharged system.*

- *Excess pressure drop in evaporator.*

- *Inadequate head pressure.*

(See Part J, *Troubleshooting, metering device*, p. 326.)

To *remove an expansion valve*, pump down the system according to procedures given in Part K:

1. Put the gauge manifold on the system.

2. Close the king valve (at the receiver outlet).

3. Pump down the system into the condenser or receiver and shut off the compressor.

4. Purge the liquid line of refrigerant down to about 0 psig.

5. Close the suction service valve.

6. When the evaporator is warm, you can assume that it is almost evacuated.

7. Disconnect and remove the expansion valve.

8. Cap the lines to keep them clean if you do not install a new TXV immediately.

Some expansion valve problems can be repaired, but others indicate a need for replacement. Follow these guidelines:

1. A clogged screen is indicated by poor system performance, or sweating or frosting near the TXV. The valve must be removed or at least purged of refrigerant before service. Remove and inspect the screen. The best cleaning procedure is to use a safe solvent and a stiff brush. Air pressure will also remove dirt. Replace the screen before closing up the valve. Do not operate an expansion valve without a screen in the liquid line entrance.

2. The sensor bulb can be removed with a large pliers and a wrench. Replace with a new element having the proper charge and design. Very carefully unwind the capillary to avoid kinking it. Make sure to make a good thermal seal between the sensor and the suction line.

3. Leaking bellows are difficult to repair. Replace the valve.

THERMAL-ELECTRIC EXPANSION VALVE

This valve uses a thermistor (a semiconductor whose electrical resistance changes with temperature) to sense temperature in the suction line. Resistance in the thermistor falls (voltage remains constant) as temperature rises, causing more current to flow in the circuit. This current passes through a bimetal element in the valve which deforms in proportion to the amount of current. This deformation causes the valve to open as long as the temperature of the bimetallic strip is high enough to keep the resistance low (see Fig. D9).

The action of the thermal-electric valve can be seen from this chart:

suction line temperature rises →	resistance in thermistor falls →	more current flows in control circuit →	bimetallic element deforms →	valve opens

A transformer supplying low-voltage current is wired in series with the transformer and valve. During the off cycle, the thermistor may get warm enough to force the valve open, balancing out the system and allowing the motor to start easily. As an alternative, the valve may be connected into the motor circuit so it only receives current when the compressor runs. In this situation, the valve will remain closed during the entire off cycle.

INSTALLING AND SERVICING

The valve body is installed in the same manner as a TXV. Mount the thermistor to the suction piping downstream from the evaporator.

Service requires an accurate voltmeter and a thermometer. When control voltage is 24 volts, the valve should be fully open. When voltage drops to 0, the valve should be fully closed. Connect the voltmeter to the valve terminals and watch the thermometer to set the superheat.

Using a continuity meter, check the heater which warms the

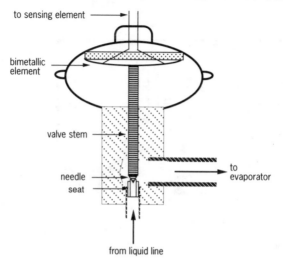

to sensing element

bimetallic element

valve stem

to evaporator

needle

seat

from liquid line

Fig. D9 Thermal-electric expansion valve

bimetallic element in the valve head. If the heater is burned out, the valve must be replaced. Check the thermistor with an ohmmeter. The resistance should change as the thermistor is heated and cooled by refrigerant gas. Otherwise, replace the thermistor.

If all factors are working, then the valve is probably jammed. Pump down the system and inspect the valve. Then repair or replace as necessary.

LOW-SIDE FLOAT (LSF)

A low-side float keeps a constant level of liquid refrigerant in the evaporator. The float pan floats on the liquid refrigerant and actuates a needle valve to regulate refrigerant flow into the evaporator. As refrigerant evaporates, the float opens and admits more into the

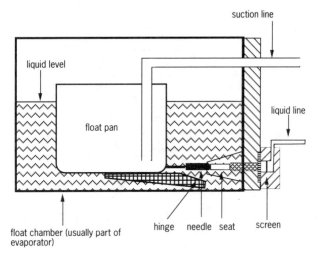

suction line

liquid level

float pan

suction line

liquid line

float chamber (usually part of evaporator)

hinge   needle   seat   screen

suction line is placed in float pan to return oil to compressor

Fig. D10 Low-side float

evaporator. The float is used in a critical charge system having a flooded evaporator (one that always contains liquid refrigerant).

A low-side float will float on top of oil as well as refrigerant, so provisions must be made to allow oil to return from the evaporator to the crankcase. With a pan-type float, the suction line extends to the bottom of the pan to ensure that oil is removed.

The LSF can be used with either a pressure or a temperature motor control, in systems with one or several evaporators. The liquid receiver must be large enough to hold all system refrigerant in case a pump-down is needed (see Fig. D10).

INSTALLING AND SERVICING

Excess or inadequate cooling both indicate a need to check the float. If there is too little cooling, the float may be stuck closed or the charge may be too low. If there is too much cooling, the float may be stuck open or the motor control does not shut the compressor down at the right time. Remember, excess refrigerant in the evaporator should be avoided because it can cause floodbacks.

The adjustment screw may be accessible outside the float chamber. If not, shut valves on both sides of the evaporator or float chamber, evacuate the chamber or evaporator, and make an adjustment. Unfortunately, you cannot see what your adjustment has done until the machine is recharged and operating again. The mating services of some low-side floats may be replaced without pumping down the system. This is accomplished with a replaceable cartridge which is factory-assembled and tested for tightness.

HIGH-SIDE FLOAT (HSF)

A high-side float controls a flooded system by operating a needle valve separating the high and low sides of the system. The float can be located in a float chamber or a receiver. This metering device is commonly used with centrifugal compressors. As liquid leaves the vessel containing the float and enters the evaporator, the liquid level and the float fall, closing the valve and stopping the flow. As more liquid refrigerant enters the float vessel, the float rises, the valve opens, and flow into the evaporator resumes.

The level of liquid refrigerant on the high side remains relatively constant, as does the pressure difference between the high side and the low side. Liquid refrigerant is stored in the evaporator, making this a critical-charge system. The system can use either a pressure or a temperature motor control.

Oil does not cause as much of a problem with a high-side float as with the LSF because oil is likely to dissolve in the liquid refrigerant. However, the evaporator must have an oil return line to the compressor to prevent oil from gathering and starving the compressor of oil.

INSTALLING AND SERVICING

The float should be located as close to the evaporator inlet as possible. If the float must be installed far from the evaporator, you may need to install a weighted valve near the metering device to

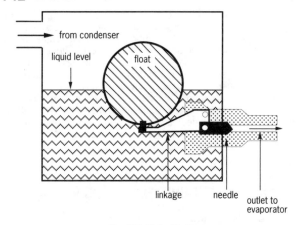

Fig. D11 High-side float

prevent flash gas from occurring in the line between the float and the metering device (see Fig. D11).

High-side floats in high-tonnage centrifugal compressors are installed in the casting of the condenser or evaporator. Otherwise, mount the float horizontal in both directions and check that the float moves freely when it is installed.

Problems in high-side float systems can arise from contamination of the system. Dirt can clog the needle valve or damage the seat. If the valve must be repaired, the charge must usually be removed from the system. With a high-temperature refrigerant with a vacuum in the evaporator, the pressure must be brought to atmospheric pressure before repairs can be attempted.

CAPILLARY TUBE
(METERING DEVICE)

A capillary tube has an accurate inside diameter which serves as a constant throttle on the flow of liquid refrigerant. Five factors determine the rate of flow through a capillary tube: length, inside diameter, configuration, operating temperature, and pressure differential across the tube.

Pressure in a capillary tube system equalizes during the off-cycle, and the charge level is critical. An undercharge may cause the system to run constantly, while an overcharge will cause frosting on the suction line. As with the thermostatic expansion valve, the operation can be assessed by measuring superheat, although the tube cannot be adjusted. A thermostatic motor control is used with a capillary tube.

A capillary tube has two big advantages: it has no moving parts to malfunction, and it allows pressure to balance during the off-cycle. The tube is subject to clogging, but tubes are now being made with a larger inside diameter, reducing the clogging problem (although a longer tube must be used in a given application). A filter or filter-drier is often used at the inlet to prevent clogging and vapor-lock (flash gas inside the tube which reduces its capacity).

INSTALLING AND SERVICING

Although they are simple and have no moving parts to break, the ID of capillary tube must remain at the correct size. Capillary tubes are subject to bending, kinking, freezing, and obstruction. Any of these conditions will cause the refrigerant to gather in the condenser and raise head pressure. If this occurs, you may also see the following conditions:

- *Some frost will appear on the evaporator.*
- *The condenser will be cool.*
- *The compressor cycling on overload.*

If plugging is suspected, start the system and listen near the point where the capillary tube enters the evaporator. If you do not hear a hissing sound, the tube is plugged. Warm the tube with a hot rag. If it opens, ice was the problem.

The following is an alternative method of checking a cap tube metering device (see Fig. D12):

1. Hook the gauge manifold with both manifold valves closed.

2. Crack the service valves off the backseats to get a reading.

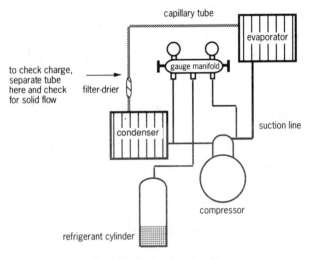

Fig. D12 Checking flow of capillary
tube metering device

3. Hook a service drum to the middle opening of the manifold to provide some pressure.

4. Open both gauge manifold valves.

5. Disconnect the cap tube at the flare near the filter-drier and pull it away.

6. Open the drum valve to pressurize both sides of the system.

7. Hold your hand at the disconnection to check that refrigerant is flowing from both sides. If not, the side without refrigerant is plugged.

Some obstructions may be cleared from cap tubes. Use a capillary tube cleaner to force refrigerant or oil through the tube. Carbon dioxide may be forced under pressure in the opposite direction to refrigerant flow.

TABLE D2

Capillary Tube Application

a) Tubing Specifications

100 ft. Coil Prod. No.	Diameter	
	I.D.	O.D.
122	0.026	0.072
110	0.031	0.083
111	0.036	0.087
112	0.042	0.093
113	0.044	0.109
123	0.049	0.099
114	0.050	0.114
124	0.054	0.106
115	0.055	0.125
125	0.059	0.112
116	0.064	0.125
117	0.070	0.125
118	0.075	0.125
119	0.080	0.145
120	0.085	0.145
121	0.090	0.145

COURTESY OF WATSCO COMPONENTS, INC.

If the tube must be replaced, make sure to use the proper size and length of tube (see Table D2). Do not damage the new tube during installation. Do not cut cap tube with a tubing cutter, as this can crimp the ID. Instead, cut it part way through with a hacksaw and bend it back and forth to finish the break. Capillary tubes are usually brazed into place. Some capillary tube connectors deform when they are tightened, so be sure to replace the connectors when installing a new tube. The cap tube may be fastened to the suction line for cooling. Take care not to solder it shut or allow solder into the tube, and do not kink or otherwise damage the tube.

TABLE D2 (Cont)

For b), c), and d): Condensing Temperature: 130°F for R-22 and 125°F for
R-12 and R-502. Length Indicated is Per Circuit

b) Freezers

Low Temp. Compressor	−10°F Evaporator	−10°F Evaporator		0°F Evaporator	
H.P.	Refrigerant	BTUH	Cap. Tube	BTUH	Cap. Tube
0.5	12	2700	95″ #115	3350	69″ #115
0.5	502	2700	45″ #112	3300	80″ #114
0.75	12	4100	80″ #116	5200	60″ #116
0.75	502	4050	45″ #114	5100	50″ #115
1	12	4900	70″ #116	6200	60″ #117
1	502	4800	60″ #115	6100	78″ #116
1.5	12	6900	105″ #119	8800	72″ #120
1.5	502	6800	60″ #116	8700	55″ #117
2	12	10700	70″ #121	13300	50″ #117(2)
2	502	10600	80″ #119	13200	85″ #121

CAPILLARY TUBES IN OTHER CONTROLS

A capillary tube can also be used to connect a sensor to a controlled device. Capillary tubes are prone to failure if not treated properly. Follow these guidelines:

1. Keep vibration and flexing to a minimum to avoid metal fatigue. Do not route the tube across vibrating surfaces. Controls mounted directly on the compressor should be allowed to vibrate with the compressor. For capillaries that must run from a stable component to the compressor, install a vibration coil to allow the inevitable movement.

2. Almost all capillary tubes will sense the coldest surface which they contact. Unless special capillary tube is used, make sure

TABLE D2 (Cont)
c) Refrigerators

Med. Temp. Compressor		0°F Evaporator		+10°F Evaporator		+20°F Evaporator		+30°F Evaporator	
H.P.	Ref.	BTUH	Cap. Tube	BTUH	Cap. Tube	BTUH	Cap. Tube	BTUH	Cap. Tube
0.5	12	2850	90" #115	3600	80" #125	4100	60" #125	4800	68" #116
0.5	502	2800	100" #114	3550	63" #114	4050	75" #124	4750	52" #114
0.75	12	4260	57" #125	5300	90" #117	6550	55" #117	7200	95" #119
0.75	502	4200	48" #114	5250	75" #125	6500	72" #116	7150	57" #116
1	12	5300	90" #117	7100	95" #119	8600	62" #119	10000	65" #116(2)
1	502	5250	48" #115	7050	60" #116	8550	64" #117	9950	60" #118
1.5	12	9500	50" #119	11500	75" #117(2)	14000	102" #119(2)	16800	70" #119(2)
1.5	502	9400	45" #117	11400	63" #119	13900	80" #121	16700	50" #111
2	12	10000	65" #116(2)	12000	68" #117(2)	15000	90" #119(2)	17500	60" #119(2)
2	502	9900	40" #117	11900	57" #119	14900	78" #121	17400	56" #117(2)
3	12	16000	76" #119(2)	19500	90" #121(2)	24000	52" #121(2)	27000	105" #121(3)
3	502	16600	50" #121	19400	43" #117(2)	23800	58" #119(2)	26800	59" #110(2)

COURTESY OF WATSCO COMPONENTS, INC.

TABLE D2 (Cont)
d) Coolers

High Temp. Compressor		+20°F Evaporator		+30°F Evaporator		+40°F Evaporator	
H.P.	Ref.	BTUH	Cap. Tube	BTUH	Cap. Tube	BTUH	Cap. Tube
0.5	12	3800	70″ #125	4500	85″ #116	5300	90″ #117
0.5	502	4200	68″ #124	5030	53″ #115	6000	86″ #116
0.5	22	4200	94″ #123	5030	70″ #114	6000	48″ #124
0.75	12	5800	75″ #117	6950	105″ #119	8200	70″ #119
0.75	502	6300	76″ #116	7550	50″ #116	9000	51″ #117
0.75	22	6300	70″ #124	7550	53″ #115	9000	83″ #116
1	12	7400	92″ #119	9000	115″ #119	10800	70″ #121
1	502	8075	56″ #117	9650	67″ #118	11500	64″ #119
1	22	8425	98″ #116	10050	62″ #116	12000	68″ #117
1.5	12	10900	62″ #121	13600	110″ #119(2)	16200	71″ #119(2)

TABLE D2 (Cont)

1.5	502	12300	52" #119	14500	77" #121	17500	44" #121
1.5	22	12650	61" #117	15000	60" #119(2)	18000	83" #116(2)
2	12	16000	75" #119	19500	84" #121	23200	82" #119(3)
2	502	16500	51" #121	19700	65" #118(2)	23500	67" #119(2)
2	22	16850	72" #119	20100	80" #121	.24000	55" #121
3	12	21000	102" #119(3)	31300	80" #119(3)	31300	80" #119(4)
3	502	24500	75" #120(2)	29350	71" #121(2)	35000	44" #121(2)
3	22	25275	52" #117(2)	30200	60" #118(2)	36000	56" #119(2)
4	12	28700	100" #119(4)	35700	58" #119(4)	43000	62" #119(5)
4	502	33000	52" #121(2)	39400	65" #120(3)	47000	63" #121(4)
4	22	33700	50" #116(3)	40250	62" #116(4)	48000	68" #117(4)

Remote Mounting

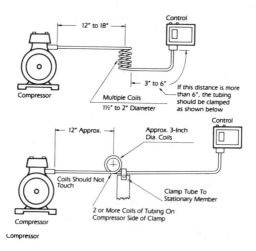

Fig. D13 Mounting capillary tubes

the tube does not pass through ambient temperatures lower than the area whose temperature is being sensed.

3. Coil extra capillary tubing in a 3-inch (7.5-cm) minimum diameter coil. Secure the coil and prevent it from rubbing against itself.

4. Install a soft grommet to protect a tube against abrasion where it penetrates a partition.

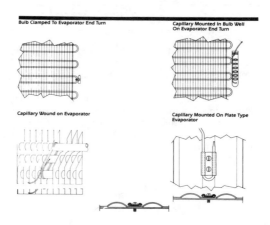

Fig. D14 Mounting sensing bulb on evaporator

5. Do not bend or stretch the tube more than necessary, as this will workharden it.

Follow these guidelines to use a capillary tube to sense temperature in various locations:

1. To measure the temperature of a liquid, submerge at least 4 inches (10 cm) of tube in the liquid.
2. To sense evaporator temperature, secure at least 6 inches (15 cm) of tube to the evaporator.
3. To sense the temperature of an air stream, make an air coil with at least 18 inches (45 cm) of tube.
4. To sense the temperature of a close-fitting well, form at least 10 inches (25 cm) of tube into a bulb and make sure it has direct contact with the well.

Safety Controls

Compressors must be protected from any reasonable source of trouble. All types of compressors are subject to damage from floodbacks of liquid refrigerant through the suction line. This is because they are designed to pump compressible vapor, not uncompressible liquid, and their pistons or valves may break from attempting to pump liquid. Devices are also used to prevent motors from operating during conditions that might damage the motor, compressor, or other system elements. These devices include the high-pressure and low-pressure cutouts, the internal relief, motor thermostat, and oil safety switch.

FLOODBACK SAFETY DEVICES

These devices are designed to prevent liquid from entering the compressor:

A *suction line accumulator* is a tank that allows liquid refrigerant to settle. (see Part E, *Suction line accumulator*, p. 192).

A *heat exchanger* between the liquid line and the suction line ensures that any liquid refrigerant vaporizes before reaching the compressor. (see Part E, *Heat exchanger*, p. 175).

An *electric heater* on the suction line can be actuated by a thermostat. When the line is excessively cold, indicating the presence of liquid refrigerant, the heater is turned on.

A *temperature sensor* in the suction line may be connected to an alarm or a compressor shut-off switch. A fast-acting sensor, such as one employing a thermistor, is helpful in this application.

TESTING SAFETY CONTROLS

The following safety controls are found on most large units: high-pressure cutout, low-pressure cutout, internal relief, motor ther-

mostat, and oil safety switch. These controls are sometimes called
"limits" because they prevent the system from exceeding safe
operating limits. Smaller systems usually have some, but not all,
of these limits. For more on motor safety, see Part F, *Overload and
overheat protection*, p. 196.

Safety controls on large units should be checked at least once a
year during routine maintenance. Testing generally requires you to
force the system to create the unsafe condition and check that the
switch does its intended job. Use care—this procedure may put the
system in some danger.

NOTE FOR HPCO AND LPCO

*The bellows and the capillary or ¼" copper tube leading to it in the high-
pressure and low-pressure cutouts are subject to oil logging, a filling with
oil that reduces accuracy. A self-draining hookup will allow oil to drip
from the tube during the off cycle. The control should be mounted above
the connection for the same reason, and in no case should the lines be
connected to the bottom of the tubes. A large diameter capillary tube,
combined with proper installation, can reduce oil logging.*

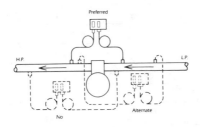

Courtesy of Ranco Controls

Fig. D15 High + low pressure cut-out installation

HIGH-PRESSURE CUTOUT

The high-pressure cutout (HPCO) shuts off the compressor when head pressure exceeds the limit, which is usually about 20 percent above normal operating pressure. The cutout prevents dangerous pressure from building up in the system and prevents the motor from overloading. The cutout has a bellows connected to the high side of the system. When high side pressure exceeds the limit, the bellows pushes a plunger which shuts off power to the compressor.

In air-cooled condenser systems, failure of the fan or blockage of the condenser can both cause excess head pressure. In water-cooled condensers, excess head pressure indicates loss of cooling water or clogged or fouled condenser tubes.

Both automatic and manual resetting cutouts are available. Manual resets are preferred because repeated cycling on the high-pressure control can damage the compressor. However, automatic reset has the advantage of resetting during unattended operation, which can prevent product deterioration. Some controls may be set for automatic or manual during installation.

Head pressure limit settings:

	Water-cooled		Air-cooled	
Refrigerant	psi	kPa	psi	kPa
R-12	150–160	1138–1206	250	1827
R-22	260–270	1896–1965	400	2861
R-500	190–200	1413–1482	300	2172
R-502	280–290	2034–2103	450	3206

The cutout pressure can be quite high on air-cooled equipment, so observe all safety precautions during testing:

1. Install the gauge manifold and crack the the discharge service valve off the backseat to get a gauge reading.

2. a. With an air-cooled condenser, shut off the condenser fan or block the air flow.

   b. With a water-cooled condenser, shut off the water supply by closing a valve and/or stopping the pump.

3. Start the compressor and let pressure build up until the cutout opens and stops the compressor. Keep one hand on the disconnect and your eye on the head pressure in case the cutout does not work.

4. Compare the cutout point to manufacturer's specifications or those listed above.

LOW-PRESSURE CUTOUT

The low-pressure cutout (LPCO) shuts down the compressor when suction pressure drops below the setpoint. The cutout can be used as either an operating control or a safety control or both. See *Operating controls*, p. 115, for information on using the LPCO as an operating control.

When used as a safety, the LPCO protects a hermetic compressor and motor (which are cooled by suction line refrigerant) from overheating due to lowered gas density and/or increased gas temperature. Low suction pressure also increases the pumping ratio, leading to overheating and oil or refrigerant breakdown. In addition, it raises compression ratio, decreasing compressor output because only a small mass of gas can enter the cylinder during each intake stroke. Low suction pressure is usually due to inadequate refrigerant level or a restriction in the suction line.

The LPCO is tapped into the suction side of the compressor. Some LPCOs have automatic reset, but manual-resetting controls are preferable because tripping an LPCO is an indication of big trouble in the system. Ideally, the situation should be investigated before the system is returned to service, but an automatic reset may be used in a system that cools perishables. The LPCO may incorporate a time delay to prevent premature tripping of the safety.

Test the LPCO with the following procedure:

1. Install the gauge manifold and run the system for a few minutes.

2. Shut the suction service valve and note at what pressure the unit stops. (The pressure might drop rapidly, so it's important to watch the gauge closely.)

3. If the LPCO is an operating control, compare the pressure to the desired evaporator temperature with a pressure-temperature chart to make sure the setting is correct. If the LPCO is only a safety control, refer to system specifications or compressor manufacturer's literature for the proper setting.

OIL PRESSURE CUTOUT

The oil pressure cutout (OPCO) is a pressure-differential limit switch wired in series with the holding coil and designed to shut down the compressor when oil pressure drops below what is needed to lubricate the compressor. The cutout is generally found on large units with forced lubrication. Because the oil pump must pump against low side pressure (a positive pump pressure that is still less than crankcase pressure is not enough), the cutout compares oil pump discharge pressure to low side pressure. If the oil pressure is not sufficiently higher than low-side pressure, oil will not flow properly and cutout will shut down the compressor (see Part E *Oil control system*, p. 180).

The shutoff may be accomplished by a solid-state device or a bimetallic strip. The limit should be set to allow a brief delay during which oil pressure can return to normal. To understand the operation of an oil pressure limit, refer to Fig. D16:

Notice that two bellows are linked to an assembly that compares crankcase pressure to oil pressure. The net pressure is transferred to the pressure switch A. In normal operation, switch A is open and thus no current flows through heater B. Switch C remains closed, allowing current to flow to the starting coil D.

If oil pressure drops, switch A closes, allowing current to flow to heater B, which warms up the bimetallic strip E. If element E stays warm long enough (reflecting sustained low oil pressure), it bends and releases the pressure holding switch C together. This opens the circuit to the holding coil and shuts down the motor. It may be necessary to reset the limit switch manually after it trips. If pressure returns to normal before the contacts open, the heating circuit will open and the bimetallic strip will cool, preventing a compressor shutdown due to a transient oil pressure drop.

The time delay may be adjusted by changing the position of the potentiometer in the delay control adjustment F. The greater the resistance, the smaller the current flowing through the heating element, and the slower the element will warm the bimetallic element. Thus the potenitometer can be used to set the limit to shut down the compressor faster or slower after a reduction of oil pressure. The time delay is usually set at between 90 and 120 seconds.

To check the amount of time from pressure loss to cutout of

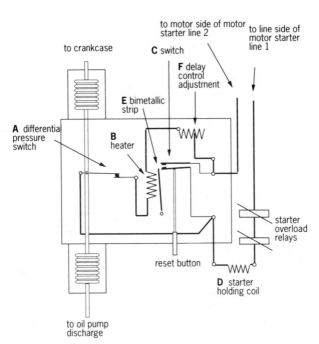

Fig. D16 Oil pressure cutout
(shown in cutout position)

motor and the overall operation of an oil safety switch, follow these steps:

1. Shut off the compressor main disconnect.

2. Disconnect the run windings from the load side of the starter, making sure to remember their hookup so you can reassemble them.

3. Get out your watch and start timing when you reclose the disconnect. The starter should pull even though the compressor will not run.

4. After a short time (the delay setting) the starter will drop back out if the switch is working correctly.

5. After the test, open the main disconnect and reconnect the wires, making sure connections are tight.

Refer to manufacturer's instructions for setting these switches, but never set them below 10 lb. (69 kPa) differential—any less and the compressor will not have enough oil pressure.

INTERNAL RELIEF

An internal relief valve prevents overpressure—if the high-pressure cutout fails—by routing refrigerant from the high side to the low side. The location varies according to compressor design, although the device is commonly found inside the discharge service valve.

Check the relief when you inspect the low-pressure cutout. If suction pressure rises quickly after the LPCO shuts the compressor down, discharge pressure is probably reaching the suction side through the internal relief. Some reliefs reseat themselves—in which case suction pressure should stop rising when the relief reseats. Rupture-disk type reliefs must be replaced after blowing.

MOTOR THERMOSTAT

Motor thermostats, also called winding thermostats, are buried in the windings of large motors. Since you cannot cause the motor to overheat, you must test this thermostat indirectly. First see that it is functioning with a continuity meter. Then disconnect the thermostat from the control circuit and check that it is actually wired in (some have been disconnected and offer no protection).

Make this check by attempting to run the system with the thermostat disconnected.

Motor thermostats that open due to overheating will reclose automatically, but due to the mass of the motor, this might take some time. During the cooling period, check the motor for opens, shorts, and grounds (see Part F). If none are found, and the motor still does not run after it has cooled, look for a second set of contacts (low-voltage wires) in the motor control box. These may be connected to a second thermostat in the windings. Connect these wires to the control circuit and try to restart the motor. If it still does not run, or there is not a second thermostat, consult the motor manufacturer. Because it is difficult or impossible to measure motor temperature directly, you should look for signs of poor cooling or excessive current draw when attempting to determine whether the motor is shutting down due to overheating.

In addition to compressors and controls, modern comfort cooling and refrigeration systems require a variety of other components to accomplish their goals. Some, such as the evaporator and condenser, are found in all vapor-compression systems, while others, such as fans, heat exchangers, and oil control systems, are used in special situations.

Condenser

The condenser is the high-side component which allows the hot, high-pressure refrigerant gas to lose its latent heat of condensation to the environment. This loss of heat causes the gas to condense into a high-pressure liquid which can be piped to the metering device. The heat rejected by the condenser enters the system in the evaporator and the compressor. Due to inefficiencies and other heat gains, a condenser in an open system must dispose of about 1.25 times the heat gained in the evaporator. Condensers in hermetic systems must also dispose of heat from the motor windings.

Many types of condensers are used, depending on the function, shape of the piping, and the means of disposing of heat. The two basic categories—water-cooled and air-cooled—are classified by the medium used to remove heat. The basic design goal of a condenser is to remove the most heat at the lowest cost, complication, and space requirements.

Water and air are both are plentiful and economical condensing media. Water can remove large amounts of heat quickly, which allows the condenser to be relatively small and makes water-cooled condensers more economical when cheap, suitable water is available. However, water may be scarce or chemically unsuited for condenser use. In addition, water-cooled condensers are subject to scale, fouling, freezing, and corrosion.

Air-cooled condensers must be larger than water-cooled units, but are not subject to freezing or water problems. Air cooling is used when water is expensive or chemically unsuitable.

In a combination air-and-water condenser, air cools under normal conditions, but water is used as the condensing medium when the ambient air is too warm.

Fins, wires, or plates may be fastened to condenser tubing to increase the surface area and the ability to dispose of the heat of condensation. Fans or pumps are commonly used to increase the flow of the condensing medium. Such enhancements increase the subcooling of the refrigerant, increase the rate of heat transfer, and decrease the overall size of the condenser.

AIR-COOLED

Air-cooled condensers rely on air to remove heat from their fins. In external-drive systems the fan may be powered by the compressor motor or crankshaft. In hermetic systems, a separate motor is needed for the fan.

In "static" condensers, air is circulated across the condenser solely by the force of convection. In "forced" condensers, a fan blows air across the condenser to increase the cooling action. Because of the increase in cooling ability, practically all large condensers are of the forced variety.

Shrouds are used to increase fan efficiency by directing all the air flow across the condenser tubes. Many types of fins can be used to increase the surface area of the condenser. Proper heat transfer in air-cooled condensers can be achieved only if the condenser surface is clean. The condenser must be engineered to work in the hottest ambient conditions, when heat transfer will be the slowest and the cooling load is likely to be the greatest.

Double condensers can be used to cool the compressor head. In this system, the hot discharge gas is cooled in the first condenser, piped through the cylinder head to pick up heat, and piped into the second condenser, where it condenses before travelling to the receiver.

Outdoor condensers in cold weather present a special system design challenge (see Part H, *Cold weather operation*, p. 279).

WATER-COOLED

If water is readily available and suited to use in a condenser, a water-cooled condenser is preferable due to its greater ability to remove heat. If water cools the compressor and the condenser, it should enter the condenser first to ensure that the refrigerant receives the maximum cooling.

Water velocity should be between 7 and 10 feet per second in a water-cooled condenser. Faster flows will strip off the oxide coating protecting the copper tubing from corrosion, and slower flows may cause scaling or fouling.

Water-system components such as solenoid, modulating, or hand valves should be fitted with a stand-pipe having an air pocket to protect against water hammer. Do not locate solenoid or pressure-operated valves between the condenser and the drain—place them between the water supply and the condenser. If the water pressure is above condenser operating pressures, install a pressure-reducing valve in the supply to the condenser.

Three types of water-cooled condensers are available: shell and tube, shell and coil, and tube-within-a-tube. The first two serve as receivers and are similar enough to be considered in one section.

SHELL AND TUBE OR COIL

A shell and tube condenser is a large cylinder with a water manifold at each end. Water circulates through the large cylinder. Hot refrigerant vapor enters the inlet manifold and flows through the cooling tubes and exits the discharge manifold.

The shell and coil style is also a cylinder with two manifolds, but the refrigerant flows through coiled tubes instead of straight ones. Due to their shape, the coils must be cleaned with chemicals, not brushes.

TUBE-WITHIN-A-TUBE

In this model, the outer tube contains refrigerant and the inner tube contains water. The two fluids flow in opposite directions so the incoming, cold water contacts the refrigerant that is just about to flow to the receiver. This ensures the greatest temperature reduction in the refrigerant. The wall between the two fluids may be shaped to increase its area and the rate of heat transfer. The tube-within-a-tube type has too little space to store refrigerant and cannot serve as a liquid receiver, unlike the first type of condenser. Consequently, the tube-within-a-tube type is easy to overcharge, which reduces the space available for heat transfer and can cause erratic cooling.

COOLING TOWER AND EVAPORATIVE CONDENSER

Heat from a water-cooled condenser may be transferred to the surroundings through a cooling tower or an evaporative condenser.

1. A *cooling tower* contains apparatus which sprays the condenser water through a blast of air (some designs rely on the wind created by the spraying itself; others use fans). Some of the water evaporates and loses the latent heat of vaporization. The remaining water drips to the bottom and is returned to the condenser for reuse. Chemicals may be needed to control rust, algae, fungus, and the organism that causes Legionnaire's disease, which grows inside cooling towers. (See *Water problems and treatment*, below.)

   During operation, a cooling tower receives enough condenser heat to keep it from freezing. The system must be able to empty itself of water when not in use to prevent freezing. An alternative is to supply electric heat during shutdown.

2. An *evaporative condenser* also uses evaporation to remove heat. In this device, the condenser water flows through a heat exchanger which is under a spray or drip of water. Fans blow air across the condenser during operation. Buildup of scale is visible in this device.

WATER PROBLEMS AND TREATMENT

Water-cooled condensers are subject to four types of water problems: corrosion, scale, fouling, and microbial action.

Corrosion, the oxidation of metal, can degrade metal and cause it to fail and leak (see Part B, *Corrosion*, p. 78).

Scale is the deposition of alkaline material, chiefly calcium carbonate (lime) and magnesium compounds, on the inside of a tube or container. Chemicals that form scale are frequently dissolved in water and may not cause problems until they precipitate out of the water. The rate of scale formation is greatly dependent on water acidity. The biggest culprit, calcium carbonate, is much more soluble in acidic water than in alkaline water and will scale out much more slowly in acidic water. Scaling rate is also affected by water temperature, the concentration of the alkaline compounds, and the presence of other chemicals that affect scaling rate. Scale can be controlled by reducing the concentration of the alkaline chemicals, boosting water acidity (although this may increase the rate of corrosion), making mechanical changes (such as speeding up the water flow), and treating with scale-preventing chemicals.

Fouling is the deposition of substances other than scale on the walls of vessels. Fouling can result from loosened corrosion particles, dirt, masses of microbes, and other materials.

These factors increase the rate of fouling:

- *contaminated water*
- *corrosion*
- *slow water flow*
- *high temperature*
- *the presence of microbes*

Fouling can be prevented by keeping contaminants out of the cooling water during startup, by filtering the water during operation, and by using antifouling compounds.

Microbial growth results from the multiplication of single-celled organisms. The primary problem is slime formed of mats of microbes and their waste products. Slime can interfere with water flow and insulate surfaces, reducing heat transfer. Another hazard of microbes is the possible presence of pathogens such as the bacteria that causes Legionnaire's disease.

Microbe growth requires the presence of:

- *Atmosphere—either oxygen or carbon dioxide.*
- *Nutrients—such as hydrocarbons.*
- *Temperature—slime organisms thrive between 40°F and 150°F.*

Microbes can be chemically controlled, but they must be identified first. Warning signs of the presence of microbes include rotting wood, slime, and corrosion (which some microorganisms accelerate). Three types of chemical agents may be used to control or kill microbes: 1) Oxidizing biocides, such as chlorine or bromine, are effective against a wide array of organisms. 2) Non-oxidizing biocides are used if the oxidizing biocides are ineffective. 3) Biodispersants do not kill the organisms but are used to loosen their deposits for removal by flushing or scraping.

Crankcase Heater

A crankcase heater warms the crankcase to prevent excess refrigerant from dissolving in the oil. If the crankcase is the coldest part of the system, the refrigerant will migrate there and mix with the oil. Oil absorbs refrigerant more readily at cold temperatures than at warm temperatures. When the compressor starts up, the oil-refrigerant mix will boil away as the pressure falls, leaving the compressor without lubrication. A heater may prevent these problems, but it will not be effective if ambient temperatures are too cold.

Large compressors, especially those operated in low ambient temperatures or subject to frequent on-off cycles, are often fitted with crankcase heaters, either at the factory or as a retrofit. The heater may be set to operate whenever the compressor is off or be thermostatically-controlled to run only in cold temperatures. In comfort cooling systems, the crankcase heaters should be turned on at least four hours prior to spring startup.

Defrost Controls

Defrost controls must operate the defrost cycle as often as necessary for the required amount of time. Excessive defrost cycles will reduce comfort or storage quality and reduce operating efficiency. Factors which increase the severity of frosting include:

- *Cold operating temperature.*
- *High relative humidity in the cooled space.*

- *Frequent opening of doors between the cooled area and surroundings.*
- *Frequent drafts across open cases.*

The defrost cycle must be long and warm enough to thoroughly defrost all evaporators. The defrost control may perform some or all of these functions:

1. Operate solenoid valves in hot-gas defrost systems.
2. Shut off evaporator fans to prevent warming of stored products.
3. Shut off or operate the compressor.
4. Connect a circuit to energize defrost heater elements in the evaporator.
5. Heat the receiver to prevent it from acting as a condenser during the defrost cycle.

A mechanical, electric, or electronic device can be used to determine the timing and duration of the defrost cycle. The cycle can be initiated based on time, pressure, or temperature in the evaporator.

Timers may be wired in series with the compressor motor to register running time, or set to start a defrost cycle after a certain number of hours or at the same time every day.

Other defrost controls use a temperature or low-side pressure sensor to measure frost buildup. The devices compare the temperature of air entering the evaporator with that of air leaving it. Temperature differences in the range of 20 to 30°F (11 to 17°C) will generally trigger the defrost cycle. These sensors also detect when frost has melted (TD falls back to normal) and the normal cooling cycle should resume. Thermistors are often used in this sensing application.

Pressure-operated switches are also used to terminate the defrost cycle. In many cases, a timer is included as a failsafe measure (see *Operating controls*, p. 115).

In large systems, controls may control the functions of several motors, fans, and valves. Different evaporators may be shut off at different times. Programmable timers, used to control multiple functions of the system, are usually repaired and adjusted by specialists.

Distributor, Refrigerant

Refrigerant distributors convey refrigerant from a TXV and feed it to different parts of a large evaporator, or to several evaporators. The tube from the TXV to the distributor is connected by soldering, brazing, a flared fitting, or a flange. The distributor has from two to twenty-four or more female fittings which connect to the evaporator feed tubes. Poor distributor design or installation can cause excessive hunting by the thermostatic expansion valve, impaired evaporator performance, and floodbacks to the compressor.

INSTALLING AND SERVICING

Brazing is often required for the outlet tube connections. Heat the distributor uniformly and allow the body to cool slowly to avoid cracking. After brazing, disassemble the distributor and inspect. If this is impossible, use a probe wire to be sure all the branches are clear of solder (a pressure test will not reveal plugged tubes). When soldering a distributor to a TXV, direct the heat away from the valve and do not overheat the joint. Leak test the system before operating. Plugging some distributor outlets is not recommended, but if it is necessary, plug them symmetrically.

Drier (See Filter-Drier)

Evaporator

The evaporator is the place where the refrigerant boils and absorbs the latent heat of vaporization from the cooled space. Evaporators that cool air are commonly called coils, blower coils, or cooling coils; evaporators that cool water are called chillers.

As liquid refrigerant enters the evaporator, the pressure drops and its temperature also drops as the gas laws require. Due to the TD between the boiling refrigerant and the surroundings, the refrigerant absorbs the latent heat of vaporization from the surroundings. This additional heat continues the boiling process. During this change of state, the refrigerant remains at a stable temperature—the saturation pressure-temperature of that refrigerant under that evaporator pressure. Depending on the application, the evaporator can remove sensible heat (by reducing the temperature of the load) and/or latent heat (by dehumidifying air).

The rate and nature of refrigerant flow in the evaporator is determined by:

- *the metering device*
- *the high-side pressure*
- *the compressor drawing on the suction line*
- *the length, inside diameter, and configuration of the tubing*
- *the viscosity of the refrigerant*

The actual amount of cooling in a dry evaporator will depend on the quantity of air blown past the coil, the dry- and wet-bulb temperatures of the air, the saturation temperature of the refrigerant, and the amount of coil surface area.

Evaporators are rated by heat removed (in Btus) per degree of temperature difference (TD). If the evaporator will operate at 10° F TD, multiply the specification amount of BTUs by 10 to find rated capacity of the evaporator in that application. Using the SI system, multiply the TD in degrees Celsius by the rating in joules to find the expected capacity of the evaporator in an application.

Although a high TD will allow use of a smaller evaporator, the rate of condensation or freezing on the coils increases along with TD. Thus, a high TD greatly reduces the relative humidity of the cooled space. In some cases, such as with meat or produce cases, low relative humidity will cause unsightly and expensive shrinkage. For this reason, a relatively small TD is often chosen for fresh food installations, although this increases the evaporator size requirement. A small TD has another benefit. Because the suction gas will be relatively cool and dense, the compressor will pump more efficiently.

TABLE E1
Evaporator TD and Relative Humidity

For evaporators in a temperature range of 25°F to 45°F

Desired Relative humidity	TD (coil to air in cooler)
90%	8°F to 12°F
85%	12°F to 14°F
80%	12°F to 16°F
75%	16°F to 22°F

COURTESY OF COPELAND CORPORATION

Proper superheat adjustment can prevent excess liquid refrigerant in the evaporator, which could flood back to the compressor. Liquid refrigerant in the suction line can also be vaporized by a heat exchanger or trapped by an accumulator between the evaporator outlet and the compressor.

Refrigerant velocity in the evaporator must be high enough to ensure oil circulation. Rapid refrigerant flow scrubs oil and refrigerant droplets from the walls, preventing them from reducing heat transfer through the evaporator tubes. Excess pressure drop, caused by many bends, excess refrigerant velocity, or inadequate tubing diameter, will slow the vapor and cause oil logging which cuts performance. Several circuits may be provided to give the correct refrigerant capacity and prevent the problems associated with pressure drop and oil logging.

FLOODED OR DIRECT EXPANSION

The two basic categories of evaporator are wet ("flooded") and dry ("direct expansion"):

* *Some liquid refrigerant is always present in a flooded evaporator, which chills water flowing through or past the evaporator tubes or coils. A wet system uses a high- or low-side float as a metering device. Instead of using a receiver, the system may be configured to pump down refrigerant to the evaporator during service operations. Wet systems are usually large.*

* *Most of the refrigerant is in vapor or droplet form in a dry evaporator. A dry evaporator may have plates, fins, or coils to chill the air. The metering device must supply only enough refrigerant to create the desired temperature while leaving the evaporator dry. The metering*

device may throttle down or shut off during the compressor off-cycle. Dry evaporator tubing may be an integral part of the wall of the cabinet.

FORCED OR STATIC COIL

Forced-air evaporators ("blower coils") have a fan to circulate air across the coils, allowing the evaporator to be relatively small. This design can lead to rapid drying unless special measures are taken, such as using a slow air speed and a small TD between the evaporator and the cabinet.

The blower may run continuously or be controlled by evaporator or cabinet temperature. Drainage may be needed to allow condensed water to leave the fixture. Because blower coils tend to be compact, with narrow passages between the fins, frost must not be allowed to clog the passages.

FROST CONTROL

Dry evaporators are classified by their system of preventing or removing frost. The goal of a defrosting system is to minimize increases in cabinet temperature, thus reducing product damage and energy use, while still removing all frost from the coils.

Frost is undesirable because it:

- *reduces the rate of heat transfer from the cabinet to the evaporator*
- *withdraws moisture from air in the cabinet and increases dehydration*
- *clogs passages, causing mechanical damage*

(See Part H, *Defrost system*, p. 273).

NONFROSTING EVAPORATOR

Nonfrosting evaporators operate down to 33 to 34°F (.5 to 1°C). At these temperatures, frost will not build up appreciably. Any slight frost that does form will rapidly melt when the compressor shuts down. Baffles may be used to collect condensate and prevent it from dripping into the cabinet. These evaporators maintain a high relative humidity in the cabinet, and thus can store produce with little dessication.

FROSTING EVAPORATOR

This evaporator has no provision for defrosting, so the equipment must be shut down occasionally to manually defrost the evaporator with the application of external heat. However, frosting evaporators which run near water's freezing point may defrost without additional heat if they warm up enough when the compressor shuts down for the frost to melt. This could be considered a type of defrosting evaporator.

DEFROSTING EVAPORATOR

Defrosting evaporators operate at temperatures that cause the accumulation of frost, but upon shutdown the temperature rises enough to defrost the evaporator. The temperature rise may be accomplished by hot gas defrost system, electric heating elements, or another means of supplying heat to the inside or outside of the coil. This system leaves air within the cabinet relatively humid and aids food preservation. The installation must have good drainage or the melted frost will puddle at the evaporator bottom and freeze when the unit cools down.

Defrosting evaporators come in many styles. They are especially useful when the evaporator temperature is low or its fins are closely spaced.

TROUBLES

Evaporators are subject to a few troubles:

If the coil is just below freezing, and there is no defrost cycle, clear ice will build up because humidity in the air condenses before it freezes. If the coil is much colder, the humidity will freeze directly and form crystals of frost on the coil. Ice conducts heat better than frost, but both ice and frost should be removed before they build up enough to cut evaporator capacity.

Coils should be protected from mechanical damage.

If the evaporator fan motor is not running, check it with the VOM. Bypass the switch to see if the fan is receiving power. Some fans are self-oiling while others need occasional oiling.

Fans

Fans are used to cool air-cooled condensers and to force conditioned air through ductwork. Fans are classified by application and design:

Exhauster	Has inlet duct only
Booster	Has both inlet and discharge ducts
Blower	Has discharge duct only

The two major categories of fans used in cooling systems are axial (or propeller) and radial (also called centrifugal). Either type may be powered by direct drive or belt drive. Large, slow fans are more likely to be driven by belts.

Axial fans force air along the axis, or shaft, of the fan. They are best suited to moving large air flows against low resistance. Axial fans are lighter and require less space than comparable centrifugal fans. Tube axial fans are mounted in a cylinder. Vane axial fans are mounted in a cylinder and have vanes to guide the air flow. Applications of axial fans include cooling condensers, humidifiers, and in cooling towers.

Centrifugal (radial) fans push air away from the shaft and use a housing to direct the air in the desired direction. This housing, also called a scroll, has an air inlet near one bearing of the fan shaft. Centrifugal fans are used to push air against large resistance, so they are often used to force air through ductwork in air-handling systems.

Fans are described by:

Volume: cubic feet of air handled per minute at specified outlet conditions.

Total pressure: the rise in pressure between inlet and outlet.

Velocity pressure: the pressure created by the velocity of the air flow.

Static pressure: total pressure minus velocity pressure.

Fan inlet area: the inside area of the fan inlet.

Fan outlet area: the inside area of the fan outlet.

Fan noise is related to tip speed, blade shape, and the number and angle of the blades. From the point of view of building occupants, fan noise is also dependent on ductwork design and construction. However, in any given installation, the higher the air speed, the louder the fan noise.

When selecting a fan, consider these factors:

1. Nature of the load.
2. Volume required in cubic feet per minute.
3. System resistance to flow.
4. Mounting arrangement.
5. Type of drive needed.
6. Tolerable sound level.

Filter-Drier

A filter-drier is used to clean up moisture and contaminants from a system. Cleanliness is vital for efficient, long-lasting systems, and refrigerant and oil must be free of moisture, sludge, acid, varnish, and metallic particles. Moisture can combine with oil to form sludge and acids that damage bearings (and motors in hermetic units). Moisture can also freeze and clog a system. Refrigerants and oil can break down if the discharge temperature is excessive and can form acids and sludges. Dirt, scale, sludge, solder, and other metallic particles can clog valves or damage compressors.

These steps will help ensure system cleanliness:

1. a design which prevents overheating and offers sufficient places to remove contaminants;
2. installation procedures, which permit minimal moisture and dirt to enter the system,
3. a filter-drier in the liquid and/or suction lines to catch contaminants which remain after installation or are created during operation,
4. operating procedures which prevent contamination by controlling discharge gas temperature.

Filter-driers combine an absorbent chemical, such as activated alumina or silica gel, with a screen or filter. The drier can only absorb a certain amount of moisture, so a moisture indicator may be used to detect moisture levels. This indicator may be incorporated in the filter-drier or be a separate component.

Adsorbing-type driers are more able to adsorb moisture when they are cold. If a system runs well when cool but the moisture indicator indicates wet as the system warms, the drier element may be waterlogged and in need of replacement. Because new drier elements are more stable, the devices should be installed in the direct flow of the system, at least in the liquid line. In the suction line, the drier may still be placed in a bypass to allow full flow of vapor to the compressor.

Filtering and drying functions may accomplished by separate units. Activated alumina elements can reduce system acidity. Some filters and driers are fitted with sight glasses for detecting refrigerant level. Service connections are handy for recharging the system or checking pressure drop across the filter-drier. Removable filter cartridges simplify replacement. A filter-drier can be used on a temporary or permanent basis to clean up the system, especially after a burnout.

Filter-driers in the liquid line prevent dirt and moisture from entering the refrigerant control and plugging or damaging it. A liquid line filter-drier may cause enough pressure drop to create flash gas at the metering device. A filter-drier directly in front of the compressor in the suction line offers protection from low-side contaminants. Such a filter-drier must present only a small resistance to flow.

TABLE E2
Pressure Drop for Filter-Drier
Maximum recommended pressure drop for suction line filter-drier:

	Permanent Installation				Temporary Installation			
Refrigerant	R-22 & R-502		R-12		R-22 & R-502		R-12	
Pressure	psi	kPa	psi	kPa	psi	kPa	psi	kPa
Air-conditioning	3	20.7	2	13.8	8	55.2	6	41.4
Commercial	2	13.8	1.5	10.3	4	27.6	3	20.7
Low temperature	1	6.9	0.5	3.5	2	13.8	1	6.9

COURTESY OF SPORLAN VALVE CO.

It is important to realize that the various halocarbon refrigerants have different capacities to absorb moisture. Absorbed moisture does not cause as much harm as moisture which is carried in the refrigerant but not absorbed. Therefore, manufacturers specify maximum refrigerant moisture levels for the various refrigerants. Thus a drier used, for example, with R-502 must be much larger and more effective one those used for other refrigerants.

INSTALLING AND SERVICING

Filter-driers are chosen based on system operating temperature, refrigerant type, amount of contamination present, allowable pressure drop, bursting pressure, and the ability of the filter-drier to trap and retain liquid and solid contaminants. Flow ratings are measured on clean systems, and the rate of flow will drop as dirt accumulates. Thus, the unit should be slightly oversize to ensure that it will operate properly after dirt accumulates.

A liquid line filter-drier should be placed directly upstream of the metering device or moisture indicator because it works most effectively at low temperature. This installation also provides the greatest protection for the metering device. A suction line filter-drier is placed near the compressor inlet.

Have the system ready to receive the filter-drier before opening the package of the device. Evacuate and dry the connecting lines and make the connection quickly to prevent excess moisture from entering the system. (See *Moisture indicator*, next page.)

Heat Exchanger

A heat exchanger is mounted between the suction line and the liquid line to exchange heat from the liquid refrigerant to the suction vapor. The effect of the device is to superheat the vapor in the suction line and subcool the liquid in the liquid line. A heat exchanger can increase operating efficiency, especially in medium- and low-temperature systems.

The device has four benefits:

1. To reduce the incidence of flash gas (the sudden change of liquid to gas) in the liquid line. Flash gas can: reduce capacity of the metering device; damage the metering device; or cause pressure drop, excessive noise, or erratic operation.

2. To regulate suction gas temperature to the optimum level to prevent floodback.

3. To allow the TXV to take full advantage of the evaporator, without worrying about floodback.

4. To reduce sweating on the suction line by warming the suction gas.

The heat exchanger can be a manufactured device or can be fabricated by soldering or taping the suction and liquid lines together. In some systems, subcooling is achieved by passing the liquid line in front of an air stream instead of using a heat exchanger. Whatever the design, the device should allow the fullest possible fluid flow in both lines.

A heat exchanger in a hermetic or semi-hermetic system can cause trouble if it warms the suction gas so much that it cannot cool the compressor and motor adequately.

Two other measures that will help ensure cooling in hermetic or semi-hermetic systems are providing accurate (not excessive) superheat setting on the TXV, and insulating the suction line to prevent the suction gas from warming before it reaches the compressor.

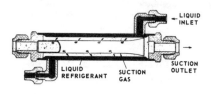

Fig. E1   Heat exchanger

Courtesy of Mueller Brass Co.

Liquid Line

The liquid line, on the high side of the system, connects the condenser, receiver (if used) and metering device. The line is commonly copper tubing and is connected by brazing, soldering, or flared fittings. The liquid line may contain valves, a filter-drier, and moisture indicators as required. Liquid lines that run through warm areas may need insulation to prevent warming of the liquid refrigerant.

Oil return is not an issue because oil and liquid refrigerant mix well and the oil will be carried along in the refrigerant, even though the velocity is relatively low. However, the liquid line should be sized large enough to prevent pressure drop and flash gas.

A system with a great deal of vertical lift in the liquid line must be designed to account for the resulting static pressure loss (see Table D1, p. 131).

Moisture Indicator

A moisture indicator is often placed in the liquid line to detect unacceptable levels of moisture in a system. It does not give exact readings but merely shows whether the level is safe or not. Excess water can cause many problems, such as icing of metering devices, rust, corrosion, refrigerant decomposition, and sludge in the oil. Some refrigerants, such as R-21 and R-22, are much more able to dissolve water than others, such as R-12. In addition, cold refrigerants dissolve less water than warm ones. Thus, a cold system using a refrigerant such as R-12 is much more prone to icing than a warm system using R-22, and would thus need greater precautions against moisture.

A filter-drier may be used for removing moisture from a system, but a moisture indicator should be installed as a safety precaution.

Moisture indicators have a reversible chemical which can indicate wet or dry as conditions in the liquid line change. Some moisture indicators are suited only to particular refrigerants, although others work with several. Temperature greatly affects the reading. An indicator might read "dry" at 75°F (24°C) and 125°F (52°C), even though the higher reading would indicate two or three times as much moisture. An exact temperature reading is not needed, but an approximate one will help you interpret the reading. Moisture indicator manufacturers provide color scales to help you assess the reading, both in terms of temperature and refrigerant in the system.

INSTALLING AND SERVICING

A moisture indicator should be connected in the liquid line in a location which ensures a positive flow of refrigerant through it. On a large system, the indicator may be installed in a bypass line, which should, if possible, be parallel to the main line and connected with 45° fittings. Keep the indicator cool during brazing.

Indicators may be sensitive to moisture in the air and read wet during installation. It is recommended that you wait several hours before reading a newly-installed indicator.

If a large amount of water enters the refrigerant, the water can dissolve the indicating salts, the sensing element or the whole indicator will need replacement. Excess oil may also call for replacement. After a hermetic motor burnout, do not install a moisture indicator until 48 hours after restart. This allows the filter-drier to remove acid from the system and prevent it from damaging the indicator. Dye-type leak detectors and dehydrating additives such as methyl alcohol may also interfere with the indicator.

Motor Drive

Compressors and fans are driven by motors with the aid of belts and pulleys, or shafts connected by a flexible coupling.

BELTS

Flexible belts are frequently used to connect motors to fans or open-drive compressors. Most belts are constructed of layers of fabric, rubber, and cord which are formed into the desired shape.

V-belts, which are tapered to fit the pulleys, are the most common type. The power is transmitted as the V shape is forced into the grooves of the pulley by the tension on the belt. Both standard and narrow V-belts are used in comfort cooling and refrigeration applications. Synchronous belts, with teeth that engage depressions in the pulley, are used when exact timing of the driven equipment is required. Multiple belts are used to transmit larger amounts of power because belts are subject to turning over if they are asked to transmit loads greater than their capacity.

The pulley on the motor is the "driver" and the pulley on the compressor or fan is the "driven" pulley. Most drives allow the motor to run faster than the compressor, which increases the torque and allows the machinery to operate at its optimum speed.

A pulley, also called a sheave, may be simple (one belt per sheave), compound (several belts per sheave), or variable pitch. The width of the groove on a variable pitch sheave can be altered, allowing you to change its effective diameter, and thus the driven shaft speed, without replacing the sheave. Pulleys are affixed to the shaft with a key secured by a set screw. Shafts for fractional-horsepower motors are commonly ½, ⅝, or ¾ inch in diameter.

Multiple belts should be matched so each has the same tension and carries the same percentage of the load. If a new belt is installed, the entire set should be replaced.

For optimum service, belts should be sized correctly. Belts are described by outside length and widest width, either in a lettering system or in inches. "A" width belts are up to ¹⁷⁄₃₂ inch (1.35 cm) wide. "B" width belts are between ½ inch (1.27 cm) and ¹¹⁄₁₆ inch (1.75 cm) wide.

For alignment, inspection, and tensioning procedures, see Part K, *Drive system service*, p. 349. For information on troubleshooting, see Part J, p. 312.

BELT SAFETY

Observe the following restrictions when installing, maintaining, and working around belt drives:

1. Turn the power off and lock the switch before working on a belt drive.

2. Check the equipment to be sure it is in a safe position before working.

3. Wear safe clothing. Neckties, loose sleeves, or any other clothing that can catch in a belt are not to be worn in the vicinity of a belt.

4. Keep the area around the drive clear of debris and clutter. Floors must be dry and free of oil.

5. Keep drive guards in place except when working on a drive. A proper guard encloses the drive completely, allows good ven-

tilation, has access panels for inspection, can easily be removed and replaced, and protects the drive from weather, damage and debris if necessary.

FLEXIBLE COUPLINGS

Flexible couplings can be used to drive a compressor from a motor. Alignment must be within .004 inch (0.1 mm) in both directions, although many manufacturer specify a closer alignment. See Part K for information on aligning.

MUFFLER

A muffler is used to reduce the transmission of discharge noise from the compressor to the piping system. A muffler is a cylinder with baffle plates inside. Because noise level can be difficult to predict, you may need a bit of trial and error to find the most effective way to control noise in an installation. High pitch noises do not travel as far in a building as low pitch noise.

In general, mufflers which create a large pressure drop are more effective than those with less restriction. Both the volume and density of gas flow through the muffler affect muffler performance. Some mufflers are adjustable to various applications.

Mufflers are usually placed inside hermetic units. Good vibration isolation is also important in controlling noise from compressors (see *Vibration absorber*). Another good measure is to hang pipes so they cannot directly contact the building. This prevents the building from becoming a sounding board for system noise.

Lubrication and Oil Control

Oil must lubricate compressors and hermetic motors during all operating pressures and temperatures. Liquid oil is soluble in liquid refrigerant, but the vapors do not readily dissolve each other. Three types of problems are associated with oil:

1. Oil can break down and lose its ability to lubricate, especially

at high discharge temperature or in a dirty system. Filter-driers can reduce acidity and contamination.

2. Oil that is diluted by refrigerant loses some lubricating capacity. The problem may be caused by oversize expansion valves, inadequate superheat, or incorrect piping.

3. Excess oil in the system oil, often caused by an oversize suction line, may reduce crankcase lubrication, clog the metering device, and reduce efficiency by 5 to 15 percent.

Excess system oil can cause these problems:

Component	Problem
Condenser	Coats walls, reducing heat transfer and volumetric efficiency; may alter condensing temperature.
Filter-drier	Plugs filter or screen; may coat dessicant.
Metering device	Forms gummy deposits; in expansion valves may restrict the orifice, alter evaporator pressure, cause hunting, or lead to unneeded replacement; clogs capillary tube.
Evaporator and suction line	Reduces volumetric efficiency and heat transfer; interferes with sensing bulb accuracy; increases TD between on and off cycles; may rob compressor of oil.
Heat exchanger	Insulates walls, interfering with ability to subcool and superheat refrigerant.
Compressor	Liquid oil may return as slugs, causing hydraulic jack; may overload motor; low oil may reduce lubrication.

NET OIL PRESSURE

Because the oil pump outlet is inside the crankcase, net oil pressure equals pump outlet pressure minus crankcase (suction) pressure. An oil pressure cutout (see Fig. D17) registers net oil pressure and allows startup during brief periods of low-pressure

Oil pump outlet pressure	80
Crankcase pressure	-40
Net oil pressure	$\overline{40}$

Note that if suction pressure is below atmospheric pressure, net oil pressure is greater than pump outlet pressure. Net oil pressures in the range of 30 to 40 psi (207 to 275 kPa) are normal, although many systems work on pressures as low as 10 psi (69 kPa).

OIL SYSTEMS FOR COMPRESSORS

Reciprocating compressors use two types of lubrication systems:

1. The splash system uses the crankshaft to splash oil; oil reaches the main bearings by flowing through channels. Bearings may be noisy because the system produces a small oil cushion.

2. The pressure system uses an oil pump driven by gears in the crankcase; oil is forced into channels in the connecting rods, main bearings, and piston pins. This system does a better job of ensuring lubrication and quiet operation, but has a higher initial cost. The pump must have an overload relief to prevent dangerous pressures. A safety switch may monitor oil pressure and shut down the compressor if pressure drops below a safe level.

Rotary compressors require a film of oil on the cylinder, blades and roller. Some machines propel the oil by the sliding action; others use a pump.

Centrifugal compressors operate at high speed and may have elaborate oil control systems, with a pump, separator, reservoirs to lubricate bearings during coast-down, filter, relief valve, and oil cooler.

Helical compressors need oil to cool, seal, and silence the rotors; they generally have a forced lubrication system. A positive displacement pump may operate independently of the compressor, ensuring complete lubrication at startup. Oil is separated, piped to a sump, cooled, and delivered to bearings and ports for injection into the compression chamber. The sump has a heater to prevent oil dilution during the off-cycle.

Note on adding oil: When starting a system for the first time, expect a certain amount of oil migration to lower the crankcase oil level. Adding oil once is normal during a startup, but if you must continually add oil, the system has a problem.

Three devices are used in industrial systems to control system oil: an oil separator, an oil level regulator, and an oil reservoir. Other elements, such as oil strainers and valves, may be needed to complete the system. Oil test kits are also used to detect damaging acidity in the oil.

PROMOTING OIL RETURN

Oil in direct expansion or dry evaporators, must be swept back to the compressor by the flow of refrigerant, with the amount returned depending on oil viscosity and refrigerant velocity in the evaporator. In horizontal lines, a velocity of about 700 feet (214 m) per minute is sufficient; in vertical lines, about 1500 feet (457 m) per minute may be needed.

Several measures will help increase oil return in dry evaporators. Slope the suction line toward the compressor. Install a trap to prevent slugs of liquid from reaching the compressor. Ensure adequate refrigerant velocity in the suction line by making it proper size, not oversize.

Remember that high-viscosity oil (as measured in evaporator conditions) is more resistant to return by refrigerant flow. Oil that dissolves a great deal of refrigerant remains more fluid than oil without refrigerant. (Oil with no refrigerant is about as thick as molasses at 0°F, or −18°C.) The amount of refrigerant dissolved in the oil varies according to pressure and temperature conditions in various parts of the evaporator, and the nature of the two fluids.

Oil return is difficult in low-temperature evaporators, because the oil is so viscous. High compression ratios also decrease oil return, because the suction gas is less dense. Thus adequate suction line velocity is especially important in low-temperature evaporators.

Oil will not be swept back to the compressor in a flooded evaporator, so an oil return line is required. In some systems, a special chamber is connected to the evaporator to allow refrigerant to be boiled from the oil before the oil is returned to the compressor (see Part J, *Troubleshooting, Oil control systems*, p. 331.)

OIL SEPARATOR

An oil separator is a container with a series of baffles or screens placed in the discharge line. The fog of oil is forced to turn corners and collide against the baffles or screens, allowing droplets of oil to combine into larger drops which drip to the sump at the bottom. The sump allows sludge and contaminants to settle out and may have a magnet to attract ferrous particles. When sufficient oil has gathered in the sump, it lifts a float and flows back to the crankcase, propelled by the oil pressure in the separator.

Oil separators are most often found on large and low temperature systems. They are mandatory on ammonia systems.

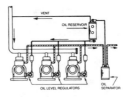

Courtesy of AC&R Components, Inc.

Fig. E2   Oil control system

INSTALLING AND SERVICING

Follow compressor manufacturer's recommendations when sizing and installing oil separators. In addition, consider these suggestions:

- *Install close to the compressor outlet.*

- *Mount in the proper orientation, usually vertical.*

- *The small oil return line must be connected to the proper location on the compressor (the oil filler plug or an oil regulator on the compressor may have a fitting). Do not install a shut-off in the return line.*

- *Do not install the separator near something which could cool it, such as a fan or evaporator, as this will interfere with the separating action. Separators located in areas colder than the evaporator may need a strap heater to prevent refrigerant from condensing in the separator.*

- *If the separator is below the condenser, route the discharge line above the condenser and pitch it downward, so refrigerant that condenses in this line will drip to the condenser, not the separator.*

- *Increase the oil charge in the system to account for the amount that will remain in the separator sump.*

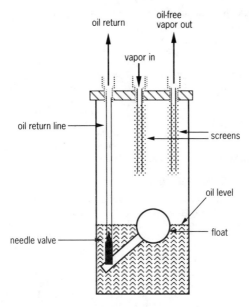

Fig. E3   Oil separator

In operation, the oil return line should be alternately hot and cold. Hot indicates that the float valve is open and oil is returning to the crankcase, and cold indicates oil has stopped flowing.

- *If the line remains hot, the float may be stuck open due to malfunction or foreign matter on the needle. If the float is operating properly and the return line remains hot, the compressor may be pumping too much oil.*

- *If the return line is always cold, the refrigerant may be condensing in the separator due to low temperatures there. This can be corrected by insulating the outside of the separator or installing a heater on it. Before insulating the separator, heat the sump to drive refrigerant out of the oil. Otherwise, the condensed refrigerant will be returned to the crankcase and cause foaming and other problems.*

Check the separator after a compressor burnout and clean or replace it.

OIL RESERVOIR

An oil reservoir maintains a supply of oil so the proper level can be maintained in the crankcase under all operating conditions. The reservoir has three tubing connections: 1) from the oil separator, 2) to an oil level regulator mounted on each crankcase, 3) to the suction line (to prevent high-side pressure from damaging the reservoir). See Fig. E3. Sight glasses on the side of the reservoir show the oil level. A float and needle valve inside the reservoir control the oil level and allow the regulators to draw oil from the reservoir when the crankcase level gets low.

INSTALLING AND SERVICING

To allow gravity flow of oil, the reservoir should be installed about 6 feet above the regulators. Oil may be added to the reservoir by closing the valve on the line to the separator. Open the valve after filling. Similarly, the outlet valve may be used to drain oil from the system.

When starting a new system, fill the reservoir to the upper sight glass port. You can expect some oil to be absorbed by the refrigerant at first. After about two hours, recheck the oil level and refill to the upper sight glass again. Repeat this procedure after two days, at which point the system should be balanced. Do not add more oil unless the level falls below the lower sight glass.

If you install a new oil control system to an existing system, the separator will withdraw some oil that was previously in the system. There is a danger of overfilling the system if you fill the reservoir to the upper sight glass. Instead, fill it to the lower glass and wait about one day to check the level. Then adjust the level accordingly.

OIL LEVEL REGULATOR

An oil regulator may be mounted on each crankcase to control oil level with the aid of a float and valve. The regulator has a sight glass for checking the oil level. Some regulators may be adjusted while the system is in operation, while others require a shutdown. In parallel-compressor systems, a small equalization tube may be used to balance pressure in all crankcases even when some compressors are shut down. This reduces or prevents oil siphoning from idle compressors.

INSTALLING AND SERVICING

A regulator is mounted on the side of the compressor on the three-hole sight glass opening. An adaptor may be needed to fit a regulator to a particular bolt pattern. The oil line is connected from the oil reservoir to the regulator. A shut-off valve may be installed to allow servicing one unit while the rest of the system operates.

The oil reservoir must have a positive pressure toward the regulator to allow oil to flow. A pressure valve on the reservoir may be used to regulate pressure. A gravity feed may be adequate if the reservoir is high enough. If satellite compressors are used, a higher pressure must be provided to force oil to flow to them. Charts are provided by regulator manufacturers to guide you in setting an adjustable regulator.

OIL TEST KIT

Acid in a system usually is picked up by the oil, so tests of oil acidity can reveal the extent of system contamination. Oil test kits are designed to be used only with specific refrigerants; using one with the wrong refrigerant will give a false reading. Old oil may be too cloudy to detect the indicator color clearly, so some test kits allow you to separate a clear solution from the oil before testing.

After testing the oil condition, make the necessary repairs: replace filter-drier elements, refrigerant, or oil as indicated. If the moisture indicator failed to show excessive moisture, it may need servicing or replacement because system moisture is a primary cause of oil acidity.

PUMP, WATER

Water pumps are used to circulate condenser water, chilled water or brine in air-conditioning and refrigeration systems. Pumps are also used to circulate fluids in absorption machines. Either centrifugal or reciprocating pumps may be used. Many types of motors can be used to power a pump, as long as the starting torque and other specifications are correct.

CENTRIFUGAL

A centrifugal pump uses a rotating impeller to accelerate the fluid by centrifugal force (similar to the action of a centrifugal compressor). The centrifugal design is suited to pumping large amounts of water against moderate pressure. The pump must be primed before operation by submersion or another method.

Because the pump has no pistons or other positive action parts, it has a limited ability to pump against resistance. A single-stage pump will operate against about 100 feet of pressure. If the head exceeds the pump's capacity at a given operating speed, the pump will just churn the water in the housing.

Due to its simple design and scarcity of moving parts and close tolerances, this design is economical and widely used. Centrifugal pumps can be placed in the pipe line and supported by the pipe, or connected to a branch.

RECIPROCATING

Many types of reciprocating pumps are available, but because they are more complex than centrifugal pumps, they are not used as frequently. Reciprocating pumps are best applied to situations with high resistance in the piping.

Receiver

The receiver is a vessel used to store liquid refrigerant on the high side of some systems. Some receivers are built into the condenser. The receiver has these advantages:

- *it eliminates the need for an exact refrigerant charge.*

- *it is a handy place to store refrigerant during servicing.*

- *it helps prevent flash gas by ensuring that liquid refrigerant remains subcooled.*

- *it can hold the refrigerant during automatic pumpdowns, such as for defrosting or when some evaporators are shut off.*

Liquid receivers are common in low-side float and expansion valve systems but not in high-side float or capillary tube systems.

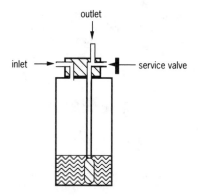

Fig. E4   Liquid receiver

If a partial pumpdown is part of the cooling cycle, a liquid line solenoid at the receiver outlet closes in response to a command from the operating control and the compressor pumps down into the receiver until the low-pressure cutout opens. The refrigerant remains in the receiver until the next on-cycle, when the liquid line solenoid opens, admitting refrigerant to the evaporator (see Part H, *Pumpdown cycle*, p. 278).

Valves on both sides of the receiver are used to shut off the receiver during service work. Sight glasses may be provided to monitor the refrigerant level in the receiver. As an alternative, two petcocks can be installed. When the charge is correct and the compressor is running, liquid refrigerant will flow from the lower petcock and vapor refrigerant from the upper one.

To prevent over-pressure in a receiver, a pressure- or temperature-sensitive safety device must be connected to a vent line to the outside (see *Valve, relief, p. 241*).

Refrigerant Level Control

A refrigerant level control may be found on receivers, intercoolers, surge drums or other places where liquid refrigerant is allowed to gather. Some of these controls merely signal when the level is incorrect. Others will automatically withdraw some refrigerant from the system when the level is too high or add it when the level is too low.

Sight Glass

A sight glass, usually in the discharge line before the metering device, will allow you to diagnose problems such as low charge or excessive moisture. A steady stream of refrigerant in the glass while the unit runs indicates a sufficient charge. See-through glasses have two openings, allowing you to put a flashlight to the opposite side for a better view.

If possible, mount the sight glass upstream of a filter-drier. Any restrictions in that unit will cause a pressure drop that will create bubbles that can be mistaken for low charge.

Some sight glasses incorporate a moisture indicator that turns color when the refrigerant is excessively moist. Moisture indicators may take as long as eight hours to give an accurate reading after system conditions change. Moisture indicators are temperature-dependent (see *Moisture indicator*, p. 177).

An electronic "sight glass" can be clamped on the line to detect bubbles by ultrasound. This device emits a sound when it detects bubbles and can be used temporarily or left in place permanently. Charge can also be assessed on liquid receivers with two petcocks. The charge is correct when liquid refrigerant flows from the lower petcock and vapor from the upper one.

Suction Line

The suction line completes the circuit by returning refrigerant from the evaporator to the compressor. The suction line is at low pressure and low temperature, and for this reason is usually insulated to prevent sweating and energy loss.

In some systems heat exchange between the suction and liquid lines is desired to increase superheat and/or subcooling. This contact can be achieved by allowing the two lines to contact each other, by soldering them together, or by installing a heat exchanger between them.

Suction line pressure drop can significantly raise evaporator temperature, especially at low temperatures. For example, if R-12 with no pressure drop was running at $-40°F$ ($-40°C$), a drop of 2 psi (13.8 kPa) would raise the temperature to $-32°F$ ($-35.6°C$). Thus any restrictions (such as filter-driers, bends) should be designed and installed to minimize the restriction and pressure drop.

The suction line must be designed to help oil to return from the evaporator to the compressor. A reverse trap should be installed in the top of the suction riser to prevent oil from returning down the riser to the evaporator. Slugs of oil that reach the top of the riser must fall into the suction line beyond the reverse trap so they can return to the compressor.

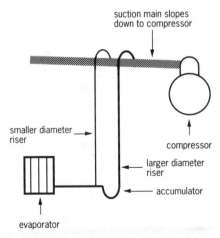

Fig. E5   Double riser-suction line

The double riser suction line system is used only with capacity-controlled compressors. The large riser has about twice the capacity of the smaller riser. During full-load operation, both risers carry refrigerant. If a slug of oil forms in the lower trap (or accumulator) it is pulled up the large line as usual. When the compressor unloads, there is no longer enough velocity to pull the slug of oil up the larger line, and slugs in the trap will close the line. However, the small line will still have enough capacity to handle the part-load flow and return both oil and refrigerant to the compressor.

A p-trap may be used at the bottom of a vertical suction line to promote oil return. Some manufacturers state that a p-trap enables good oil return with vapor velocities as low as 160 feet per minute. Depending on the vapor velocity, the oil can return as a mist, as a rippling film, or as a colloidal dispersion.

Suction Line Accumulator

A suction line accumulator is a small reservoir used to prevent slugs of liquid refrigerant from reaching the compressor. The accumulator is generally, but not always, located inside the cabinet. The typical accumulator has an outlet at the top so only vapor can return to the suction line. The unit should be sized according to the system design and capacity, evaporator temperature, and refrigerant.

Suction Line Pressure Alarm

The low-pressure cutout may include an alarm to announce that suction pressure has risen above a safe level, indicating excessive evaporator temperature. The alarm may have a delay to prevent it from triggering during defrosts. When the timer is energized, it waits a certain period—commonly 45 to 60 minutes—before allowing the alarm to go off.

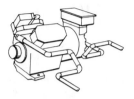

Fig. E6 Stress relief in compressor piping

Vibration Absorber

Both the suction and discharge lines transmit vibration from the compressor to other cooling system components and the building. This vibration can cause unwanted noise and deterioration of tubing, leading to leaks of refrigerant and capillary tube control fluids. (See Part D, *Capillary tubes in other controls*, p. 146).

On a small system with small-diameter soft copper refrigerant lines, the vibration absorber may consist of a coil of tubing. Flexible metallic hose, with an ID at least as large as the connected tubing, is preferable for larger systems. This section of tubing may be terminated by flanges or threaded male ends. Refrigerant travelling too quickly along the convoluted inner diameter of the absorber may cause whistling.

Vibration absorbers are not designed for compression or extension, so they must be oriented parallel to the crankshaft, not at right angles to it. If the absorber is mounted improperly, it will resist the rocking of the compressor instead of flexing along with it. For maximum control of vibration, two absorbers should be placed in each line, one for horizontal movement and the other for vertical movement. Do not stress, compress or twist the absorbers during installation.

Electric motors are used to drive the vast majority of compressors and fans used in cooling systems. Motors are very reliable but they can suffer from troubles that originate elsewhere. For example, a burnout, the ultimate form of motor trouble, may result from contamination or a failure of a limit switch, rather than a motor problem. A failure of a control or relay may seem like motor trouble even though the motor is intact.

Actual motor trouble, on the other hand, is not something the average cooling system technician is trained or equipped to handle. Nevertheless, to pinpoint trouble and correct problems in motor circuits and controls, you must understand the principles of motor operation and troubleshooting.

The degree of service you can perform also depends on the system configuration. Motor-compressors in small hermetic systems must be replaced after a motor failure. But, controls may be located outside the hermetic housing for accessibility. Motors in large hermetic and semihermetic systems may be replaced in the field.

Electric motors convert electrical energy to magnetic energy and then to kinetic energy. The rotation is caused by repeated attractions and repulsions between electromagnets located in the motor housing and induced magnets rotating on the armature. Practically every motor used in a commercial cooling system operates on alternating current because the wavelike magnetic field of AC induces a current in conductors whether or not they are moving in relation to each other. (See Part B, *Electromagnetic energy*, p. 3)

Electric motors have two basic parts: the stator (or the housing or field) and the rotor (or armature) which spins on a shaft inside the housing. When electricity passes through the stator windings, they become an electromagnet whose field strength rises and falls with the AC waves. This induces a current in the rotor, causing it to become a magnet. The motor would not rotate if the opposite poles were positioned next to each other, so motors are designed so the magnetic fields can never rest in this condition. Due to magnetic attraction and repulsion, the rotor tends to spin, and as it does, the magnetic fields shift position to cause the attraction or repulsion to continue.

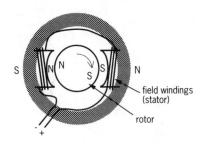

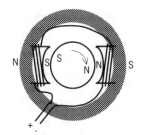

Fig. F1 Elementary/electric motor

As the AC wave increases in strength during the start of each half of its cycle, the induction of magnetism in the rotor lags slightly. By the time the rotor is fully magnetized, the stator is already starting to change polarity due to the change in the AC wave, so the fields can never line up with north opposite south.

Electric motors can respond to changes in demand. As the rotor slows down as a result of increasing load, more current is induced in the rotor, increasing the strength of its magnetic field and thus the motor's output.

The simplest AC motor has a single magnet in the field windings and is called a two-pole motor. Each change of the AC wave causes half a revolution of the rotor. Thus a two-pole motor running on 60 hz (60 cycles per second) current rotates 60 times per second or 3600 revolutions per minute. This is termed synchronous speed, although motors actually "slip" behind synchronous speed, generally to about 3450 rpm. A four-pole motor (with two magnets in the field windings) operates at half this speed because each reversal of the AC produces ¼ turn of the rotor. Synchronous speed for a four-pole, 60 hz, motor is 1800 rpm and the normal running, or "operational," speed is 1750. Four-pole motors are common in compressor drives.

Nameplate Information

All electric motors should have a nameplate listing vital data about installation and operation.

- Required voltage and frequency *(in Volts and hertz, or hz.—1 hz = 1 cycle per second)*
- Service factor *describes the motor's ability to withstand overload. A motor rated at 1.0 cannot sustain an overload without dangerous overheating; one rated at 1.15 can handle a 15 percent continuous overload without damage.*
- *Locked rotor kVA.* The number of kilovolt-amperes drawn when the rotor is locked or starting. Used to diagnose trouble.
- *Time rating.* The amount of time the motor may run without overheating. The rating may be continuous or a certain number of minutes.
- *Frame size.* Used primarily when sizing motors for installation.

Overload and Overheat Protection

Motors must be protected from two related conditions: overload—an excess current draw for any reason, and overheating, which can result from overload or other reasons. Overloading and overheating can cause melted contacts, burned insulation, and burnout. Motors are protected against these perils with a combination of fuses or circuit breakers (to prevent overload) and temperature-sensing devices coupled with shut-offs (to prevent overheating).

A motor overload protector, in the form of a circuit breaker or a fuse, must be installed on each motor circuit. Unlike other circuit breakers, this protector must allow a temporary overload because motors draw up to 600 percent of the running current during startup. To prevent motor damage, the protector must trip under a sustained current more than about 25 percent above rated amperage.

The motor safety may be combined with another device. For example, the starting relay may offer overload protection in the form of a bimetal strip and a resistance heater. Excessive current will warm the heating element, heating the bimetal strip and causing it to bend and open the circuit.

Overheating can result from inadequate refrigerant (in hermetic systems), poor air flow near the compressor (in open systems), a locked rotor, or excessive head pressure during startup. Motor temperature in general should not exceed 72°F (40°C) above room temperature—or about 150° F (66°C). The motor cooling system should receive attention during routine maintenance.

All compressor motors should be supplied by separate circuits, to prevent a problem with another circuit from shutting off power to the compressor motor. The National Electric Code requires that motors have a disconnect installed within sight of the motor control. This disconnect must disconnect both the motor and the control from all ungrounded supply wiring. This disconnect may be incorporated in the overload protective device.

The following devices are used to protect motors from overloading and overheating:

A *fuse* (or circuit breaker) must be found on all electric circuits to protect against excess current. In a motor circuit, a fast-acting fuse can open too quickly during the large draw of a normal startup. A time-delay fuse allows a brief period of excess current before opening, but might not open quickly enough during a true overload. A fourth type, the current-limiting fuse, puts a ceiling on the current allowed into the circuit but does not blow.

Circuit breakers are classified in the same general manner as fuses. Breakers are preferable to fuses because they can be reset after they open. A circuit breaker or fuse that continually blows indicates trouble in the circuit or that the protection device itself is undersized. Do not install an oversize breaker or fuse—correct the problem in the circuit instead.

A *bimetallic overload device* senses temperature or current and opens a circuit if the value exceeds a safe limit. These devices may be buried in the motor windings in hermetic systems—a protection system designated "internal overload protected." The protector should have a snap action so it opens the points quickly and prevents arcing.

A *thermistor* is an electronic device used to sense motor temperature and shut off the flow of current to the motor relay. As temperature rises, resistance increases in a "positive temperature coefficient" thermistor. As temperature rises, resistance decreases in a "negative temperature coefficient" thermistor.

(See Part D, *Testing safety controls*, p. 152.)

Start Winding Relay

The starting winding relay supplies current to the start winding during startup and shuts it off when the motor approaches about 75 percent of operating speed. The relay is mounted outside hermetic housings for easy service.

In open drive equipment, a centrifugal switch may replace a starting relay. This governor-type device is mounted on the motor shaft and also cuts off the start winding current when the motor nears operating speed.

Each type of relay can be tested according to manufacturer's instructions, or it can be replaced by a relay known to be good. A motor-starting relay tester can be used if it is available, or you can test the current in each part of the relay to diagnose the trouble.

When replacing a relay, make sure to reconnect the wires to the correct terminals. A roll of masking tape and a marking pen are handy for labelling wires.

Four types of starting relays are used to control current to the start winding on hermetic and semihermetic systems:

1. A *current relay* is a magnetic switch that senses the current in the run winding. This current is highest when the rotor is stationary or rotating slowly, both indications that the motor is starting. The relay stays closed and energizes the start winding whenever the run winding current is above the setting. When the run winding current falls, a weight or a spring overpowers the magnet, causing the switch to shut off current to the starting winding.

2. A *potential relay* is a magnetic switch that senses voltage in the starting winding. As the motor gains speed, start winding voltage increases, strengthening the electromagnet in the relay. At the set point, the relay opens and current to the start winding is shut off. Because the relay contacts are closed during the off cycle, there is no danger of arcing across the points during start-up.

3. A *thermal relay* warms up in response to current. Two versions are possible:

   • *Separate bimetallic strips open and close circuits to each winding (see Fig. F2d). A heating wire near the bimetallic strip is in series with the run winding. During startup, both windings are energized. When the motor nears operating speed, the heating wire warms the start winding strip and causes it to break contact, shutting off current to the start winding.*

   The device can also serve as a motor safety device. If the run winding draws excess current during operation, the heating wire will warm the bimetallic strip controlling the run winding and shut the motor down.

   • *The heating wire is attached directly to the contacts, and the wire is designed to hold the contacts closed when the wire is cold. When the motor reaches operating speed, the starting winding wire warms and relaxes, breaking contact. This type of relay can also serve as a safety cutout.*

4. Electronic relays of various designs can also be used to control current to the starting winding. These relays sense motor voltage and perform the cutout function.

a) current relay position in circuit

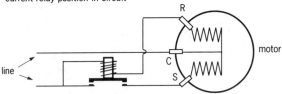

b) potential relay position in circuit

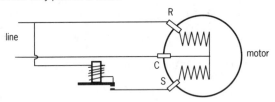

Fig. F2 Starting relays

Contactor and Motor Starter

A contactor is a type of relay used to make and break electric circuits with the aid of an electromagnet. In contrast to a start winding relay, a contactor handles the full line voltage being fed to the motor. Using a contactor eliminates the need to route large currents or voltages to the motor control, thus cutting costs and increasing safety. The control circuit in the contactor is completed in response to signal from a thermostat or another control, energizing the contactor's electromagnet and pulling the armature to close the contacts. The motor circuit remains closed as long as the control energizes the contactor.

c) current or potential relay in run position

armature pushes movable contact when current or potential in magnet is high enough

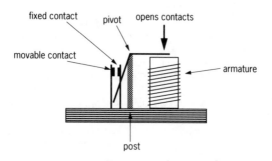

d) thermal relay—run winding energized

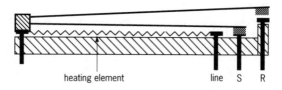

Fig. F2 Starting relays (cont)

A motor starter contains the relay described above, as well other elements, such as overload protectors, disconnects, and whatever else is required to operate a large motor in a complex system.

Enclosures

Four types of motor enclosures may be used for open motors, depending on the application:

- *The* open *motor is cooled by air circulating over the windings. This type may be used in areas with cool temperatures that are relatively free of dust and moisture.*

- Totally-enclosed fan-cooled *motors have a double shell and a fan to circulate air from the inner chamber to the outer chamber. This type is useful in dusty conditions.*

- Splashproof *motors are suited to outdoor installations because they are protected from rain.*

- Explosion-proof *motors are totally enclosed and suitable for use in an explosive atmosphere.*

Bearings

Motors depend on quiet, efficient bearings on the shaft for proper operation. Open motor bearings are lubricated with one of the following:

1. Wicks are used to hold lubricant against the shaft. Wicks should be oiled with the correct non-detergent, medium viscosity oil about twice a year. A wick may become plugged if it is singed, dirty, or lubricated with sludgy oil.

2. A slip ring is designed to dip into a pocket of oil to lubricate a bearing.

3. Oilless bearings are made of porous bronze material impregnated with oil at the factory. They should not need service. Tolerance in oilless bearings is very tight and a bearing may become noisy as it wears. These bearings are most effective when the shaft is rotating continuously and wear relatively quickly with frequent cycling.

Ball bearings can carry a large load but need proper care. Some ball bearings must be replaced in pairs. Ball bearing life span is reduced by rapid rotation, increased load, and dirt, which can scratch the races. Overheating of a bearing may result from incorrect oil grade, dirty or old oil, over-tight belts, a pulley rubbing against the bearing, or improper alignment of the drive. (see Part K, *Drive system service*, p. 349).

BEARING INSTALLATION

Bearing installation must be done correctly or the bearing will never do its job. Do not drop bearings, as they are brittle. Prevent contamination by keeping the bearing, your hands, and the work area clean.

Bearings must be pressed out with special tools, taking care not to damage the motor endplates. Before installing the rotor, the bearing must be reamed in the correct alignment with a special reamer.

Do not remove the rust-preventative coating from new bearings, as it is compatible with bearing grease. Use the correct grade of grease, but do not overfill, as this can cause overheating. Use a tube of grease to lube sealed bearings, as a grease gun can create enough pressure to dislodge the seals.

Support the shaft during installation to prevent pitting of the races. Make sure to align the shaft during installation.

Worn bearings may allow the rotor to contact the stator. This condition may be audible when the motor runs; it calls for immediate action as this abrasion will quickly damage the motor.

Single-Phase Motors

Single-phase motors are most common in fractional-horsepower applications. Because these motors depend on the spinning of the rotor to produce the proper sequence of attraction and repulsion, a separate start winding is needed to start the rotor spinning in the first place (and in the proper direction). The start winding (also called the auxiliary winding) is wired to repel the rotor when the motor is at rest, usually by exerting a magnetic field that is out of phase with the run winding field. Once the motor reaches about two-thirds of synchronous speed, the start winding shuts off and the run winding takes all the current.

Single-phase motors are generally described by the starting and running methods. A capacitor-start motor supplies good starting torque. An induction-run motor depends on the field to induce the proper magnetism in the rotor.

Starting capacitors must not be substituted for running capacitors because they have no means of disposing of heat. A great deal of heat builds up in a run capacitor.

The most popular single-phase motors for refrigeration systems are the split-phase, the capacitor-start, induction-run, and the permanent split capacitor. The capacitor start-capacitor run motor may sometimes be seen on large systems.

A *split-phase* motor has a starting winding with high resistance and low inductance, which alters the phase of the current in the starting winding. These windings are physically located in a place that will provide a weak starting torque. To reverse direction, reverse the main and start windings. A centrifugal switch or starting relay shuts off the start winding when the motor reaches about 75 percent of synchronous speed. The motor is suitable to systems that balance pressure during the off cycle, such as those with a capillary tube metering device or an unloader on the compressor.

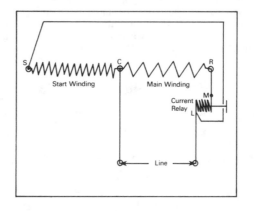

Fig. F3 Split-phase motor

Courtesy of Copeland Corporation

The capacitor-start, induction-run motor is probably the most popular single-phase motor for air conditioning and refrigeration systems. The capacitor in series with the start winding causes the motor to act as a twophase motor during startup. These motors produce high starting torque, and many are adaptable to 120 and 240 V.

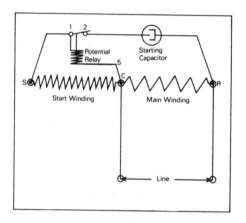

Fig. F4 Capacitor-start, induction-run motor

The *permanent split capacitor* (PSC) motor has a low starting torque so it must be used with systems that balance pressures during the off cycle. The motor requires relatively stable line voltage. No relay is used; both starting and running windings are energized whenever the power is on. Note that a running capacitor is wired between the terminals of the running and starting coils, and that no starting capacitor is used. Low voltage supply can cause over-heating so a thermal protection device is needed.

The *capacitor start–capacitor run* motor is used in large hermetic systems, using a potential relay to control power to the start windings. During startup, both the start and run windings receive electricity through a capacitor. This two-phase motor is very efficient and has a high starting torque.

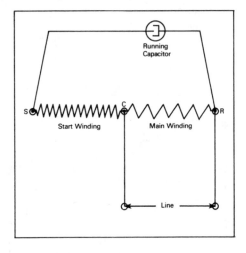

Fig. F5 Permanent split capacitor motor

Three-Phase Motors

Three-phase motors are used in larger compressors and fans because they have a higher power factor and are more efficient than single-phase motors. In addition, they require no start winding as some magnets are always in a position to repel each other.

Most three-phase motors run on voltages of 208 V and above. Because of the complicated nature of the wiring for these motors, it is best to have a qualified electrician hook them up. By changing any two leads of the connection, the direction of rotation can be reversed. Many three-phase motors can be adapted from 220 V or 440 V by changing the connections.

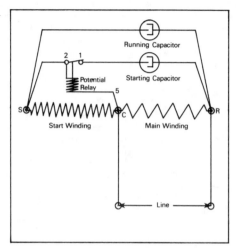

Fig. F6 Capacitor start-capacitor run motor

Most three-phase motors are protected by a circuit breaker which controls all three hot leads to the motor. If protected by fuses, each fuse will regulate a single phase of the current. If one fuse blows, the motor may continue running on the other two phases, but this is likely to overload the motor. A "phase loss monitor" can be used to detect this situation. If you suspect a loss of phase in a fuse-protected three-phase motor and no monitor is being used, test each of the three phases individually with a voltmeter. A three-phase motor should show full input voltage across each pair of input wires. The current is supplied by a heavy-duty relay having three contacts. The motor starter housing may contain a circuit breaker or other overload protection device.

Three-phase motors that draw the full line current are said to have "across-the-line starting." This can result in starting current as much as 650 percent of full load current, which may dim lights and reduce voltage to other equipment. For these reasons, some utilities restrict the use of across-the-line starting. A part-winding may be used to cut down the current surge at start-up, but this reduces starting torque. See below for a procedure for testing the voltage of three-phase motors.

TESTING VOLTAGE AND AMPERAGE

The voltage unbalance between the three legs of a three-phase motor should not exceed 2 percent when calculated with this formula: 100 times the sum of the deviations of the three voltage readings from the average (ignore the sign of the deviation) divided by twice the average voltage.

For a motor rated at 208 V, with legs reading 211, 206, and 205 V, the formula would be:

Average = 211 + 206 + 205 = 622/3 = 207.33

$$\frac{(211 - 207) + (207 - 206) + (207 - 205)}{2 * 207.33} * 100 = \frac{7 * 100}{414.66}$$

$$= 700/414.66 = 1.69\%\text{—within the 2 percent guideline.}$$

If the voltage balance is unacceptable, notify the electric utility before the motor is damaged.

Amperage on all lines should also be close to each other. If one or two legs are higher than the other leg(s), you have either an unbalanced voltage or a winding imbalance. Either check the voltage with the procedure above or:

1. Mark each supply wire and write down the amperages you have found.

2. Disconnect the supply wires from the terminals and reconnect to different ones.

3. Measure amperage during the same load conditions as when the problem was detected.

4. If the high amperage reading stays at the same line, the problem is with the supply. If the high amperage remains at the same terminal, the winding is at fault.

Motor Troubles

Motors are subject to mechanical and electrical damage. A motor with major problems must be repaired by a specialist or replaced. However, an air conditioning and refrigeration technician should be able to diagnose and repair simple motor problems. For an overall view of system troubleshooting, refer to Part J, *System*, p. 314. For specific motor troubleshooting information, see Part J, *Motors*, p. 335.

The first step in assessing whether a motor is at fault is to check the safety and operating controls and the operating conditions. Many external factors can interfere with proper operation: excessive cycling, a blown capacitor or fuse, or a faulty operating control.

Then examine the motor nameplate. Check that the electric power has the proper frequency, voltage, amperage, and phase. Voltage must be within 10 percent of the value on the nameplate. Check for loose or undersize wires or overloaded circuits, or inadequate power supply to the building. Read the actual voltage with a voltmeter while the unit runs, if it will operate. Hook up an ammeter—amperage should never exceed 120 percent of nameplate value, except during startup. Excessive current draw indicates overload or other difficulties.

IDENTIFYING TERMINALS

If you are working on a motor that has no indication of which terminal is start winding (S), run winding (R), or common (C), test the impedance across each combination of two terminals with an ohmmeter:

- *The highest resistance will be between R and S.*
- *The lowest resistance should be between C and R.*
- *The sum of resistance from C to S and C to R equals resistance from R to S:*

$$\begin{array}{r} \text{Resistance C–S} \\ + \quad \text{Resistance C–R} \\ \hline = \quad \text{Resistance R–S} \end{array}$$

WINDING PROBLEMS

Motor windings are subject to three types of problems:

- *Grounds are failures of insulation between a winding and the motor frame. A ground will generally cause motor failure.*

- *Shorts are internal insulation failures that cause part of the winding to be bypassed. The motor may continue to run, but will not reach full power. A short will increase current draw, decrease power, and lead to overheating. Resistance in the winding will be below manufacturer's specifications.*

- *Opens are windings that are incomplete, preventing the flow of current. Opens will generally cause motor failure. Because they create infinite resistance in the winding, they are easy to detect with an ohmmeter.*

MOTOR DIAGNOSIS

After confirming that the motor is not being shut down by operating or safety controls, check whether the motor has grounds, shorts, or opens with the procedure below. If the motor is hot, the internal overload protection may be interrupting the circuit. Allow it to cool, then check for short, grounds and opens:

1. Check for grounded windings. (This can be done without an ohmmeter—see the procedure on the next page.) Connect one lead of an ohmmeter to the housing and the other lead to each winding terminal in turn. Resistance should be off the scale of a standard ohmmeter.

    A better test for grounds requires the use of a megohmmeter, because some grounds will not show up unless you have a very high test voltage. Use caution with a high voltage. A hermetic motor of 1 hp or less should have resistance of at least one million ohms. Larger motors should have at least 1000 ohms per volt. Refer to manufacturer's literature or use the above guidelines. (Grounds are more likely to show up when the motor is warm, so run the motor for a few minutes first.)

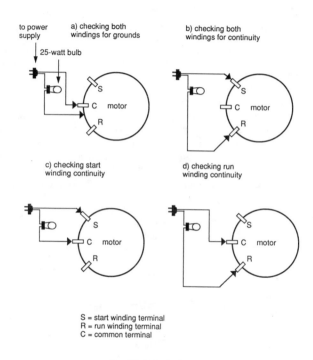

S = start winding terminal
R = run winding terminal
C = common terminal

Fig. F7 Motor test

2. Check operating and locked-rotor volt–ampere draw. Use an ammeter–voltmeter to measure whether excessive current is being drawn. Compare to nameplate values. There is no need to use a wattmeter or worry about the power factor for this test. If you have a wattmeter, measure the wattage draw during startup (one second only) and during running. Starting wattage should be much higher than running wattage. If both readings are similar, the motor is locked or has other problems.

ALTERNATE MOTOR TEST

Some motor diagnostic tests can be made without a meter. Prepare a simple continuity tester by assembling a 25-watt bulb and socket, a pair of test leads, and a standard 120-V plug as shown in Fig. F7. (Use care with the test leads as they will be carrying 120-V current.)

Disconnect the motor from the circuit and use this procedure:

1. Check both windings for ground by connecting one lead to the start terminal and the other to a clean, rust-free section of the housing. If the bulb lights, an internal ground must be repaired.

2. Check the continuity of both windings by connecting the test leads to the start and run terminals. A light indicates the windings are intact. If the bulb fails to light, continue to step 3.

3. Check the continuity of the start winding by connecting leads to the start and common terminals. If the bulb lights, the winding is intact.

4. Check the continuity of the run winding by connecting leads to the run and common terminals. A light indicates the winding is intact.

TESTING AND REPLACING CAPACITORS

The capacitor is a common source of motor trouble. The capacitor creates a slight "delay" in the current, usually to create a temporary second phase for the starting windings. Some motors use starting and running capacitors, while others use only a starting capacitor.

Test a capacitor with a capacitor tester. An easier method is to replace the suspect capacitor with an identical new one.

Do not use an undersize capacitor. When replacing a capacitor, use these guidelines if the identical item is unavailable:

- *The voltage rating must be at least as high as the original.*
- *Starting capacitors must have between 100 and 120 percent of original capacitance.*
- *Running capacitors must have between 90 and 110 percent of original capacitance.*

For capacitors in parallel, each replacement must have a voltage rating at least as high as the original. To find the total capacitance of parallel capacitors, add the ratings of each individual capacitor in the circuit.

For series capacitors, the total voltages of the replacement capacitors must equal the originals. Find the total capacitance of series capacitors with this formula:

$$C_t = \frac{C_1 C_2}{C_1 + C_2}$$

Capacitors may be connected by solder or screw terminals. Do not substitute a starting capacitor for a running capacitor, as starting capacitors cannot dispose of heat rapidly enough.

WARNING: A capacitor can hold its electric charge after the power is turned off. Be sure to discharge a capacitor by attaching a 100,000-ohm resistor across the terminals. Wet-type capacitors, which are designed for continuous duty on running windings, may contain a toxic chemical called polychlorinated biphenyl (PCB). Do not open such a capacitor. If it is dripping fluid, do not touch or breathe the fumes. Dispose of wet capacitors in accord with local environmental regulations.

STARTING A ST
HERMETIC COMPRESSOR

Some units will not start even though the motor and controls are in good condition. This may occur if the unit has been idle for a long time or has excess refrigerant. First try to diagnose motor or control problems as suggested above. Then use one of these methods to start the motor:

1. Connect a power line to the motor terminals, bypassing the starting relay.

2. *Briefly* connect a higher-voltage source to the motor terminals (see Fig. F8a).

3. Wire a capacitor in series with the running winding to run the motor backward. Connect the circuit for only two seconds (see Fig. F8b).

a) using higher voltage

b) reversing rotation

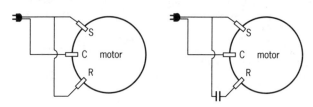

c) using a capacitor in the start winding

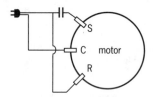

Fig. F8 Starting a stuck motor   *(apply current for 2 sec. maximum)*

4. Install a capacitor in the start winding as shown in Fig. F8c.
5. Use a hermetic analyzer to move the motor. Consult instructions for the device for the exact hookup.

PIPE, TUBE, AND FITTINGS

Pipe and fittings are the sinews joining the components of air conditioning and refrigeration systems. This section covers the major varieties of pipe and tube, fittings, and valves needed in various types of systems. It also describes procedures for handling tubing—bending, flaring, brazing, and soldering.

Piping Design

A proper piping design will help a system operate safely, efficiently, and always under control. Pipe and system design is the province of engineers, but a few pointers will help technicians install and service equipment.

The size of connections at the compressor do not indicate the size of piping needed. Pipe sizing depends on many factors that the compressor manufacturer cannot know.

The requirements of a refrigerant piping system are numerous. The ideal piping design incorporates these factors:

- **Economical use of refrigerant and energy**—*Energy should be conserved. Systems with excessive refrigerant are hard to control and operate erratically. Systems with too much capacity tend to short-cycle and this reduces equipment life.*

- **Creates little noise**—*Insufficient pipe size leads to excessive refrigerant velocity, which creates noise.*

- **Controls the refrigerant during all demand states**—*The system must be able to handle minimum expected loads as well as maximum load.*

- **Minimizes pressure drop**—*This pressure drop reduces capacity and increases power use. However, enlarging the suction line to reduce pressure drop may cut refrigerant velocity so much that oil will not return to the compressor.*

215

Pipe and Tube

Although "pipe" and "tube" are often used interchangeably, in this manual, "tubing" refers to material that is not threaded. Pipe is material that is joined with threads, primarily iron or steel pipe. However, steel pipe that is welded, as in ammonia systems, is also called pipe here. In air-conditioning and refrigeration work, the major tubing material is copper, although steel, stainless steel, and plastic are also used.

COPPER

Copper tubing is classified in two ways: by use and by manufacture. By use:

1. Plumbing (also called nominal size) tube, has an actual OD ⅛-inch (.32 cm) larger than the nominal size. This category includes both water tube and drainage (DWV) tube.
2. Air-conditioning and refrigeration (ACR) tube is described by OD, which is its actual outside diameter. ACR tube receives special handling during and after manufacture to keep it clean.

Tubing is also classified by method of manufacture and degree of hardness:

1. Hard-drawn tubing is stiff because it is not annealed after drawing. Hard tube should not be flared or bent without annealing. The best procedure is to make bends and connections with fittings.
2. Soft tubing is annealed after drawing and is more workable, so it can be flared, swaged to make a joint without a coupling, or bent. Soft tubing must have more supports on long runs than hard tubing.

Although hard tube is preferable for cooling system work, soft tubing may be used in liquid and suction lines which require flexibility, as in transport refrigeration. It is also used in capillary tubes, which must be manipulated during installation.

Age, hammering, and bending all tend to "work harden" copper, making it brittle and unsuited to bending and flaring. Anneal work-hardened (or hard-drawn) tubing by heating it to a dull red and allowing it to cool.

The three grades of copper tubing are:

- Water tube, *the type of plumbing tube used for water supply, is available in hard or soft temper. Water tube may be connected by flaring or soldering. Soft water tube must be supported at close intervals on long runs. Soft tubing is sold in 25-foot and 50-foot (7.62- and 15.24-meter) coils. The inside diameter is close to, but not exactly the same as, the nominal size.*

  Water tube is made in three wall thicknesses:

  > *Type K: heavy wall—used where corrosion is expected*
  > *Type L: medium wall*
  > *Type M: light wall*

- Drainage tube (DWV, for Drain, Waste, Vent), *another type of plumbing tube, is used for drains and vent lines. Minimum size is 1¼ inches (3.175 cm). DWV has a thin wall and is not designed for pressure applications. It is available only in hard temper.*

- ACR (Air-Conditioning and Refrigeration) tube *is used for most cooling system work. In the color-coding system used by manufacturers to mark tubing, ACR has crimson on the carton. Most ACR tubing is made hard in Type L—medium wall thickness. The designated OD equals the actual outside diameter.*

  ACR is available in 20-foot (6.01 m) lengths. At the factory, the tube is chemically cleaned, dried, filled with nitrogen to prevent oxidation in storage, and capped. This treatment allows the construction of clean cooling systems. Keep the ends sealed while storing and working with ACR tube to prevent contamination and corrosion. The nitrogen will be diluted or lost during work, but sealing the ends is better than nothing. When brazing ACR tubing, purge the lines and fill them with nitrogen to prevent oxidation inside the system, which can cause scale and corrosion problems.

  ACR can be worked with techniques usd for hard plumbing tube. However, annealing the tube (before bending or flaring) will cause corrosion, nullifying the benefit of using clean, evacuated tube. Therefore, it is best to use solder fittings instead of bending.

TABLE G1
Dimensions and Properties of Copper Tube

Line Size O.D.	Type	Diameter OD In.	Diameter ID In.	Wall Thickness In.	Surface Area Sq. Ft./Lin. Ft. OD	Surface Area Sq. Ft./Lin. Ft. ID	Inside Cross-section Area, Sq. In.	Lineal Feet Containing 1 Cu. Ft.	Weight Lb./Lin. Ft.	Working Pressure Psia
⅜	K	0.375	0.305	0.035	0.0982	0.0798	0.0730	1973.0	0.145	918
	L	0.375	0.315	0.030	0.0982	0.0825	0.0779	1848.0	0.126	764
½	K	0.500	0.402	0.049	0.131	0.105	0.127	1135.0	0.269	988
	L	0.500	0.430	0.035	0.131	0.113	0.145	1001.0	0.198	677
⅝	K	0.625	0.527	0.049	0.164	0.138	0.218	660.5	0.344	779
	L	0.625	0.545	0.040	0.164	0.143	0.233	621.0	0.285	625
¾	K	0.750	0.652	0.049	0.193	0.171	0.334	432.5	0.418	643
	L	0.750	0.666	0.042	0.193	0.174	0.348	422.0	0.362	547
⅞	K	0.875	0.745	0.065	0.229	0.195	0.436	331.0	0.641	747
	L	0.875	0.785	0.045	0.229	0.206	0.484	299.0	0.455	497

Size	Type									
1⅛	K	1.125	0.995	0.065	0.295	0.260	0.778	186.0	0.839	574
	L	1.125	1.025	0.050	0.295	0.268	0.825	174.7	0.655	432
1⅜	K	1.375	1.245	0.065	0.360	0.326	1.22	118.9	1.04	466
	L	1.375	1.265	0.055	0.360	0.331	1.26	115.0	0.884	387
1⅝	K	1.625	1.481	0.072	0.425	0.388	1.72	83.5	1.36	421
	L	1.625	1.505	0.060	0.425	0.394	1.78	81.4	1.14	359
2⅛	K	2.125	1.959	0.083	0.556	0.513	3.01	48.0	2.06	376
	L	2.125	1.985	0.070	0.556	0.520	3.10	46.6	1.75	316
2⅝	K	2.625	2.435	0.095	0.687	0.638	4.66	31.2	2.93	352
	L	2.625	2.465	0.080	0.687	0.645	4.77	30.2	2.48	295
3⅛	K	3.125	2.907	0.109	0.818	0.761	6.64	21.8	4.00	343
	L	3.125	2.945	0.090	0.818	0.771	6.81	21.1	3.33	278
3⅝	K	3.625	3.385	0.120	0.949	0.886	9.00	16.1	5.12	324
	L	3.625	3.425	0.100	0.949	0.897	9.21	15.6	4.29	268
4⅛	K	4.125	3.857	0.134	1.08	1.01	11.7	12.4	6.51	315
	L	4.125	3.905	0.110	1.08	1.02	12.0	12.1	5.38	256

With copper fittings made to fit both nominal size and ACR tube, there is a great potential for confusion. You can avoid this problem by always ordering and naming fittings, lines, and devices by OD only. The best practice is to use long-radius fittings to minimize resistance to flow.

Long runs of tubing must be designed to accommodate the expansion of copper with warming. Otherwise, the tubing assembly will be subject to breaking, buckling, leaking at joints, or it may damage the building structure. A rise in temperature of 50°F (27.8°C) will expand a 100-foot (30.5-m) tube by 0.57 inch (1.45 cm), while a 100°F (55.6°C) rise will expand it by 1.06 inch (2.69 cm). Expansion joints should be provided in long lines if the tube temperature is subject to much variation. The expansion joint can consist of a loop of tube (horizontal in a suction line to allow oil return) or other means of allowing the tube to flex.

STEEL

Although most cooling system work is done with copper pipe, ammonia systems require black standard weight steel pipe. Connections in these systems are generally made with black extra-heavy welding steel fittings.

Steel pipe is described by ID (inside diameter). Stainless steel tubing (often no. 304) is required for some food-processing applications, such as in brewing and milk handling systems.

PLASTIC

Plastic tubing is restricted by limitations on its working temperature and pressure. Plastic tubing may be used for cold-water lines and water-cooled condensers. Polyethylene tubing is the most common type of plastic tubing. Black tubing is used in outdoor applications because its pigments reduce degradation from ultraviolet light. Manufacturers will supply information about resistance of products to oil, refrigerant, and other chemicals.

Fittings

Fittings are used to connect adjacent lengths of tubing and pipe. In comfort cooling and refrigeration work, the major fitting categories are brazed and flared, although threaded fittings are used on water pipes and small ammonia pipes. Larger ammonia systems use welded steel fittings.

Copper fittings are available in short-, medium-, and long-radius configurations. In cooling system work, long-radius fittings are preferred because they have less resistance to fluid flow, thus creating a smaller pressure drop in the system. Fittings should be of the wrought variety, which resists pressurized refrigerant vapor better than the cast variety.

A vast number of fittings are made for various applications in the trade. A standard terminology has been developed to describe fittings and reduce confusion in specifying them. The safest procedure is to always specify fittings by OD (see Table G2).

1. *Flare fittings* are often used with soft copper tubing, in relatively small sizes (usually under ¾-inch (1.9-cm) OD) The flare must be a 45° flare, not the 37° flare used in some other applications. Flare fittings are described by the tubing OD, not the thread size: a ¼-inch OD flare nut connects ¼-inch OD tubing to ¼-inch OD flare fitting. Fitting nuts have hexagonal flats for a wrench.

   Special short flare nuts have been devised for cold-temperature connections because water migrates by capillary action into the gap between the nut and the tubing. Under freezing conditions this water can compress the tube and destroy it. This problem can be alleviated by 1) drilling through the flare nut, 2) using a flare nut with water passages built in, or 3) using a special, short flare nut which has too little room for frost to form.

2. *Threaded fittings* in refrigeration work are used mainly for water lines and smaller sizes of ammonia piping. Threaded fittings have either coarse or fine thread. Pipe thread (NP or National Pipe) is coarse. Fine thread is found on Society of Automotive Engineers (SAE) fittings, and is also called National Fine (NF) Thread. Fittings are described by the tubing size and NP or NF.

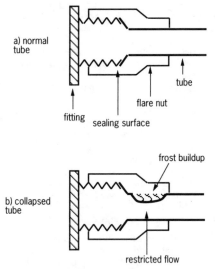

a) normal tube

tube

flare nut

sealing surface

fitting

b) collapsed tube

frost buildup

restricted flow

Fig. G1 Flared tube collapsing under frost

3. *Capillary fittings,* also called *solder, sweat,* or *wrought* fittings, are soldered or brazed to tubes. Capillary fittings are named because the filler metal flows into the joint by capillary action. These fittings are strong, easy to join, and virtually leakproof if installed properly. Capillary fittings are available in short-, medium-, and long-radius configurations. The long-radius fittings are preferred because they have less resistance to fluid flow, thus creating a smaller pressure drop. Fittings should be wrought rather than cast, because they resist pressurized refrigerant vapor better.

   A tight joint requires just enough room for the filler metal to flow, so a precise gap between the fitting and the tubing must be maintained during brazing or soldering.

4. Compression fittings can be used to connect plastic tubing to

copper tubing. (Because polyethylene is soft, tighten these fittings gently. Polyethylene fittings are not commonly used in air conditioning and refrigeration systems.)

5. A quick-connect fitting allows field connection of factory-charged systems without the need to purge and charge their lines. A precharged system using these connectors would consist of an evaporator, a compressor condensing unit, and the tubing to connect them together. Everything is precharged, and the suction line is ready-insulated.

   The quick-connect couplings are equipped with diaphragms that seal the tubing during storage and setup. A knife in each coupling cuts the diaphragm as the coupling is engaged. The connection must be made quickly. The tubes come in specific lengths. If one is too long, do not cut it, as this would allow air to enter. Make a horizontal coil of the excess tube (this is especially important in a suction line, which must allow oil to return to the compressor).

PRESSURE DROP

Fittings restrict fluid flow, causing pressure drop and reducing system efficiency. The number of fittings in a system should be minimized, and the necessary ones chosen to allow maximum flow. When engineers design piping systems, they use a technique called "equivalent length of pipe" to determine how much restriction each fitting or component will add to the total flow restriction. This calculation system assumes that each fitting has a characteristic resistance to fluid flow that equals the resistance of a certain length of tube of the same diameter.

To determine the total resistance of a piping circuit, an engineer simply adds the length of all straight runs to the equivalent length of pipe of all fittings. Then he or she could consult a line sizing table, which gives pressure drop per 100 feet of pipe of each size, to determine overall pressure drop (see Table G3 for equivalent length of pipe data for common fittings). Pressure drop in certain types of fittings, such as solenoid or pressure-regulating valves, should be listed in manufacturer's literature.

TABLE G2

Fitting Varieties

Class	Use	Common varieties	Sample identification	Comments
Extension or joining	Connect same-size pipe or tube	Coupling	7/8-inch OD solder coupling	Two female ends.
		Nipple	3/4-inch by 4inch nipple	Connects fittings—has two male ends. From "close"—all threaded, to 6 inches.
	Removable connection of tube or pipe	Union	7/8-inch OD solder union	Both ends are sweat fittings; also available with one sweat, one threaded.
Reducing or enlarging	Connect different size pipe or tube	Reducing coupling	7/8-inch OD solder by 5/8-inch OD solder coupling	
	Connects threaded pipe to sweated tube	Adaptor	7/8-inch OD solder by 3/4-inch pipe thread (NPT)	
Directional	Change direction of a pipe	Elbow (ell)	7/8-inch OD solder ell	Elbows come in three radii—short, medium or long. Long-radius should be used in refrigeration

				because they cause less pressure drop.
		Street elbow	7/8-inch OD solder street ell	Has one male end and one female end.
	Connects two sizes of tube	Reducing elbow	7/8-inch OD solder by 5/8-inch OD solder ell	
	Makes a 45° bend	45° elbow	7/8-inch OD solder 45°	Also made in street variety.
Branching	Join three or more tubes at one point	Tee	7/8-inch OD solder tee (all tubes same size)	
	Three tubes, two tube sizes	Reducing tee	7/8-inch OD by 5/8-inch OD (reducing tee with constant run)	Specify the run first and then the branching size.
	Three tubes, three tube sizes	Reducing tee	7/8-inch OD by 5/8-inch OD by 7/8-inch OD	Specify the two run sizes first and then the branching size.
Shut off or closing	Closes end on tube or pipe	Cap	7/8-inch OD cap	Female.
	For threaded only	Plug	3/4-inch plug	Male.
Flange	Connects pipe to equipment	Flange	2-1/8-inch OD solder flange	Specified by pipe OD.

MANY OTHER FITTINGS ARE AVAILABLE, FOLLOWING THIS GENERAL NOMENCLATURE.

ELBOWS, TEES, UNIONS AND 45° CAN BE USED AS SOLDER-TO-THREAD ADAPTORS. TO SPECIFY, YOU MUST DESCRIBE WHICH END IS SOLDERED AND WHICH IS THREADED. FOR EXAMPLE, 7/8-INCH OD SOLDER BY 3/4-INCH MPT (MALE PIPE THREAD).

NOTE: FOR PURPOSES OF THIS MANUAL, TUBE IS CONNECTED BY SOLDERING OR BRAZING; PIPE IS CONNECTED BY THREADS OR WELDS (FOR AMMONIA SYSTEMS).

In practice, many engineers use a compensation factor based on experience instead of using equivalent length of pipe data. Thus a standard 100-foot run might be assumed to have 20 to 30 percent restrictions (and would be equivalent to 120 or 130 feet of straight pipe). On shorter, more complicated layouts, a higher compensation factor must be used. Although equivalent length of pipe data primarily concerns engineers, it may be helpful if you suspect that the compressor is too small for the system.

TABLE G3
Equivalent Length

OD, In. Line Size	Globe Valve	Angle Valve	90° Elbow	45° Elbow	Tee Line	Tee Branch
½	9	5	.9	.4	.6	2.0
⅝	12	6	1.0	.5	.8	2.5
⅞	15	8	1.5	.7	1.0	2.5
1⅛	22	12	1.8	.9	1.5	4.5
1⅜	28	15	2.4	1.2	1.8	6.0
1⅝	35	17	2.8	1.4	2.0	7.0
2⅛	45	22	3.9	1.8	3.0	10.0
2⅝	51	26	4.6	2.2	3.5	12.0
3⅛	65	34	5.5	2.7	4.5	15.0
3⅝	80	40	6.5	3.0	5.0	17.0

COURTESY OF COPELAND CORPORATION

LIQUID AND SUCTION LINE SIZES

Engineers use pressure drop tables to size liquid and suction lines. Technicians, who are responsible for installing the designs, do not ordinarily need these tables. A simpler table listing line carrying capacity (Table G4) is enough to make a rough check of liquid and suction line sizes. Find the system refrigerant in the top row and the system Btu/hour in the left column. Read across from the Btu/hour column to find liquid line size. Find the suction line size in the proper suction line temperature column.

To do the above check, you must know the system capacity in

Btu/hour. Multiply a tonnage rating by 12,000 to find Btu/hour. You can find the capacity of a new system by examining the specifications. For old systems, check the rating of the expansion valve, read the compressor nameplate, or track down literature for that model of compressor.

The liquid line should be somewhat oversized if the exact capacity is not listed on the chart. If the suction line is not listed for your exact capacity, go down in size a bit (but not a great deal) to increase suction line velocity and help ensure oil return.

Valves

A wide variety of valves are used in cooling systems. The refrigerant piping requires shut off, solenoid, and three-way valves. Heat pumps use a four-way valve. Water-cooled condenser systems and chiller distribution systems also have plumbing valves.

NOTE: it is a good idea to "crack" all valves open when opening them for the first time. Crack a valve by opening it one-quarter turn or less and immediately closing it. This will protect you from unexpected rushes of pressure if the system has very high pressure or the valve malfunctions.

Valves can be categorized as low resistance (gate, ball, plug, and butterfly) or high resistance (globe or angle). In addition, valves are described by these important aspects:

1. *Flow characteristic* is the relationship between the setting of the valve handle and flow rate. The characteristic can be varied by altering the actuator mechanism or the internal valve mechanism.

   A linear flow characteristic exists when each turn of the handle produces the same increase in flow. In a quick-opening characteristic, the first turn opens the valve more than the second turn, and so on. This characteristic is useful for on–off valves. An equal-percentage characteristic valve increases the flow an equal percentage with each unit of opening.

2. *Rangeability* is the ratio of maximum controllable flow to min-

TABLE G4
Carrying Capacity of Pipe
Sizes of Refrigerant Lines

Btu. Per Hour	Refrigerant 12			Refrigerant 22			Refrigerant 502		
	Liquid Line	Suction Line		Liquid Line	Suction Line		Liquid Line	Suction Line	
		5°F	40°F		5°F	40°F		5°F	40°F
3,000	1/4	1/2	1/2	1/4	1/2	1/2	1/4	1/2	1/2
6,000	3/8	5/8	5/8	3/8	5/8	5/8	3/8	5/8	5/8
9,000	3/8	7/8	5/8	3/8	7/8	5/8	3/8	7/8	5/8
12,000	3/8	1 1/8	7/8	3/8	7/8	7/8	3/8	7/8	7/8
15,000	3/8	1 1/8	7/8	3/8	1 1/8	7/8	3/8	1 1/8	7/8
18,000	3/8	1 1/8	7/8	3/8	1 1/8	7/8	3/8	1 1/8	7/8
21,000	1/2	1 1/8	1 1/8	1/2	1 1/8	1 1/8	1/2	1 1/8	1 1/8
24,000	1/2	1 3/8	1 1/8	1/2	1 1/8	1 1/8	1/2	1 1/8	1 1/8
30,000	5/8	1 3/8	1 1/8	1/2	1 3/8	1 1/8	5/8	1 3/8	1 1/8
36,000	5/8	1 3/8	1 3/8	5/8	1 3/8	1 3/8	5/8	1 3/8	1 1/8
42,000	5/8	1 5/8	1 3/8	5/8	1 3/8	1 3/8	5/8	1 3/8	1 1/8
48,000	5/8	1 5/8	1 3/8	5/8	1 3/8	1 3/8	5/8	1 3/8	1 3/8

BTU/hr								
54,000	5/8	1 3/8	5/8	1 5/8	1 3/8	5/8	1 5/8	1 3/8
60,000	7/8	1 3/8	5/8	1 5/8	1 3/8	7/8	1 5/8	1 3/8
72,000	7/8	1 5/8	7/8	1 5/8	1 3/8	7/8	1 5/8	1 3/8
96,000	7/8	2 1/8	7/8	2 1/8	1 5/8	7/8	2 1/8	1 5/8
108,000	7/8	2 1/8	7/8	2 1/8	1 5/8	7/8	2 1/8	1 5/8
120,000	7/8	2 5/8	7/8	2 1/8	2 1/8	7/8	2 1/8	1 5/8
150,000	1 1/8	2 5/8	1 1/8	2 5/8	2 1/8	1 1/8	2 5/8	2 1/8
180,000	1 1/8	3 1/8	1 1/8	2 5/8	2 5/8	1 1/8	2 5/8	2 1/8
210,000	1 3/8	3 1/8	1 3/8	2 5/8	2 5/8	1 3/8	2 5/8	2 1/8
240,000	1 3/8	3 1/8	1 3/8	3 1/8	2 5/8	1 3/8	3 1/8	2 5/8
300,000	1 3/8	3 5/8	1 3/8	3 1/8	3 1/8	1 3/8	3 1/8	2 5/8
360,000	1 5/8	4 1/8	1 5/8	3 1/8	3 1/8	1 3/8	3 1/8	2 5/8
420,000	1 5/8	4 1/8	1 5/8	3 5/8	3 1/8	1 5/8	3 5/8	3 1/8
480,000	1 5/8	4 1/8	1 5/8	3 5/8	3 1/8	1 5/8	3 5/8	3 1/8
540,000	1 5/8	4 7/8	1 5/8	4 1/8	3 1/8	1 5/8	4 1/8	3 1/8
600,000	1 5/8	4 7/8	1 5/8	4 1/8	3 1/8	1 5/8	4 1/8	3 1/8

TO CONVERT BTU PER HOUR TO TONS OF REFRIGERATION—DIVIDE BY 12,000. SUCTION TEMPERATURE, CONDENSING MEDIUM, COMPRESSOR DESIGN AND MANY OTHER FACTORS DETERMINE HORSE-POWER REQUIRED FOR A TON OF REFRIGERATING CAPACITY. CONSULT ASHRAE HANDBOOK.

Courtesy of Mueller Brass Co.

imum controllable flow. The higher the rangeability, the better the control of low flows, and the higher the price.

3. *Tight shutoff* is the ability to close with virtually no leakage. Single-seated valves have better shutoff than double-seated valves.

4. *Cavitation* is the creation of bubbles in a valve due to the loss of pressure after a restriction (flash gas is a type of cavitation). The repeated formation and implosion of bubbles as they reach an area of increased pressure causes tiny shock waves that can fatigue the valve and ruin it.

5. *Maximum fluid pressure* and temperature are rated by the manufacturer to reflect all aspects of valve construction. The nominal body rating is not reliable for this purpose because some components in the valve may be weaker than the body.

6. *Pressure drop* is the difference between upstream and downstream pressure.

CONSTRUCTION

Four basic types of construction can be used in valves:

1. A *single-seated valve* is capable of tight shutoff, although more control force is required than with a double-seated valve. Single-seated valves may incorporate a diaphragm inside the valve body and between the stem and the seat. In this design, opening the stem will not open the valve if there is a vacuum in the line.

2. A *double-seated valve* is designed to minimize closing force and maximize opening area. However, it is not as good at complete shut-off as a single-seated valve.

3. A *three-way mixing valve* has two inlets and one outlet. The proportion of inlet A to inlet B is regulated by the stem.

4. A *three-way diverting valve* has a single inlet and two outlets. Any proportion of flow to either or both outlets is regulated by the stem. An example is a compressor service valve.

CHECK

Check valves allow fluids to flow in only one direction. They are used to prevent a backflow of refrigerant in hot-gas defrost cycles and during compressor shutdowns. When damaged, check valves may fail to reseat and make a hammering sound.

Courtesy of Watsco, Inc.

Fig. G1b Check valves

CONDENSER PRESSURE REGULATOR

A condenser pressure regulator (also called a holdback valve, a head pressure control, a limitizer, or a condenser limiter) is designed to maintain high-side pressure so an adequate pressure drop will occur at the metering device. The valve can be damaged by pressure fluctuation and should be protected by being located at the condenser outlet, not at the inlet.

The condenser pressure regulator is helpful for maintaining head pressure during low ambient temperatures. The valve can be set to nearly fill the condenser with refrigerant, thus reducing the area available for condensing during these conditions (see Part H, *Cold weather operation*, p. 279).

CRANKCASE PRESSURE REGULATOR (CPR)

This modulating valve limits the supply and pressure of refrigerant to the crankcase as a way of limiting the compressor loading during motor startup. The valve responds only to outlet (suction) pressure. The valve (also called the suction pressure regulator) is installed in the suction line near the compressor. The valve remains closed as long as crankcase pressure is above the valve setting. When the compressor lowers the crankcase pressure (after a defrost cycle or a normal off-cycle) the valve opens and admits suction gas to the crankcase, but only after the motor has finished starting. When the compressor shuts down, pressure in the compressor rises and the valve closes.

Three factors influence the choice of a crankcase pressure regulator: 1) design suction pressure, 2) maximum allowable suction pressure, and 3) pressure drop across the valve.

An equal amount of inlet pressure is exerted on the top of the seat disk and on the bellows so the valve can be controlled by the relationship between the adjusting spring pressure and the outlet pressure on the bottom of the seat disk. This allows the valve to modulate crankcase pressure as designed.

EVAPORATOR PRESSURE REGULATOR (TWO-TEMPERATURE VALVE)

This valve controls pressure and temperature in the warmer evaporators in a system with several evaporators. The regulator is used to prevent the compressor from creating excessive vacuum in the warmer evaporator. A two-temperature valve is especially useful 1) when several evaporators operate at different temperatures, 2) to balance pressures among several evaporators running at the same temperature but with different loads, and 3) to maintain desired pressure during minimum load conditions.

Most evaporator pressure regulators, (also called two-temperature, constant-temperature, or pressure-reducer valves) are installed in the suction line of the warmer evaporators. These valves close off the suction line when evaporator pressure drops below the set point. A second type of regulator (type 4), is located in the liquid line of the warmer evaporator. This valve uses a solenoid to shut off supply of refrigerant when the evaporator reaches operating temperature.

The two-temperature valve uses a needle and seat to control suction. Some varieties have service fittings to allow pressure

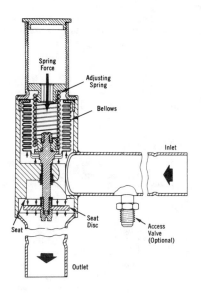

Fig. G2 Crankcase pressure regulator

readings to be taken from the warmer evaporator. Two-temperature valves sense evaporator pressure or temperature; they are usually operated by system pressure. The liquid line model, (type 4), below, is opened by electricity and closed by pressure.

PRESSURE-OPERATED

Pressure-operated two-temperature valves use a bellows or diaphragm to detect pressure in the warm evaporator. This valve comes in two basic varieties:

1. A metering-type valve throttles the opening in the suction line in response to pressure variation in the evaporator. A spring is the only adjustment mechanism. Because the valve has no differential, it responds directly to pressure without any lag. In larger systems, this valve uses a solenoid to open and close a pilot line because the pressure differential is too small to move the sealing faces.

2. The snap-action valve opens and closes without intermediate steps. The valve is commonly used with fixtures with similar temperatures or in systems which require defrosting in each cycle.

TEMPERATURE-OPERATED

Temperature-operated two-temperature valves use a sensing element to detect air or surface temperature in the warmest cabinet. These valves are divided into two basic categories, according to location:

3. a. The sensing bulb is connected by capillary tube to the valve bellows in a mechanism similar to the thermostatic expansion valve. Decreasing temperature at the bulb causes the plunger to close the suction line. As the evaporator warms, increasing pressure in the capillary tube forces the bellows to open the valve, allowing the compressor to again pull down evaporator pressure and temperature. Thermostatic valves are modulating valves that are capable of throttling the opening.

   b. An electronic version of the thermostatically-operated two-temperature valve is now available. This device contains a solenoid-operated valve to modulate the suction pressure. A line from the high-side may provide actuating power to the valve (see Fig. G5). Several electronic two-temperature valves can be controlled by a panel board, which can in turn accept input from a defrost timer.

4. A solenoid two-temperature valve is connected to a thermostat in the cabinet. Unlike other two-temperature valves, this valve shuts off the supply of refrigerant to the evaporator. The motor runs as long as any fixture in the system needs cooling. The supply to each evaporator is shut down by a separate solenoid valve as it reaches proper temperature. When all fixtures are

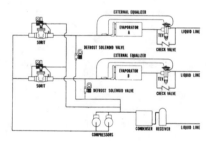

Courtesy of Sporlan Valve Co.

a) pressure-operated

b) solenoid-operated

a) with parallel compressors. Pressure-operated modulating-type valve. The pilot line reads suction pressure.

b) With hot-gas defrost system. Temperature-sensing, solenoid operated valve.

Note: "ORIT" indicated "open on rise of temperature"
"SORIT" indicates "solenoid-open on rise of temperature"

Fig. G3 Pressure-operated two-temperature valve in system

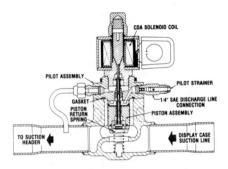

Pilot assembly throttles valve when solenoid opens valve.

Fig. G4 Electronic two-temperature valve

properly cooled, the motor shuts off. The solenoid in this valve is a normally-closed type. When the temperature rises, the thermostat energizes the solenoid coil, causing the valve to open.

Check valves should be used in the suction line to keep high-pressure gases from other evaporators out. The liquid line two-temperature valve should be mounted near the metering device.

ADJUSTING THE ELECTRONIC, THERMOSTATICALLY-OPERATED PRESSURE-REGULATING VALVE

Use the following procedure to adjust this valve after installation in the suction line. This procedure as written must be performed on a warm system:

1. Insert the diagnostic board (if one is used) into the panel controlling the valve. Check that all systems are operational and not defrosting.

2. Set the valve thermostat to the desired temperature.

3. Start the compressor and place a thermometer in the return air stream of the "control fixture" (the fixture containing the thermostat for this valve).

4. Allow the system to operate for at least one hour. If the air temperature is more than 3°F (1.7°C) off from the setting on the thermostat, adjust the thermostat and retest.

5. After the thermostat is set, you may have to readjust the thermostatic expansion valve. Do this with the thermostat for the pressure-regulating valve disconnected.

6. Reconnect the pressure-regulating valve thermostat and retest to confirm that it correctly controls the temperature.

REPAIRING PRESSURE-OPERATED TWO-TEMPERATURE VALVES

A shutoff and gauge opening in the suction line are great conveniences for repairing a pressure-operated two-temperature valve. The opening permits you to measure pressure in the suction line during the adjustment.

Two-temperature valves are subject to four types of problems:

1. Leakage past the seat will reduce the temperature in the warmer evaporator (this can also be due to maladjustment). If the valve was not adjusted recently and has just lost its ability to prevent low temperature, you can assume that a leak is the problem.

2. The valve may stick closed. This is indicated by a warm evaporator when the other evaporators are cooling properly. A clogged screen can also cause this problem.

3. The valve may go out of adjustment. Readjust by turning the adjusting nut half a turn at a time and monitoring the results for 15 minutes before making another adjustment.

4. A valve in a cold location may accumulate frost on the bellows, interfering with proper operation. To fix, move the valve to a warmer location and/or coat it with grease to inhibit frost.

Various elements of an electronic pressure-regulating valve may be tested with electrical meters. Consult the manufacturer for details.

REPAIRING THERMOSTATICALLY-OPERATED TWO-TEMPERATURE VALVES

These valves are subject to the same type of trouble as thermostatic expansion valves: pinched capillary tubes, poor contact between the sensor and the evaporator, loss of sensor charge, frosted bellows, and maladjustment. Repairs should be based on the nature of the problem.

HEAT PUMP FOUR-WAY VALVE

A heat pump uses a four-way valve to change its operation from heating to cooling, so the hot gas can be directed to the proper heat exchangers according to the demand. The four-way valve must also change its position to direct hot gas to the exchanger for de-icing in winter.

The slide in the four-way valve shown in Fig. G5 is actuated by a solenoid-operated pilot valve which directs compressor pressure or vacuum to the slide. The pilot valve is connected to the suction line and sometimes the discharge line as well. If the four-way valve has bleed holes in the slide, it need only be connected to the suction line. In operation, an electric signal to the pilot valve causes it to direct suction pressure to the slide of the main valve. Because the main valve has discharge pressure inside it, the slide is forced to move. This movement allows the valve to direct compressor discharge to the desired heat exchanger.

DIAGNOSING PROBLEMS

A few quick checks can help isolate problems in a four-way valve:

1. *Check tube temperature.* In a functioning valve the discharge line from the compressor and the line from the valve body to the heat exchanger that is serving as condenser should be hot. The line from the current evaporator to the valve, and the suction line, should be cold. The two capillaries from the pilot valve to the valve body should be about as warm as the valve body.

2. *Inspect for damage.* Check for pinches or other problems in the capillaries. Inspect the valve body for dents, deep scratches, or signs of overheating during installation.

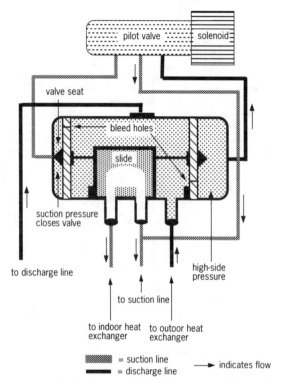

Fig. G5a 4-way valve heat pump in cooling mode

3. *Check electrical supply to the pilot valve coil.* The valve may require energy during heating or cooling, depending on system design. Pilot valves that are energized during the cooling mode will also be energized during defrost. You should be able to hear a click when the valve is energized.

4. *Check system charge.* Undercharge can prevent proper operation.

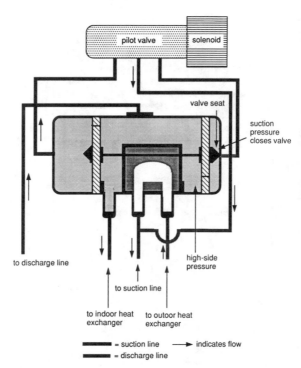

Fig. G5b 4-way heat pump in heating mode

If the pilot valve operates correctly, the four-way valve may still fail to operate due to dirt in a bleeder hole. Deenergize the solenoid, increase the head pressure, and reenergize the solenoid to blast the dirt out. If this does not work, take the valve apart and wash it. Use air pressure to check operation before reinstalling. Add a strainer in the tube feeding the valve.

If the pilot tubes are plugged, raise the head pressure and operate the valve a few times. If this does not work, replace the valve. If the valve starts to reverse but is unable to complete the stroke, check the operating pressures and charge. A valve with smaller ports may be needed.

PRESSURE LIMITER

A pressure limiter is a safety device to prevent evaporator pressure from exceeding a ceiling value. The limiter is used in special applications such as systems with one compressor feeding several evaporators running at different temperatures (as in freezers and refrigerators on a single compressor).

RELIEF

A relief valve will open when pressure or temperature in a vessel exceeds safe levels due to fire, electrical or control problems, or any other reason. Dangerous pressure can build up quickly in components which are flooded with liquid refrigerant. Flooding can occur even in vessels which normally contain a large percentage of vapor (such as receivers, flooded evaporators, and liquid-line driers with a bypass). These vessels are subject to explosive forces of thermal expansion.

The relief valve is usually installed on a receiver, although it may be located on a condenser or flooded evaporator. Do not place a hand valve between the vessel and the relief valve, as this would defeat the purpose of the safety device. All relief valves should be connected to lines to carry escaping refrigerant to the outdoors. In ammonia systems, the relief should be piped to a water tank to absorb the ammonia and prevent it from escaping.

Three types of relief valves are used: 1) fusible plug, 2) rupture disk, and 3) spring-loaded. Valves are rated by cubic feet or pounds discharge rate.

Relief valves are required in units above certain capacities by the National Refrigeration Code and many local codes. The ANSI/ASHRAE 15-1978 standard requires that pressure relief devices be capable of protecting against over-pressurization. Sizing of pressure relief devices is given in the *American Society of Mechanical Engineers Boiler and Pressure Code, Refrigeration Handbook*, Section 8, Division 1:

- *No device is required on a pressure vessel with a capacity of 3 cubic feet (85 liters) or less if the inside diameter is less than 3 inches (7.62 cm).*

- *Devices with internal gross volume of 3 cubic feet or more require protection. These devices may not use fusible plugs for protection.*

- *A pressure vessel with a capacity of at least 10 cubic feet (283 liter) requires a three-way valve connected to two pressure relief valves, each of which is large enough to vent the system by itself.*

- *Rupture disks or relief valves may be used on vessels of any size.*

- *No stop valve is permitted between the relief valve and the vessel, except in systems with multiple reliefs. In such a case, the stop valve may not be installed where it can shut off all relief valves at once.*

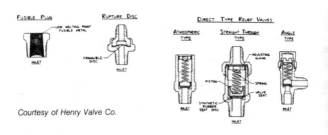

Courtesy of Henry Valve Co.

Fig. G6   Relief valves

The various types of reliefs are described below:

1. Fusible plugs contain a compound which melts when the receiver temperature exceeds a safe level. When the plug melts, all the refrigerant escapes to the air.

2. A rupture-type device (also called a rupture disk) usually contains a disk of silver which is designed to rupture when pressure exceeds the rating. Disks are available with ratings between 175 and 1000 psi (1310 to 6997 kPa). Rupture disks should be chosen to blow at 50 percent above static system pressure or 100 percent above pulsating system pressure.

3. A spring-loaded, or "pop," valve, has springs which counteract system pressure. The advantages of these valves are low cost, simplicity, high discharge capacity, and the ability to reclose after the pressure drops, thus saving some refrigerant. Closing pressures may be 10 to 20 percent below opening setting. After adjusting the valve to the desired setting, wire the valve seal tight to prevent tampering. Spring-loaded valves are affected by back pressure in their discharge line, so a rupture-disk cannot be installed at the outlet of a spring-loaded relief. Diaphragm-type spring-loaded relief valves use an indirect linkage, so system pressure pushes on the diaphragm rather than directly on the valve. The action is not affected very much by back pressure, and this valve may be set to discharge into the low side of the system, saving refrigerant in case of an overpressure. A diaphragm valve has a relatively high initial cost and lower discharge capacity than a comparable pop valve.

A three-way valve connected to two relief devices is required on larger vessels. The valve allows you to place one relief in service and remove the other for inspection or repair. During normal operation, the three-way valve is set so one relief is in service and the other is in reserve.

A periodic maintenance program is recommended for a relief system, with regular replacement of rupture elements and return of relief valves to the manufacturer for inspection and resetting.

INSTALLING AND SERVICING

A relief-valve installation should meet the following requirements:

1. The relief valve should be suitable to the refrigerant and have enough capacity to meet code requirements.

2. The discharge tube must meet code requirements for length and inside diameter.

3. The valve should not be discharged during installation or pressure testing of the system.

The difference between opening pressure and reclosing pressure is called "blowdown." The ability of a valve to reseat after discharge depends on system cleanliness, because foreign matter is likely to impair reseating. (Filters or screens are not permitted between the vessel and the relief.) Thus, relief valves may need cleaning, repair, or replacement after discharge.

SERVICE

Service valves are used in diagnosis, repair, recharging, and other service operations. Both one- and two-way valves are used. One-way valves, which open and control the flow between two ports, are used to shut off parts of the system to remove or repair components. An example is the king valve at the condenser outlet. Two-way valves have one inlet and two outlets. Either one or both outlets can be open to the inlet, depending on the valve setting. Examples are the discharge and suction service valve.

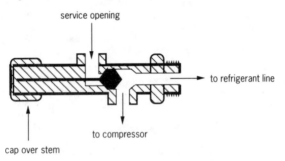

service opening

to refrigerant line

to compressor

cap over stem

Fig. G7 3-way service valve shown backseated

Protective caps and plugs should protect the valve stem area from contamination.

Service valves are mounted at the suction and discharge ports on compressors in open and some hermetic systems. The valves are fully open when the system is running normally. Most service valves are "backseating" types—meaning that the valve is seated against the rear seat in operating position. This helps prevent leaks through the valve packing.

Service valves are sometimes found on the receiver, where they are used to isolate the refrigerant during repair or system pump-down. Other possible locations include the evaporator liquid line or suction line.

In a system without service valves, a line-piercing valve may be installed for service operations. These valves clamp to the line, pierce the tubing, and allow installation of a gauge manifold or charging hose. Some clamps have a positive stop to prevent over-piercing. After service, the valve is closed and left on the line.

Courtesy of Imperial Eastman

Fig. G8 Line piercing valve

USING A SERVICE VALVE

To use a service valve, remove the cap, loosen the packing nut one full turn, and clean and oil the valve stem. Then crack the nut about one-eighth turn. This will prevent a rush of fluid which could damage gauges, flush excess oil, or cause personal injury. Do not crack the valve with a ratchet wrench, as you want to be able to quickly close the valve if necessary. Oil hose threads before fitting them to the valve. When finished, seat the valve and retighten the packing nut before replacing the cap.

If you anticipate severe corrosion of the valve, fill the valve body with the system oil before refitting the plug.

SOLENOID

Solenoid valves are magnetically-operated valves designed to in-crease the actuating power or work by remote control. The actual valve can be a shut-off or a three-way valve. A solenoid consist of wires wound around a core to make an electromagnet. Inside the coil is a plunger made of a magnetic material, usually iron. When electricity flows through the coil, the magnet attracts the plunger and pulls it toward the center of the coil. When the current is removed, the plunger responds to other forces, such as a spring, fluid pressure, or gravity (see Fig. G 9).

The plunger in a solenoid valve is connected to the valve needle or another apparatus to control fluid flow. The two basic types of solenoid valve are normally open (NO) and normally closed (NC). A normally open valve is open when power is off, and closed when power is on. The reverse is true of a normally closed valve. In some valves, a manual stem may be provided to operate the valve when electric current is absent.

In small systems, a simple, direct-acting solenoid valve may be used if the magnet is strong enough to operate the valve. In large systems, a pilot-operated solenoid valve is often used. In this device, the solenoid closes a pilot valve, which causes discharge pressure to pressurize a diaphragm and close the main valve.

Solenoid valves should be selected based on these considerations:

- *The fluid in the system*
- *Operating temperature*
- *Pipe capacity*
- *Maximum operating pressure differential (inlet pressure minus outlet pressure)*
- *Electrical control system (AC or DC, hertz, and voltage)*
- *Valve maximum pressure (must be above system working pressure)*

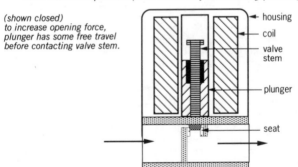

Fig. G9 Solenoid valve

Solenoids must be installed so the flow direction conforms to the arrow on the body. A strainer is helpful for keeping foreign matter from the valve. When brazing, keep the valve body as cool as possible by using a low flame and draping wet rags or chill blocks over the valve. Do not over-torque the valve during assembly.

TUBING PROCEDURES

Tubing is the basic means of connecting most refrigeration components. Technicians must be able to cut, bend and join this tubing. Observe the guidelines shown in Fig. G10 when installing copper tubing.

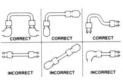

PRECAUTIONS

Avoid straight line connections wherever possible, especially in short runs.

Design piping systems symmetrically. They are easier to install and present a neat appearance.

Care should be taken to eliminate stress from tubing lines. Long tubing runs should be supported by brackets or clips. All parts installed on tubing lines such as heavy fittings, valves, etc., should be bolted down to eliminate tubing fatigue.

Before installing tubing, inspect the tube to see that it conforms to the required specifications, is of the correct diameter and wall thickness and is not out of round.

Cut tube ends reasonably square and lightly deburr inside and outside edge. Chamfer on outside edge will destroy bearing of tube end on the fitting seat.

To avoid difficulty in assembly and disconnecting, a sufficient straight length of tube must be allowed from the end of the tube to the start of the bend. Allow twice the length of the nut as a minimum. Tubes should be formed to assemble with true alignment to the center line of the fittings, without distortion or tension.

Courtesy of Imperial Eastman

Fig. G10 Tubing do's and don'ts

MEASURING AND CUTTING

Pipe can be cut by laying out the pipes and fittings and marking the cuts, or by using dimensions from plans. Dimensions are more accurate and should be used if available. Plans show the centerline of each tube and fitting, and list center-to-center measurements. You must convert center-to-center dimensions to actual pipe measurements before cutting.

To find the amount of tube to cut from one end when given the center-to-center measurement AB (6 feet 0 inches) between the fittings in Fig. G11, make this calculation:

Center-to-center AB	6 feet 0 inches	183 cm
− Center-to-face of fitting BC	− 2 inches	− 5.08 cm
+ Face to pipe end CD	+ 3/4 inches	+ 1.9 cm
Net length after subtracting (for one end only)	5 feet 10-3/4 inches	179.82 cm

Then make a similar calculation for the other end. If it has the same type of fitting, merely cut off twice as much as in the above calculation. Otherwise, make sure to subtract from the shortened length (not the original center-to-center measurement) in the second calculation.

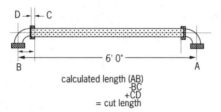

calculated length (AB)
-BC
+CD
= cut length

Fig. G11 Cutting pipe to length

To find the cut length from the calculated length, for threaded fittings on pipe up to 2 inches in diameter, use this rule of thumb: center-to-center measurement − (diameter of pipe × number of elbows) = cut length (for threaded fittings only).

For a 2-inch (5.08-cm) pipe having a center-to-center measurement of 48 inches (122 cm) ending in two elbows, the calculation would be:

$$48 \text{ inches } - (2 \text{ inches } \times 2) = 44 \text{ inches}$$
$$122 \text{ cm } - (5.08 \text{ cm } \times 2) = 111.84 \text{ cm}$$

WELDED FITTINGS

To calculate the subtraction from center-to-center measurement cut length when using a 90° welded elbow, subtract 1.5 times the pipe ID from the center-to-center length.

For a 45° welded elbow, multiply the pipe ID by 0.625 (⅝) and subtract this amount from the calculated length.

CUTTING

Once the length is determined, mark the tube with a pencil and cut it. Small, soft tubing is usually cut with a tubing cutter. After using the cutter, ream the end to prevent restriction in the flow. A hacksaw is more commonly used to cut hard and large tubing. A

32-tooth per inch (13-tooth per cm), wave-pattern blade is best. Prevent chips from entering the tube by stuffing a rag into the tube and withdrawing it after cutting.

To prevent dirt and moisture from entering tubes while idle, caps, or plugs should be inserted in the ends. Soft tubing can be pinched to keep it clean.

BENDING

Tube must be bent in many installations, although fittings are preferable for tight bends. Avoid pinching or kinking the tube or making a bend too tight. A good guideline is to make the minimum radius five to ten times the tube diameter. Tighter changes in direction must be accomplished with the help of a fitting; hard tube is resistant to bending and should use fittings instead.

Both internal and external bending springs can be used. External springs are used for bends in the middle of a long line because internal springs cannot be removed. If you plan to use an external spring, bend first and flare afterward. Internal springs can be used after a flare has been made. To remove an external spring after bending, twist it while extracting. Another suggestion is to take the bend slightly beyond the desired angle, and to relax it slightly while removing the spring.

FIGURING OFFSETS

An offset is a change of direction to allow a tube to pass an obstruction. The offset typically terminates in pipes that are parallel with each other. The angled piece is termed the offset.

Use the following procedure to determine the length of a 45° offset to bypass the obstruction shown in Fig. G12.

1. Determine the distance A between the centerlines of pipes B and C (use 15 inches or 38.1 cm for this example).

2. Multiply A by 1.41:

   $15 \times 1.41 = 21.15$ inches ($38.1 \text{cm} \times 1.41 = 53.72$ cm)

   This is the calculated length of the offset.

3. Now subtract an allowance for the elbows (see *Measuring and Cutting*, p. 247) to find the cut length of the offset.

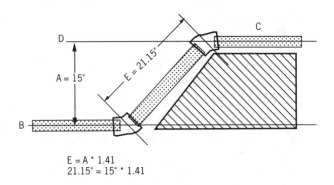

$$E = A * 1.41$$
$$21.15" = 15" * 1.41$$

Fig. G12 Figuring offset bend with 45° elbow

FLARING

Refrigeration systems often use flared joints between copper tubes and fittings and valves. Flares offer an easy-to-make connection that can be pulled apart much more readily than a soldered or brazed joint. The flare must have the correct angle (45°) and offer a full seat to achieve a proper seal. Flares may be single-thickness and double-thickness, also called a "double-flare." Double-flares are stronger and more reliable when properly constructed, and are used with tubing 5/16 inch (7.9 mm) and larger. Some flaring blocks have adaptors allowing them to be used for both single and double flares.

Copper tubing is flared to a 45° angle. Because steel tubing is less malleable than copper, it is usually flared to 37°. Separate tools must be used to make each angle.

Soft tubing is easier to flare. If hard tubing must be flared, anneal it first to prevent cracking. Annealing is also suggested before flaring old, brittle copper.

Use this procedure to make a single flare:

1. Cut the tube to the proper length and square the end with a file. Prevent filings from entering the tube.

2. Remove the burr left by the file with a reamer (this is essential for a good contact between the flare and the fitting).

3. Slip the coupling nut over the end of the tube.

4. Clamp the tube in the flaring block, making sure that about one-third of the height of the flare protrudes. Excess protrusion will make the flare too large for the fitting. Inadequate protrusion will leave the flare with too small a seating surface.

5. Place the yoke of the flaring tool around the shoulders of the block and insert the cone into the tube. Add a few drops of refrigerant oil where the flaring cone meets the tube—otherwise the tube is likely to grow thin and brittle.

6. Screw the cone to make contact, then one-half turn further, back off one-quarter turn, then advance three-quarter turn and back off one-quarter turn. Repeat this motion until the flare is completed. Do not overtighten the tool. (The back-and-forth motion is intended to limit the amount of work-hardening in the tube, which could weaken the joint.)

7. Remove the tool, clean the flare, and assemble the joint.

Use this procedure to make a double flare:

1. Clamp the tubing in the block.

2. Insert the female punch into the tubing and hammer it down. This will preform the double flare.

3. Remove the female punch and insert the male punch.

4. Hammer down the male punch to force the flare into its final form.

BRAZING AND SOLDERING

Brazing and soldering are two similar techniques for joining copper and brass tubing and fittings. Brazing can be done with steel piping as well. Both soldering and brazing are methods of applying a "filler material" to a hot, but not molten, base metal. They are distinct from welding, which melts and fuses similar metals. Welding is also a localized operation that proceeds from one end of a joint to the other. Soldering and brazing are usually performed on the whole joint at once. Welding is more likely to cause heat damage (warping or burnthrough) than the cooler techniques of brazing and soldering.

Although brazing is sometimes called silver brazing or silver soldering, this confusing terminology should be avoided. In both procedures, the filler metal is drawn into the joint by capillary action. Capillary action works best when the clearance is between 0.002 inch to 0.005 inch (.051 to .13 mm).

Soldering occurs below 800°F (426°C), and brazing above this temperature. Both techniques are able to bond unlike materials. Soldering is not as heat-resistant as brazing and is used extensively for water lines and drains. Soldering can be used for refrigerant lines which will not exceed the solder's maximum operating temperature. Brazing is used if the operating temperature is expected to exceed 250°F (121.1°C). Brazing filler metal is either 1) copper alloyed with 30 to 60 percent silver, or 2) copper alloyed with phosphorus.

SOLDER TYPES

The strength of soldering depends greatly on the solder chosen (the strength of brazing depends more on joint design). 95/5 tin–antimony soft solder contains 95 percent tin and 5 percent antimony and melts at 450°F (232°C) and becomes fluid at 465°F (241°C).

Silver solders (either hard or soft) are recommended for joints that will be exposed to high or low temperatures and pressures. Silver solders usually contain 5, 15, or 45 percent silver. However, circumstances calling for silver solder lend themselves to brazing, which takes no more time and results in a stronger joint.

CLEANING THE JOINT

Soldering and brazing must be done on metal that is free of oxides or contaminants. Follow these directions for cleaning a joint:

1. The tube must be cut square and clean, so it reaches the bottom of the fitting.

2. Ream the tube to remove burrs on the inside.

3. Clean the joint. Degrease first if necessary. Remove oxidation from the exterior with sandpaper or sandcloth. Clean only the tubing that will be in or near the joint. Use a steel brush to clean interiors of valves and fittings. Prevent filings and dirt from entering the tubing or fitting. Do not touch a cleaned area, as acid from your skin causes oxidation that will reduce bonding. Blowing on the clean area will moisten it and should also be avoided.

4. Immediately flux the joining surfaces to prevent new oxidation. Do not overflux, as flux should be kept from the system.

SOLDERING PROCEDURE

Soldering depends on establishing a good mechanical joint first. Use this general procedure:

1. Clean the tube and fitting (see above).

2. Immediately apply flux to the joint with a clean rag or brush. Apply flux to the outside of the tube and inside the fitting. Remove the excess flux with a rag. Do not use acid fluxes or acid-core solder, as they degrade metal.

3. Assemble the joint, using a slight twist to spread the flux. Make sure the parts fit tightly but have clearance for the solder to flow. Use supports if needed to keep the parts lined up.

4. Heat the joint evenly with an air acetylene or propane torch. Test the joint with solder to see when it is hot enough. (Overheating will cause flux to fail, allowing the metal to oxidize. If the joint gets overheated, take it apart, clean it, reapply flux and resolder.)

5. Remove the flame and apply solder to the joint. Solder should flow towards the hottest spot. Reapply the flame to the far side of the joint, and let the heat draw the solder into the joint. Then remove the torch and add more solder. A clean, well-fluxed joint at the proper temperature will quickly fill with solder. Use extra care when soldering large fittings. Tap the fitting occasionally with a hammer to break surface tension that can inhibit solder flow.

6. Wipe the joint with a rag to smooth the molten solder.

7. Allow the joint to cool.

8. Remove excess flux, which can corrode the tube over time.

(Making the last joint in a system can present problems because once the system is closed, heat will cause pressure to build up and force the molten filler from the joint. You can prevent this problem by opening a service valve to vent the system while making the last joint.)

BRAZING PROCEDURE

Brazing is performed at temperatures of 1000 to 1500° F (538 to 816°C) and requires an air-acetylene or oxyacetylene torch. Use a neutral or slightly reducing flame, never an oxidizing one. A blue cone with a bit of reddish-purple fringe indicates a neutral flame. A large torch tip is preferable because it creates a large, hot flame with mild gas pressure. Smaller torches run near maximum heat output will create a localized point of extreme heat which is likely to burn through the base metal. For large fittings, a multiple-tip torch may be used.

Make sure not to ignite anything with the torch; if in doubt, use sheet metal or another shield to cover flammable areas.

Select the filler metal according to manufacturer's recommendations for the metals in the fitting and tubing, and according to the operating temperature of the system. The two categories of filler material are 1) copper–silver alloys (designated the BAg series in product descriptions) and 2) copper–phosphorus alloys (BCuP series). Filler will flow inside a joint by capillary action as long as the clearance is at least .003 inch (.072mm). Excessive clearances will reduce the strength of the joint. Filler will flow toward the source of heat.

Be careful not to overheat the fittings and components. Some devices can be disassembled so the delicate parts need not be subjected to heat. Otherwise drape the fitting with a water-soaked rag to keep it cool.

Purge air from the system before brazing with a non-reactive gas such as nitrogen or carbon dioxide. This will control the amount of oxidation and prevent oil inside the joint from warming, vaporizing and exploding. A nitrogen tank feeding 20 cubic feet (557 liters) per hour should be enough for most systems. Purging is especially important when using the higher-temperature silver-bearing filler metals. Do not fill the system before brazing with refrigerant or compressed air, as they are all reactive at brazing temperature. **Never** introduce oxygen into any system to clean, purge, or pressurize it, as the combination could be deadly. Oil is hydrocarbon and will explode when pressurized with even small amounts of oxygen.

Follow this general procedure for brazing:

1. Start with a clean joint (see page 253). Degrease the joint if necessary. Clean the joint thoroughly with stainless steel wool or a stainless steel wire brush.

2. Fit the parts together. If necessary, repair or cut off dented sections of tube. Square the tubing end with a file. Remove burrs. Make sure the fit is tight and the tube extends squarely to the bottom of the fitting. Support the parts during the brazing if necessary, choosing props that conduct little heat.

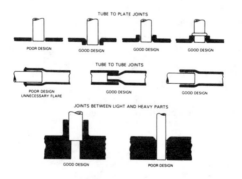

Courtesy of Handy & Harman

Fig. G13 Good and bad brazing joints

3. Select flux to match the filler material, and apply it according to manufacturer's directions. Prevent flux from entering the refrigeration system, because it is hard to remove.

4. Evenly heat the joint to the correct temperature. Move the torch around to heat all parts evenly, using a sweeping motion to avoid overheating. Filler will flow toward the heat, so you can heat a certain part of the joint to induce the filler to flow toward it. When brazing a small mass to a larger one, concentrate the heat on the larger one. When brazing copper to steel, concentrate on the copper, which conducts heat more readily from the joint. Flux will turn from a milky liquid to a clear liquid around 1100°F (593°C), which is close to brazing temperature. Brazing alloys melt at about 1120°F (604°C) and flow at about 1145°F (618°C). A slight green flame should be visible at brazing temperature.

5. Move the torch tip to another part of the joint and apply filler. Do not heat the filler with the torch and make sure the alloy flows freely. Continue heating by waving the torch across the joint. A continuous fillet of filler should be visible around the edge of the joint when done.

6. Cool the joint. After the joint has air cooled briefly, you can wet it with warm (120°F or 50°C) water, to break up the flux. Wrought fittings can be cooled quickly, but cast fittings need more time to cool before wetting.

7. Brush flux off the exterior because remaining flux can cause corrosion or hide flaws in the joint. Difficulty removing flux indicates that not enough was used, or that the joint was overheated. Overheated flux is saturated with oxides, and generally green or black in color.

8. Inspect the cold joint to look for dark, cup-shaped areas which can mark poor adhesion of braze alloy.

| | **Brazing Problems** | |
Trouble	Cause	Solution
Filler does not flow or balls up	Oxidation on the base metal or insufficient heat	Disassemble and clean the joint or add more heat
Oxide forms on joint during heating	Inadequate flux	Cool, clean, add flux and reheat
Filler does not enter the joint but flows on outside	One part was underheated	Add heat to the cooler part

SOLDERING AND BRAZING SAFETY

Fumes, fire, and explosion are the major hazards of soldering and brazing. Follow these guidelines for safety during both operations:

1. Use adequate ventilation in confined areas. Respirators with an air supply may be necessary. Do not breathe or allow fumes to contact your eyes.
2. Do not use brazing filler metal containing cadmium, which makes poisonous fumes when heated.
3. Flux is particularly harmful to the eyes. Do not apply it with your fingers, as it can damage your skin.
4. Clean the base materials. This is necessary for a tight joint, and also removes unknown contaminants that can cause hazardous fumes or degrade the flux.
5. Use enough flux to prevent oxidation of the base metals and resulting fumes.
6. Heat the joint broadly, preventing hot spots, flux burnout, and fuming. Do not heat filler, which can cause fuming.
7. Learn to recognize galvanized (zinc) and cadmium coatings. These metals produce dangerous fumes. Remove them before heating.
8. Use adequate ventilation when working on lines which have held halocarbon refrigerant, which breaks down into a toxic gas (see Part L, *Safety, torch*, p. 410).

REPAIRING A LEAKING JOINT

To repair a leaking solder joint, you must disassemble it and resolder. Although it is tempting to just resolder the joint, this will fail because you must clean oxide from the mating surfaces first. (If the joint leaked when the system was running, oil must be cleaned out as well.) Use the following procedure:

1. If the area contains refrigerant, pump down or otherwise evacuate the system.
2. Saw through the leaking fitting and drain remaining refrigerant from it.
3. Heat the leaking joint and quickly pull it apart.

4. Inspect the inside of the joint to determine the cause of the leak—such as an unclean spot or a deformed fitting. Then use the normal procedure to solder or braze.

DETECTING LEAKS

After a system is assembled, you must test it for leaks. Read the compressor installation instructions to determine the testing procedure. Manufacturers may specify that a certain pressure be sustained for a specific period before a system is considered leaktight.

Check the instructions for your leak detector, noting especially whether you must balance the detector to the atmosphere before each use (some detectors do this automatically). While making these tests, remember that excess system pressure can damage some components.

NEW SYSTEM

Use this procedure to test a new system for leaks:

1. Install the gauge manifold and pressurize both sides of the system with nitrogen. Consult the manufacturer's specifications for the proper pressure. Generally, water-cooled equipment should be tested at 250 psi (1724 kPa), and air-cooled equipment at 350 psi (2413 kPa).

2. Watch for a drop in pressure that would indicate a leak. Make sure to uniformly pressurize the entire system.

3. If the system passes this test, pressurize to 150 psi with dry nitrogen and test with soapsuds.

4. If the system is still tight, blow out the nitrogen and add refrigerant to 30 psi (207 kPa). Pressurize the refrigerant to 150 psi (1035 kPa) by adding nitrogen. Test for leaks with a halide torch.

5. If the system still checks out, use an electronic leak detector to make the final check, (electronic detectors are so sensitive that they will read "positive" several feet from a big leak—too far to tell the exact source of the leak).

OLD SYSTEM

If you suspect that a leak is responsible for system trouble, make your test before disassembling the system. Otherwise, the atmosphere may become so contaminated with refrigerant that the leak will be difficult to find. Some leaks will show themselves with a sludge of oil near a fitting, but a good test with a leak detector is the surest means of finding a leak.

When testing for leaks on a running system, briefly increase discharge pressure by blocking the air or water flow to the condenser (remember that this can damage the system if you run it too long). It is difficult to raise the pressure in the suction line. An electronic leak detector is quite handy for these tests. Red dye may be used to find a sneaky leak. Or wrap a suspect area with household plastic wrap and wait a few hours. If the joint is bulging, you have isolated the leak.

PART H
WHOLE SYSTEMS

Air-conditioning and refrigeration systems are more than individual components—they are systems which must work as a whole. Part H deals with typical systems. The absorption cycle is explained and compared to the more familiar vapor-compression cycle. Some common varieties of the vapor-compression system are presented, along with descriptions of defrost systems, the pumpdown cycle, and cold-weather operation. Hints for selecting and installing components are given. Part H concludes with information on comfort cooling and commercial refrigeration systems.

Absorption

The absorption cycle uses heat instead of mechanical compression to energize the cooling cycle. Absorption systems usually have two interconnected loops: one for the absorber and another for the refrigerant. The absorber loop runs from the generator through the separator and the absorber and back to the generator. The refrigerant loop runs from the generator through the separator, condenser, evaporator, and absorber before returning to the generator.

The two major absorption systems use 1) ammonia as the refrigerant and water as the absorber, or 2) water as refrigerant and lithium bromide as absorber. The following table lists normal operating conditions for these systems:

Component	Pressure-temperature ammonia		Pressure-temperature lithium bromide	
Generator	290 psi 290°F	2103 kPa 143°C	1.5 psia 210°F	10.34 kPa 99°C
Condenser	290 psi 122°F	2103 kPa 50°C	1.5 psia 115°F	10.34 kPa 46.1°C
Evaporator	52 psi 36°F	462 kPa 2.2°C	29.6″ Hg 40°F	1.1 kPa 4.4°C
Absorber	52 psi 190°F	462 kPa 87.8°C	.15 psia 105°F	1.03 kPa 40.6°C

The heat supply to the boiler can come from steam, fossil fuels or, less commonly, electricity. Ammonia systems typically operate at pressures up to 400 psi (about 2800 kPa), so welded steel is the preferred construction method. Ammonia reacts with copper, so copper cannot be used in components or tubing.

Ammonia-water absorption systems are used in comfort cooling and refrigeration. The lithium bromide-water system works at very low temperatures and pressures and is used primarily in industrial applications. Both systems have similar actions and components, although the details vary with the manufacturer and application.

Capacity control is simple. A thermostat senses the temperature of the chilled air or water leaving the evaporator. As the temperature nears the set point, the heat is gradually reduced at the generator, resulting in a weaker solution being pumped from the concentrator to the absorber. This weaker solution is less able to absorb the refrigerant vapor coming from the evaporator so the supply of warm vapor refrigerant to the condenser is reduced.

TERMINOLOGY

Understanding the terminology of absorption systems will help you work with them. In absorption work, "strong" and "weak" refer to the ability of a fluid to absorb refrigerant. Components are described as being on the high or low side of the system; technically this would apply only to systems with a pressure differential, but the distinction is helpful for understanding the principles nonetheless.

COMPONENTS

Absorber—The low-side vessel in which the low pressure refrigerant vapor dissolves in the strong solution of absorber. Some heat of dissolving is dissipated to the surroundings or the cooling water.

Condenser—The high-side vessel in which the refrigerant condenses and loses the heat of condensation to the surroundings.

Evaporator—The low-side vessel in which the liquid refrigerant evaporates and cools the load before flowing to the absorber.

Generator—The high-side vessel in which the strong solution is heated and forced to the separator. Also called the boiler.

Separator—The high-side vessel in which refrigerant vapor is liberated from the weak solution. High-pressure vapor refrigerant flows toward the condenser; weak solution of absorbent flows toward the absorber. The separator may be a part of the generator or separate.

Solution pump—An optional device (one or several may be used) to move strong solution from the absorber to the generator. Divides the high and low sides.

FLUIDS

Ammonia—A toxic, nonflammable chemical used as the refrigerant in conjunction with water as absorber.

Hydrogen—A light, insoluble, and flammable gas found in a circuit between the evaporator and the absorber in some systems. Used to increase the boiling of ammonia by taking advantage of Dalton's law of partial pressures. Not used in lithium bromide systems.

Lithium bromide—A nontoxic, nonflammable, stable substance used as the absorber in conjunction with water as refrigerant. Becomes corrosive in contact with air and is harmful to eyes, skin, and mucus membranes.

Strong solution—Solution of cool absorber which has great (strong) ability to absorb refrigerant. Flows from the absorber to the generator.

Weak solution—Solution of refrigerant and absorber which has little (weak) ability to absorb refrigerant. Flows from the generator to the absorber.

To understand the absorption cycle, it helps to compare its components with those of the vapor-compression cycle. A fundamental difference is that the absorption cycle has far fewer moving parts than the vapor-compression cycle, and it may operate at uniform pressure throughout the system.

THE ABSORPTION SYSTEM COMPARED TO THE VAPOR-COMPRESSION SYSTEM

Cycle	Energy source	Energy input	Heat removed	Refrigerant
Vapor-compression	Electricity	Compressor	Compressor and condenser	Halocarbon or ammonia
Absorption	Fuel, steam or electricity	Generator (boiler)	Absorber and condenser	Ammonia or water

WATER-AMMONIA

This system cycles solutions of water (the absorber) and ammonia (the refrigerant) (see Fig. H1). The water dissolves the ammonia at low temperatures; at higher temperatures the ammonia is driven from solution. Absorption cycles have two interlocking loops of fluids: one for ammonia, and another for water. A third loop sometimes contains hydrogen gas. The system disposes of unwanted heat from the absorber and the condenser.

The cycle begins in the generator, also called the boiler, where a cool, strong solution of ammonia in water is heated and driven by convection to a separating device. As the solution warms, it becomes a weak solution (warm liquids can dissolve less gas than cool ones). In the separator (which may be part of the generator or a separate vessel) the ammonia leaves solution and enters the condenser. There, the ammonia loses the heat of condensation to the condensing medium and condenses, just as refrigerant vapor does in a mechanical refrigerator. The liquid ammonia enters the evaporator after passing through a liquid trap that keeps hydrogen gas in the evaporator and out of the condenser.

In the evaporator, the liquid ammonia enters an atmosphere with a high concentration of hydrogen. According to Dalton's law of partial pressures, the total gas pressure is the sum of the pressures of hydrogen and ammonia. Therefore even though pressure on the ammonia may be the same as elsewhere in the system, it is low enough for the ammonia to evaporate. This evaporation reduces the temperature of the gas, and heat from the surroundings warms the gas, causing the evaporation to continue as in the vapor-compression cycle.

As the ammonia gas warms and evaporates, it travels to the absorber. A stream of weak solution from the separator is cooled in the absorber (or on the way to it) and gains ability (becomes a strong solution) to absorb vapor. The heat liberated during absorption is dumped to the surroundings. After the ammonia is absorbed, the strong solution flows back to the generator to repeat the cycle. Because hydrogen is virtually insoluble in water, it passes through the absorber and returns to the evaporator, flowing in the opposite direction as the refrigerant.

Some systems have a pump to create a high side (generator and condenser) and a low side (absorber and evaporator). The pump circulates strong solution from the absorber to the generator. A check valve, liquid trap, or another means is used to maintain the difference in pressures: high side 200 to 300 psi (1482 to 2172 kPa); low side 40 to 60 psi (379 to 517 kPa).

The hydrogen loop is closed on one end by a liquid trap at the entrance to the evaporator and at the other by hydrogen's inability to dissolve in water in the absorber. Hydrogen is only found between the evaporator and the absorber. The higher the hydrogen pressure, the lower the temperature produced by the boiling ammonia.

LITHIUM BROMIDE-WATER

In this system, the water is the refrigerant and lithium bromide is the absorber. With a very low system pressure, the water boils in the evaporator at a very cold temperature. Lithium bromide systems can be used in heating-cooling equipment as well as in industrial refrigeration. In other respects, the cycle parallels the water-ammonia cycle, except that water is the refrigerant instead of the absorber (see Fig. H1).

Both the absorber and the condenser are supplied with cooling water, which generally is piped to a cooling tower and recycled.

The higher the concentration of lithium bromide, the thicker the solution will be. Lithium bromide can crystallize and prevent the system from operating properly until the crystals dissolve. However, these crystals are unlikely to harm the equipment. Each manufacturer has its own method of preventing crystallization; make sure you understand the one you are using. Octyl alcohol is sometimes added to the charge to act as a wetting agent to reduce the surface tension. A lithium bromide system can use two pumps to move the solutions and create a high and a low side.

SAFETY

Ammonia-water systems operate under pressures as high as 350 to 400 psi. Ammonia is toxic, interfering with breathing and harming the skin and eyes. Hydrogen is highly flammable. Follow these hints:

- *Be especially cautious about leaks.*
- *Never cut or drill into the piping.*
- *Check the gas piping supplying fuel the generator. Use soapsuds, not a flame, to check for gas leaks.*

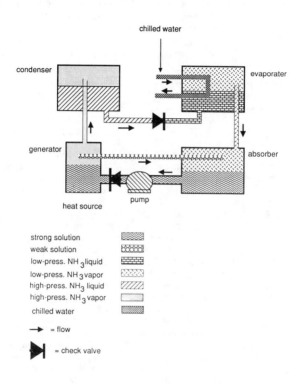

condenser

chilled water

evaporater

generator

absorber

heat source

pump

strong solution

weak solution

low-press. NH_3 liquid

low-press. NH_3 vapor

high-press. NH_3 liquid

high-press. NH_3 vapor

chilled water

$\longrightarrow$ = flow

= check valve

Fig. H1 Ammonia-water absorption system

- *Check the flame safety valve by smothering the flame and waiting for the shutoff valve to close. If it does not close promptly, repair or replace the shutoff.*

- *Place ammonia systems outdoors to prevent leaking ammonia from injuring people. For more on ammonia safety, see Part A,* Refrigerants, p. 31.

Types of Vapor-Compression Systems

Many system types can be built around the components of a vapor-compression (sometimes called "mechanical") refrigeration system. These systems can be classified as "self-contained," with all components housed within a single enclosure or "remote" or "split," with the major components in several locations.

Another important means of classifying systems is by whether the compressor and motor are inside a single housing. "Open" systems have a motor connected by a flexible coupling or belt to the compressor. "Semi-hermetic" systems incorporate the motor and compressor inside a gasketed housing that may be opened for service. A true "hermetic" system houses these two components inside a single vessel, but the vessel cannot be opened and must be replaced if it fails.

System	Advantages	Disadvantages
Open	Accessible for service; adaptable.	Crankshaft seal likely to leak and must be designed and installed properly. Must provide compressor and motor cooling.
Semi-hermetic	May be disassembled for service. No danger of crankshaft seal leaking. Good cooling to compressor and motor by suction gas. Sold as "made-up" system—easier to install.	Difficult (but possible) to open system for service.
Hermetic	No danger of crankshaft leakage; little assembly work; low cost.	Hard to service; motor-compressor is a throwaway item, i.e., for small residential units.

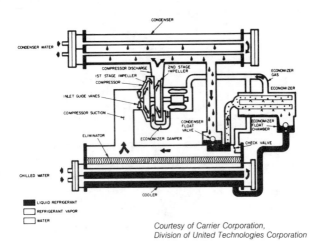

Courtesy of Carrier Corporation,
Division of United Technologies Corporation

Fig. H2 Hermetic centrifugal system

Another classification of vapor-compression systems reflects the type of metering device used to control refrigerant entry into the evaporator (see Part D, *Refrigerant Control Metering device*, p. 120).

- *A capillary tube is a tube with a small ID, which restricts the flow of refrigerant. Cabinet temperature is controlled by a thermal motor switch (thermostat) in the cabinet. The system is commonly found in small residential and commercial refrigeration and comfort cooling systems (see Fig, H3).*

  The motor need not have a high starting torque because high- and low-side pressures equalize during the off cycle. Because the capillary tube has no moving parts, the major hazard is plugging due to debris or damage. Refrigerant charge must be measured very accurately (a "critical charge") to prevent slugs of liquid refrigerant from reaching the compressor or problems due to low charge. An accumulator is often installed in the suction line to prevent slugging.

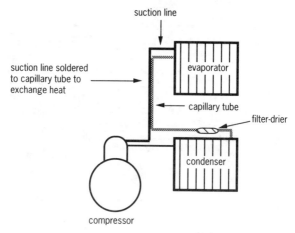

Fig. H3 Capillary tube system

- *An automatic expansion valve (AEV) between the liquid line and the evaporator maintains the desired evaporator pressure. The valve automatically opens when evaporator pressure falls as the compressor pulls on the suction line. The motor thermostat can be clamped to the evaporator near the suction line. When the evaporator is sufficiently cool, the thermostat shuts the motor down, and the motor stays off until the cabinet warms up and trips the thermostat (see Fig. H4).*

  An oil separator is not necessary in this system, but the motor must usually be able to start under load. A serious leak in the AEV may allow excess liquid refrigerant into the evaporator and cause floodback.

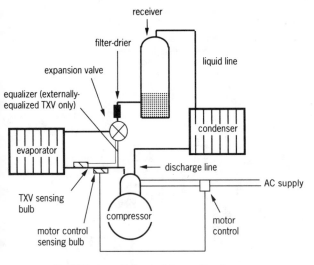

Fig. H4 System with thermostatic or automatic
expansion valve metering device

- A thermostatic expansion valve (TXV) is a very common and effective
  method of controlling refrigerant flow. The TXV is located on the
  evaporator inlet and can be considered an improved version of the
  AEV because it responds to evaporator pressure and suction line
  temperature-pressure. The motor can be controlled by a thermostat
  inside the cabinet. The motor must be able to start under load, as
  pressures do not balance during the off cycle.

- A low-side float is a valve inside the evaporator, which regulates the
  liquid level in the evaporator. Because the evaporator always contains
  some liquid refrigerant, it is said to be ''flooded,'' and it always
  cools to some extent. A low-side float is often used in large, centrifugal
  water chillers. Because the system contains liquid refrigerant in both

the receiver and the evaporator, it uses a comparatively large charge. The motor must be able to start under load (see Fig. H5).

The compressor control powers the motor when suction line pressure rises, (indicating a warm evaporator). As an alternative, a thermostat can be mounted on the evaporator (or immersed in the circulating water of a chilled water system).

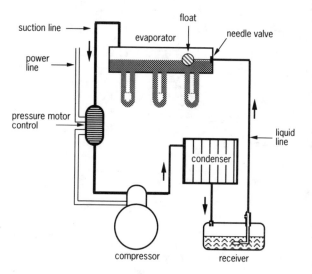

Fig. H5 Low-side float system

- A high-side float is a valve inside the receiver which controls the level of liquid refrigerant. The evaporator is always flooded with refrigerant. The compressor pumps refrigerant through the condenser into the receiver. When the preset level of refrigerant fills the float chamber, the float rises and opens the valve, allowing refrigerant to flow to the evaporator (see Fig. H6).

A thermostat in the cabinet, or a pressure sensor on the suction line, may be used to control the compressor motor. Refrigerant charge is critical. If the system has too much refrigerant, the float will open too wide and flood the compressor with liquid refrigerant. If the charge is too small, the valve will stay closed and the evaporator will be starved.

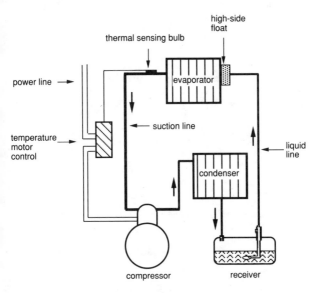

Fig. H6 High-side float system

Another way of classifying systems is by how they combine different numbers of compressors or evaporators to create extremely low temperatures, produce a great deal of cooling power, or cool different cabinets to different temperatures. These systems can range from simple to extremely complex:

- A **compound system** *has multiple compressors connected in series. The output of the first compressor discharges into the inlet of the second compressor, and so on. Aside from this, the system resembles a conventional vapor-compression system. Multiple compressors allow the system to create an extremely high vacuum in the suction line and thus very low temperature. An intercooler may be used to cool the hot vapor exiting the first compressor before it enters the second compressor. The system is regulated by a single motor control and a thermostatic expansion valve. Because the TXV does not allow the pressures to balance when the compressor is off, the motors must be able to start under load.*

- A **cascade system** *uses two separate compression systems to achieve temperatures in the range of −50°F (−46°C) for industrial processes. The only connection between the systems is that the evaporator of the primary, or "booster," compressor cools the condenser of the secondary compressor. The evaporator of the secondary system cools the actual load. Both systems use thermostatic expansion valves. A single control regulates both motors according to temperature or pressure in the secondary evaporator. Due to the extremely low temperatures in the secondary system, the refrigerant must be extremely dry. Oil separators are desirable on the lines between compressors and condensers.*

- A **modulating system** *links several compressors in parallel, with the number of compressors in operation depending on the load. A modulating system is suitable when the load varies greatly during a twenty-four-hour cycle; typical in office buildings, where the load on the comfort cooling system is usually much greater during the day than at night. A system large enough to handle the peak load might not be able to throttle down enough to cool the nighttime load.*

  The modulating system has a second advantage: a compressor may be shut down if it needs service and some cooling capacity will remain. The compressors usually all feed one evaporator, but they can have common or separate condensers.

  Modulating may also be accomplished with capacity controls by 1) holding suction valves open, preventing these cylinders from compressing the refrigerant or 2) routing refrigerant from the high side to the low side but not through the condenser (see Part D, Capacity controls, p. 111).

- **Multiple evaporator systems** *have several evaporators in different locations. If these evaporators run at the same temperature, the system can be controlled by a low-side float or a thermostatic expansion valve. If their temperatures must be different, a two-temperature valve is used to control pressures in the evaporators.*

   The system may require a check valve in the suction line of the colder evaporator to prevent refrigerant from the warmer evaporator from being sucked into the colder, lower-pressure evaporator during the off cycle.

- *A* **reheat system** *reduces humidity by cooling the air to a certain humidity and then warming it enough to be circulated at design temperature. Part of the heat may be supplied by the room air, and part may come from a furnace or the cooling system. Properly installed, a reheat system can control both relative humidity and temperature. If a reheat system delivers air that is too cool, the reheating element may be shut off. If the air is too damp or warm, there may be a problem with the cooling components or the controls.*

Defrost Systems

Frost, the freezing of moisture on a cold surface, can be a problem for any comfort cooling and refrigeration systems whose evaporator operates below water's freezing point. The basic problem is that frost transmits heat poorly, and it can lead to food dehydration. Some systems require no frost control because their evaporators run warm enough that only condensation, not frost, will form on the coil. However, almost any evaporator operating below 30°F will frost and needs either a defrost system or regular manual defrosting.

Many defrost techniques are available. The coils may be allowed to warm up during part of the cycle, or they may be heated from within or outside. Most systems require provisions to drain melted frost to avoid rotting, discoloration, refrosting, and other problems.

HOT GAS DEFROSTING

Hot gas defrost systems feed hot, discharge gas into the evaporator and can usually melt all frost in about 10 minutes. The condenser and metering device normally play no part in the defrost cycle. Units with multiple evaporators may be set to defrost each evaporator according to its needs. Solenoid valves are used to operate hot gas defrost systems. Two basic layouts of hot-gas defrost system are used, with the usual variations:

1. The system shown in Fig. H7 directs hot gas through a bypass into the evaporator, and gas returns to the compressor down the suction line in the usual direction. This is similar to the hot gas capacity control system.

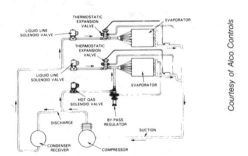

Fig. H7 Hot gas defrost system—liquid line feed

This type of hot-gas defrost system must prevent liquid refrigerant that condenses in the evaporator from flooding back to the compressor. Methods of doing this include:

a. An accumulator in the suction line traps and vaporizes liquid refrigerant. A heater in the accumulator may hasten evapo-

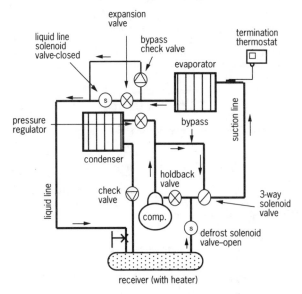

Fig. H8 Two-pipe defrost system shown in defrost mode

ration. The accumulator is helpful even if other floodback prevention techniques are used.

b. An electric heater can be switched on to heat the suction line.

c. A blower-evaporator in the suction line can be switched to operate only while the unit is in defrost cycle.

d. The vapor and condensed liquid from the defrosting evaporator may be routed to another evaporator, where the liquid will vaporize.

2. An alternative type of hot-gas defrost system is shown in Fig.

H8. As in the previous system, hot vapor is pumped from the compressor to the evaporator through a bypass. In this system, however, the hot vapor reaches the evaporator through the suction line. After exiting the evaporator, the vapor flows through the liquid line and ends up in the receiver.

REVERSE CYCLE

This defrost system is primarily used with the heat pump. It is named because the roles of the condenser and evaporator are reversed during the defrosting cycle. The defrost cycle is accomplished by briefly switching the heat pump into the summer, cooling mode during the winter.

In operation, the compressor pumps hot gas directly to the evaporator, where it condenses and melts the frost. The liquid refrigerant then passes through a check valve (piped parallel to the

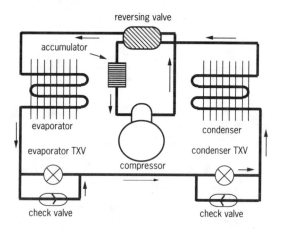

Fig. H9 Reverse cycle defrost system
(shown in defrost cycle)

metering device) and passes through a special thermostatic expansion valve to the condenser, which now serves as an exaporator. Finally, the vapor passes through an accumulator and back to the compressor (see *Heat pump*, p. 76).

ELECTRIC HEAT

Electric heaters may be used for defrosting evaporators and suction lines. A timer performs these functions at the start of each defrost cycle: a) closes a solenoid to shut the liquid line, allowing the compressor to pump the evaporator dry, b) shuts down the compressor, c) supplies current to the heating elements and blowers (if blowers are used to speed the defrost action). A thermostat on the evaporator signals the system controller when the evaporator is warm enough (indicating defrost is completed) to resume operation.

Electric heating elements may be wired into drain pans or floors to allow melt water to run off. If these elements fail, a large sheet of ice might result, so it should be part of a service routine to inspect them.

NON-FREEZING SOLUTIONS

The non-freezing solution system uses a tank (usually containing brine) which gradually absorbs heat from discharge gas or an electric heater. When the defrost timer signals, the brine is pumped through its own series of pipes to warm the coil.

DEFROST CONTROLS

Three control methods are used to defrost commercial systems:

1. A timer is set to defrost for a certain period at set intervals. This is a simple system but it cannot account for varying loads or humidity, and thus will probably result in too many defrosting cycles, which wastes energy and wears equipment unnecessarily.

2. A pressure control (commonly called a TP control) measures suction pressure. The control initiates a defrosting cycle when pressure rises, indicating a rise in evaporator temperature (ice on the coil interferes with heat transfer). This control must be installed carefully, as it tends to respond to the coldest point in the system, which may not be in the evaporator it is supposed to measure. A fail-safe may order a defrost cycle at set intervals if the TP control fails.

3. A temperature sensor registers a rise in temperature and terminates the defrost cycle when the display case reaches a set temperature, often about 50°F (10°C). A temperature control is not prone to reading conditions in remote evaporators, unlike the TP control.

Pumpdown Cycle

A pumpdown cycle is used to pump all refrigerant to a vessel in the system (commonly the receiver or condenser) during the off-cycle. The purpose is to prevent refrigerant from migrating to the crankcase, where it can condense and saturate the oil. Without a pumpdown cycle, the crankcase can fill with liquid refrigerant during a long off-cycle. At startup, the liquid refrigerant can flood the cylinders and damage the compressor much like a floodback. (Large compressors have springs on intake and exhaust valves to reduce this hazard.)

After the system has cooled the evaporator sufficiently, a solenoid valve closes in the liquid line and the compressor pumps liquid refrigerant into the condenser or receiver, where it remains until the next on-cycle. If some refrigerant escapes the vessel, it may be recovered by a recycling-type pumpdown control, which periodically restarts the compressor for a short time to refill the storage vessel. If a recycling control cannot be used, a crankcase heater may be used to keep refrigerant out of the crankcase.

Cold Weather Operation

Special precautions are needed to protect an outdoor, air-cooled condenser from low ambient temperatures. The major problem is that the refrigerant will not flow through the metering device unless head pressure is sufficient, and the cold temperatures reduce head pressure. Systems operated in cold conditions require:

1. a weatherproof housing

2. a method of preventing short cycling

3. a head pressure control if the weather will be colder than the cabinet

4. a method of preventing oil from being diluted by refrigerant

Ambient temperatures are a greater problem in areas with high winds, so it is advisable to mount the condenser in a sheltered location, as long as there is sufficient air circulation in summer.

Head pressure can be sustained by insulating and heating the receiver, to prevent the receiver from getting cold enough to act as a condenser. If the receiver is mounted above the condenser, static pressure will add to head pressure.

A second means of ensuring head pressure is to interfere with the condenser action with any of these techniques:

1. Reduce the speed of the condenser cooling fan (or cycle the fan with a temperature control that senses condenser temperature).

2. Close louvers on the condenser to reduce air flow.

3. Increase the amount of liquid refrigerant to the condenser to reduce the space in which vapor can condense. This is often accomplished by placing a condenser pressure regulator valve (see Fig. H10) in the liquid line. This setup requires a larger refrigerant charge. In cold weather, the pressure regulator raises condenser pressure by closing off the condenser outlet. This also has the effect of keeping more refrigerant in the condenser. The valve measures ambient temperature and receiver pressure. As ambient temperature cools, the valve reduces the flow through the condenser outlet, increasing head pressure and warming the receiver (see Part G, *Condenser Pressure Regulator*, p. 231).

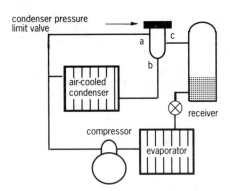

In warm weather, valve a is closed and refrigerant flows through b and c.
In cold weather, valve b throttles closed and some discharge gas bypasses the condenser.
The condenser is partly filled with refrigerant.

Fig. H10 Condenser pressure regulator

Choosing and Installing a System

System design is the province of engineers, and little effort can be made here to delve into the many complexities of design. Nevertheless, an acquaintance with the basic procedures will help those working in the field.

COOLING LOAD

Cooling load is the amount of heat that must be removed from the cooled space to maintain design conditions. Calculating cooling load can get pretty complicated. You may need to calculate cooling load when sizing equipment for a new installation or servicing a system that is not cooling enough but is otherwise operating properly.

Cooling load is a function of space heat gain and design temperature and humidity. Space heat gain is the sum of:

1. solar heat gain

2. heat conducted through interior and exterior walls, roof, and foundation

3. heat generated by activities in the building, such as people, appliances, equipment, and lighting

4. energy transfers resulting from ventilation and infiltration

5. other sources of heat

Buildings can gain both sensible and latent heat. Latent heat gain is the intake of humidity, which must be condensed from the air by removing the latent heat of condensation.

Cooling load calculations also require that you know summer and winter temperatures and humidity as well as design temperature and humidity. Calculate the temperature difference (TD) by subtracting design interior temperature from summer high temperature. Find the heat transmission factor (U) for each material or wall type used in the construction. Then, for each building element with similar construction, make this calculation: U * TD * area = heat loss. You must make separate calculations for each area having different construction (exterior and interior walls, floor, ceiling) and sum the losses together. Then add internal heat gains and infiltration.

Some equipment manufacturers offer worksheets to help calculation cooling loads (see Table H1) but the process is approximate, and it's best to allow some extra capacity rather than risk installing an undersize system.

Once you have calculated cooling load, you can search for the best way to cool that load. Sometimes, the most economical method is to insulate and weatherstrip first, because this will reduce first costs and operating costs at the same time. Then a new cooling load must be calculated before the cooling equipment can be chosen.

TABLE H1 Cooling Load

COOLING AND HEATING LOAD ESTIMATE SHEET

TRANE

COPYRIGHT 1975

LATITUDE	DESIGN MONTH		DAILY RANGE	F		DATE	JOB NO	SHEET NO
	SUMMER	OUTDOOR	INDOOR	DIFFERENCE		CLIENT		
A	DRY-BULB	F	F	F		ADDRESS		
B	WET BULB	F	F	F		CITY		STATE
C	HUMIDITY RATIO (W)	Wo	Wi			EST BY		CHECKED BY
D	WINTER	OUTDOOR	INDOOR	DIFFERENCE				
E	DRY BULB	F	F	F				
	HUMIDITY RATIO (W)	Wo	Wi					

CONDUCTION

ITEM NO.	ITEM	DIREC-TION	CLTD FROM TABLE		ADJUST FOR LATIT & MONTH	COLOR X CORR.	CORR. INDOOR-OUTDOOR "K" = (78–Ti) + (To–85)	CLTD CORRECTED		U VALUE	AREA X FT²	Q SENSIBLE BTUH	
			HR	HR	HR			HR	HR			HR	HR
1	ROOF												
2	WALL												
3	WALL												
4	WALL												
5	WALL												
6	GLASS												
7	GLASS												

ITEM NO.	ITEM	U	AREA X FT²	ΔT				
8	PARTITION WALL							
9	CEILING							
10	FLOOR							
11	FLOOR							

SOLAR

ITEM NO.	ITEM	DIRECTION	SHADE COEFF (SC)	SHGF	AREA X	USAGE	CLF	Q SENSIBLE BTUH	
								HR	HR
12	GLASS	UNSHADED							
		SHADED							
13	GLASS	UNSHADED							
		SHADED							
14	GLASS	UNSHADED							
		SHADED							
15	GLASS	UNSHADED							
		SHADED							

LIGHTS

ITEM NO.	TYPE	TOTAL HOURS ON	TOTAL WATTS	WATTS TO BTUH 3.41	USAGE %	X BALLAST X	CLF		
								HR	HR
16	FLUORESCENT								
17	INCANDESCENT								

PEOPLE

ITEM NO.	HRS. IN SPACE	NO. PEOPLE	X	Q₁ PER PERSON		CLF		
							HR	HR
18								
19								

COOLING

HEATING

SUBTOTAL

INFILT./VENT.AIR
1.085 X ΔT X CFM

PICK-UP FACTOR

TOTAL

GRAND TOTAL

HUMIDIFICATION
7 X ΔW* X CFM

*Grains of Moisture
(Wi – Wo)*

EQUIPMENT

ITEM NO.	HRS ON	HOODED YES - NO	BTUH SENS.	X CLF	Q_L
20			X	HR	HR
21					
22					
23					
24					

INFILT.

ITEM NO.				
25	CFM X 1.085 X	ΔT (DB)		HR

26   F — FACTOR = 1 — [.02 x (SUM OF U X A OF EXT WALLS, ROOF, GLASS, DOORS)) / BLDG EXTERNAL PERIMETER (FT)] = ___ F — FACTOR X SUBTOTAL.

SUBTOTAL

ROOM SUBTOTAL

27   ROOM SUBTOTAL

28   HEAT TO RETURN AIR   WATTS X 3.41 BTUH   X % TO RETURN AIR

DEDUCT FROM ROOM SUBTOTAL

29   NET ROOM SENSIBLE

NET ROOM SENSIBLE

30   VENTILATION AIR   CFM X 1.085 X   ΔT (DB)   HR

VENTILATION AIR

LATENT LOAD

	ITEM	X	Q LATENT		NUMBER
31	PEOPLE			X	
32	EQUIPMENT				
33	EQUIPMENT				

Q LATENT, BTUH

34   INFILTRATION AIR   CFM X 7   X $W_G - W$*   HR

35   TOTAL ROOM LATENT

36   VENTILATION AIR   CFM X 7   X $W_G - W$*   HR

TOTAL ROOM LATENT

VENTILATION AIR

*Grains of Moisture

COOLING LOAD SUMMARY

Q SENSIBLE

37   NET ROOM SENSIBLE (ITEM 29)

38   PLUS HEAT TO RETURN AIR (ITEM 28)

39   PLUS VENTILATION AIR (ITEM 30)

40   TOTAL Q SENSIBLE

44   TOTAL EQUIPMENT LOAD   (ITEM 40 + ITEM 43)

48   TONNAGE EQUIVALENT   (ITEM 44) OF EQUIPMENT LOAD   12,000 BTUH

*Consult either the 1977 ASHRAE Handbook of Fundamentals or the "Cooling and Heating Load Calculation Manual," ASHRAE GRP 158, for additional instructions and tabular data.

Q LATENT

41   TOTAL ROOM LATENT (ITEM 35)

42   PLUS VENTILATION AIR (ITEM 36)

43   TOTAL Q LATENT

46   SENSIBLE   =   (ITEM 29) HEAT RATIO   (ITEM 29 + ITEM 35)

47   CFM   =   (ITEM 29) SUPPLY AIR   1.085 ($T_{ROOM} - T_{SUPPLY}$)

"K" is a color correction to be applied after the month-latitude adjustment.
   Roofs: K = 1.0 Dark Color   K = .75 Light Color
   Walls: K = 1.0 Dark Color
      K = 0.5 Light Color   K = .83 Medium Color

THE TRANE COMPANY, LA CROSSE, WISCONSIN 54601

1-26.04—(8/79)

SELECTING COMPONENTS

After the load is determined and the operating conditions established, the compressor or condensing unit should be chosen. Components must be chosen to provide sufficient cooling for the application at the minimum initial, operating, and maintenance cost. The proper motor voltage, cost, personnel expertise, and other factors will play a part in the decision.

The basic rating of compressors is their output as measured in tons of refrigeration at standard condenser and evaporator temperatures. (One ton equals 12,000 Btu/hour or 3,024 kcal/hour.) Manufacturers have charts listing compressor capacity at various operating conditions. Pay close attention to the conditions stated in specifications, such as amount of superheat or subcooling assumed, when selecting a compressor. Some specifications explain how to add or subtract capacity to adjust for different superheat or subcooling conditions. Pressure drop in the system, which represents lost cooling capacity, should also be anticipated when sizing a compressor.

The compressor must be matched with the evaporator and condenser. A "condensing unit" is a built-up refrigeration machine with all major components except the evaporator and metering device. Condensing units are factory-matched and should work harmoniously. When selecting components, add a safety margin to allow for pull-down after large loads, unanticipated temperature and pressure losses, and miscalculations.

A condensing unit should be:

- *Able to handle expected maximum load safely and minimum load without short-cycling.*

- *Capable of creating the required evaporator temperature and handling the number of evaporators in the system.*

- *Provided with adequate defrost cycle and defrost controls.*

- *Able to run on available electricity phase and voltage.*

- *Able to make the best use of condenser cooling medium, according to these factors:*

- *Maximum summer air and water temperatures.*

- *Cost, quality, and availability of condenser water.*
- *Location of condensing unit and auxiliary components.*

INSTALLING THE COMPRESSOR

Select a location with enough size, ventilation, and support for the compressor or condensing unit. Ventilation requirements will be greatly reduced when a remote or water-cooled condenser is used. The natural ventilation requirements listed in Table H1 are figured for a single window; rooms with cross-ventilation may need less air volume.

Most compressors are installed on a concrete pad raised above the floor. For installations that do not rest on a basement floor, isolator rails may be used reduce the transmission of vibration to the structure. The machine or the isolator rails should be secured to the floor or concrete with bolts to prevent movement.

Reciprocating compressors require some form of isolation to prevent stresses to the piping, especially when they are affixed to a resilient mounting. A compressor will shift slightly on startup and shutdown, placing torque on attached pipes. Allow the piping to move slightly by installing one or more elbows in the lines near the compressor. Use at least 10 pipe diameters of straight pipe between the elbows (see Part E, *Vibration absorber*, p. 192).

The method of hooking up the compressor will depend on so many factors that no instructions can be given here. Exercise caution during the entire process to keep the inside of the system clean. Shortcuts that contaminate the system may return to haunt you.

PIPING INSTALLATION

Many "extras" in the piping system may be included, depending on the bid and requirements of the situation. A filter-drier in the liquid line and possibly in the suction line will help prevent burnouts and plugging of the metering device and other components. Insulating the suction line will prevent condensation and save

TABLE H2
Ventilation of Compressor

For Condensing Units with Water Cooled Condensers or Compressor Units with Remote Condensers

Motor H.P.	Natural Ventilation Room Volume Cubic Feet	Forced Ventilation CFM
3	600	300
5	850	500
7½	1100	700
10	1300	900
15	1650	1300
20	2000	1800
25	2250	2200
30	2450	2600
40	2800	3000
50	3100	3400
60	3350	4000
75	3650	5700
100	4000	7000

REPRINTED WITH PERMISSION © AMERICAN STANDARD 1989

energy. Installing service valves will save the owner money in the long run, although they are not essential in every system.

The manufacturer or engineer may supply a mechanical drawing using the symbols shown in Table H3. A key may be provided to clarify the symbols used.

Follow these guidelines for a successful installation:

Keep tubing clean and dry before and during installation. Use only sealed ACR grade tubing. Open the seals on compressors and filter-driers only as long as needed to make the connections— about two minutes maximum.

Permanent suction line filters and liquid line filter-driers are an excellent means of extending system life.

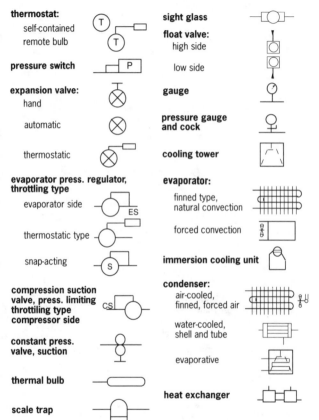

thermostat:
self-contained
remote bulb

pressure switch

expansion valve:
hand

automatic

thermostatic

evaporator press. regulator,
throttling type
evaporator side

thermostatic type

snap-acting

compression suction
valve, press. limiting
throttiling type
compressor side

constant press.
valve, suction

thermal bulb

scale trap

sight glass

float valve:
high side

low side

gauge

pressure gauge
and cock

cooling tower

evaporator:
finned type,
natural convection

forced convection

immersion cooling unit

condenser:
air-cooled,
finned, forced air

water-cooled,
shell and tube

evaporative

heat exchanger

Table H3 Mechanical symbols for refrigeration

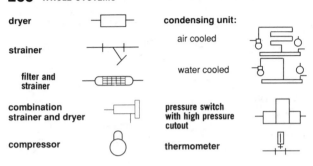

dryer

strainer

filter and strainer

combination strainer and dryer

compressor

condensing unit:

air cooled

water cooled

pressure switch with high pressure cutout

thermometer

Table H3 (cont) Mechanical symbols for refrigeration

Slope suction lines ½ inch per 10 feet (approximately 4 mm per meter) toward the compressor to promote oil return.

During brazing, fill the tubing with a nonoxidizing gas such as dry nitrogen or carbon dioxide to prevent corrosion.

Choose solder and brazing filler metal which can withstand the pressure and temperature in the system. Use no more soldering paste or flux than necessary.

Vibration absorbers must be installed in the proper orientation and position. Consult manufacturer's directions. Absorbers installed perpendicular to the crankshaft may fail because normal compressor shifting will stress their bellows.

If using quick-connect fittings, coil extra tubing horizontally to allow oil to flow, especially in the suction line.

Leak test the system before insulating the tubing.

PLACING A SYSTEM INTO SERVICE

Before running a system for the first time, you must go over all control settings and check the other components. Use the following guidelines:

1. Set the refrigerant and temperature controls according to specifications from the designer. The control differential must be great enough to prevent short cycling.

2. Check interlocks between the controls and components. This check will ensure that components designed to work together actually do so.

3. Check the following before starting the compressor:

   a. Condenser water shutoff valves: open?

   b. Compressor oil level: above center of the sight glass?

   c. Suction and discharge valves: open?

   d. Refrigerant valves: open?

   e. Liquid line solenoid: on automatic setting?

   f. Gauges for oil pressure, suction, and discharge pressure: installed?

   g. Tag identifying system refrigerant: in place?

4. Start the system, keeping a close watch on the suction, discharge, and oil pressures.

5. Check superheat if using a thermostatic expansion valve.

6. Check the running amperage and voltage of the motor. If using a three-phase motor, check the variation in voltage between the three legs of the circuit (see Part F, *Three-phase motors*, p. 206).

7. Fill out a log such as shown in Fig. H11 to record operating conditions.

8. Run the system for 72 hours, with a technician available if possible. Monitor the oil level closely.

At the conclusion of the 72-hour run-in, perform these checks:

1. Check the compressor oil. If it is low, run the compressor for a few hours at full load (to ensure maximum refrigerant velocity) checking whether the oil returns from the piping and components. If crankcase oil is still low, add more.

2. Check for a solid stream of liquid at the liquid line sight glass. If bubbles appear, determine whether they are due to a restriction

in the line or a low charge. If the charge is low, check for leaks. Add refrigerant if needed.

3. Check the temperature of the liquid line on both sides of the filter-drier. If there is much temperature drop, the drier element is restricted. Remove and replace it.

4. Measure the superheat and adjust if needed.

5. Observe operating pressures. If they do not match specifications, determine the cause and correct it. If correct, backseat the service valves, remove the gauge manifold from the system, and plug the valves. If gauges are permanent parts of the system, close the valves leading to them, as continual service shortens gauge life. Record operating conditions on the log.

6. On an open system, shut off the compressor and check for leaks at the shaft seal with a leak detector. Also check the alignment of the motor shaft. Lubricate the motor if necessary.

7. Clean all strainers in condenser circuits.

8. Check and re-tension all fan belts.

9. Check that air filters are clean.

After one week, return to perform these services and turn the system over to the owner:

1. Replace the filter-drier element.

2. Tighten the motor-compressor coupling (on an open system).

3. Watch the system cycle once or twice, looking for irregularities.

4. Check:

   - *System pressures*
   - *Compressor oil*
   - *Liquid line sight glass*
   - *Condenser operation*

After the check-out period, gather the operating specifications, parts lists, and other pertinent information. Make a permanent data sheet for the installation. Save one copy for your files and give another to the owner. The sheet should include:

1. Manufacturer, model, and serial or part number of compressor,

PLANT ________ MACHINE SERIAL NO. ________ MACHINE SIZE ________

Time	COOLER					CONDENSER				COMPRESSOR						THERMAL PURGE				Operator's Initials
	GPM ______					GPM ______							OIL			Purge Pressure for Pump Operation		Time Between Pump Starts	Refrig. Level	
				WATER TEMPERATURE				WATER TEMPERATURE								Starts	Stops			
																COMPRESSION PURGE				
Time	Vacuum or Pressure	Refrigerant Temperature	Refrigerant Level	In	Out	Vacuum or Pressure	Condenser Temperature	In	Out	Vane Position Indicator	Main Bearing Temperature	Level	Temperature	Pressure	Motor Amps	Suct. Press.	Disch. Press.	Oil Level	Refrig. Level	Operator's Initials
1	2	3	4	5	6	7	8	9	10	11	12	13	14	15	16	17	18	19	20	21

REMARKS: Indicate shut-downs on safety controls, repairs, made, oil or refrigerant added or removed, and water drained from purge. Include amounts.

Fig. H11 Refrigeration log

Courtesy of Carrier Corporation, Division of United Technologies Corporation contactor, starter, protection device, and all related electrical components.

2. Electrical data for both line and control circuit: current, voltage, phase, hertz, wire size. Electrical diagram.

3. Make, model, size, and serial number for other equipment in system: evaporators, condensers, receivers, filter-driers, defrost timer, fans, and pumps.

4. Refrigerant piping diagram.

5. Refrigerant number and initial charge size.

6. Design operating temperature and pressure.

7. Defrost cycle information.

8. Settings on all operating, safety, capacity, and refrigerant controls.

SERVICING

A residential central air system should receive some service each year, either from the homeowner or a contractor. The crankcase heater must be energized 24 hours before start up to drive refrigerant from the oil. Other services should include:

1. Check duct dampers and balance if needed.

2. Inspect and replace filters.

3. Clean condenser and fan.

4. Lubricate bearings on motor and fan.

5. Inspect fan belt. Replace if cracked or glazed.

As with other cooling systems, pressures, operating controls, refrigerant charge, suction line sweating, voltage and full-load amperage should be checked occasionally. Check for condensate drainage inside the furnace, which can cause corrosion if it escapes from the drain pan.

Comfort Cooling (Air Conditioning)

Properly speaking, air conditioning is the treatment of air to control temperature, humidity, cleanliness, and distribution. Thus, it includes both heating and cooling of air. What is commonly called "air conditioning" is known to the trade by two names. "Comfort cooling" is cooling used to make human beings comfortable. "Process conditioning" is cooling used for the benefit of an industrial process, such as a computer room, a candy factory, or the like.

To service comfort cooling systems, you must have knowledge of heating and air distribution systems, as in many buildings, the same equipment that moves cooled water or air in summer handles heated water or air in winter. And in the case of the heat pump, one system does both jobs.

Central comfort cooling may use either an air- or a water-cooled condenser. The general practice is to locate the condenser outside and return liquid refrigerant to the evaporator inside the building, but in some cases ducts are used to bring condenser air into the building instead. The evaporator must be chosen to fit inside the furnace being used.

RESIDENTIAL CENTRAL AIR CONDITIONING

Residential central air systems, like all other cooling systems, must be matched to the load. An undersized system will be unable to supply enough cooling, while an oversized system will be expensive to install and will have a shortened operating life due to short cycling.

To avoid noise problems, an outdoor condensing unit should be located away from neighbors and bedroom windows. To promote air circulation, it should be beyond the roof overhang, not in a building's inside corner, and at least two feet from walls. A four-inch concrete slab is often poured to hold the condensing unit. Make sure to provide at least 5 feet (1.5 m) of clearance above the condensing unit fan to allow air circulation. About 10 inches (25 cm) should be allowed on all sides of the unit, with 18 inches (45 cm) clearance near the access panel.

If the condensing unit is installed above the evaporator, slope the suction line downhill and install a U-bend in it to aid the oil return.

The method of installation will reflect one of three basic configurations:

1. The system can be built up of individual components. This procedure is cumbersome, expensive, and requires a great deal of engineering knowledge.

2. The system can be ordered completely assembled, which requires minimal work at the assembly site, primarily uncoiling the tubing and placing the evaporator and condensing unit in their places and connecting the electric and control circuits. However, the tubing must be carefully handled and is subject to kinking.

3. The system can be built up from a completely charged condensing unit and evaporator that are shipped separately and joined at the job site. This technique probably offers the greatest flexibility in relation to price. The attachments may be made with sweat or flare fittings or quick couplings.

After the parts are delivered, the condensing unit should be placed on a concrete pad according to the guidelines above. The evaporator is installed in the building air-handling system, typically in the furnace plenum. Blankoff plates may be installed to ensure that all air passes through the coil. The evaporator must be installed level to ensure that the condensate drainage can flow out the tube provided for that purpose. This drainage can be combined with the furnace condensate tube or routed to a floor drain, sump, or sewer, or it can be pumped to the outside.

The suction and liquid lines are installed and connected, and the electrical wiring is hooked up. The controls are wired and adjusted as well as possible before startup. For more information on starting a system, see *Placing a system into service*, p. 288.

AIR CIRCULATION

Air circulation equipment enables an air conditioning system to deliver the proper amount of cooled, conditioned air to where it is wanted. Depending on the system, air may be propelled by a fan located in the furnace, the cooling unit, room units, or ductwork. The ability of a fan to move air depends on the fan size, speed, and design, and the pressure differential between the intake and output (see Part E, *Fans*, p. 172).

A good air distribution system will:

- *Mix cooled or heated air well enough and deliver it in a manner that does not expose occupants to drafts or obnoxiously warm or cold air.*

- *Limit noise from air flow and equipment.*

- *Provide some turbulence in the living area to promote air movement.*

- *Operate reliably under all conditions.*

PRINCIPLES OF DUCT DESIGN AND INSTALLATION

Although duct design is beyond the scope of this manual, a few principles of design will assist those who must oversee duct installers, work alongside them, or install the ducts as part of a larger comfort cooling installation:

1. Air should be delivered as directly as possible, using minimum amounts of material, space, power, and money.

2. To avoid noise problems, air should not flow faster than maximum recommended velocities.

3. Do not install sharp elbows or turns in the ducts.

4. The angle of divergence in enlargements should not exceed 20°. The angle or convergence in contractions should not exceed 60°.

5. Round ducts have the highest capacity per square foot of metal. Square-section ducts have the greatest capacity of any rectangular ducts. The maximum ratio of long side to short side in a rectangular duct should be 6 to 1.

6. Long runs require expansion joints to give the metal room to expand without buckling.

7. Bracing must be secure enough to prevent movement.

8. Duct insulation prevents heating and cooling losses and also reduces sweating and noise problems.

9. Each branch should have a damper for balancing the system.
10. Ducts should be tight, with laps formed in the direction of flow.
11. If mechanical or electrical apparatus is located in a duct, provide an opening to service it.

Airflow through a duct can be calculated by multiplying duct size in square feet by air speed in feet per minute (fpm). The "free area," or actual opening, of a grille should be listed in manufacturer's catalogs; it is usually between 60 and 85 percent of the overall size.

Ducts must be sized correctly. You can calculate the amount of air flow needed to cool a room by figuring that each cubic foot of air flow per minute (cfm) will remove about 30 Btus (one liter will remove 1116 joules). Divide the cooling load of a room by 30 and you will find the approximate air flow in cfm needed to cool it. In the SI system, divide the heat load in joules by 1116 to find the air flow in liters needed to cool it.

Use a manometer to measure pressure in a duct. An inclined-tube manometer is more precise than a U-tube model. The manometer may be used to compare pressure at two areas of a duct, or to find the pressure drop across a filter, coil, or a long run. It may also be used to measure absolute pressure (the total pressure at one point in the duct), if the day's barometric pressure is known. To find absolute pressure, one manometer tube is left open to the atmosphere and the other hooked into a duct.

When connecting a manometer into a duct, be sure not to confuse static pressure with velocity pressure. Static pressure results from the pressure on the fluid, while velocity pressure results from the movement of the fluid. (Static pressure + velocity pressure = total pressure.) Unfortunately, both static and velocity pressure are created when a fan runs, but generally only the static pressure is wanted for a duct analysis. To measure only static pressure, use a probe with holes drilled in it and a closed end, instead of an open-end probe. Be cautious because certain areas of a duct, such as behind obstructions, will have eddies that prevent accurate measurement.

Balancing ductwork is the process of assuring that each room receives the desired amount of conditioned air. The procedure should wait until the system and controls are working right. Begin by examining the duct setup to see which damper controls what room. Then open all dampers and begin closing those closer to the fan first. Continue checking the results and adjusting dampers. Each adjustment will affect the entire system, so the process can take some time.

WATER CIRCULATION

Comfort cooling systems that distribute their cooling with water are termed "chiller" systems. As with air-distribution systems, a chiller system can be integrated with the heat distribution system to save first cost and building space. Chilled water piping can range from simple to complex. Simple systems save first cost but offer less control and flexibility than more complicated piping.

The most basic water circuit is the *series loop system*, in which chilled water passes through a single loop of pipe and every heat exchanger device. All the heat exchangers are connected in series. Slightly more complex is a *one-pipe system*, in which a single pipe circulates all the cooling water, but tee valves are used to divert some water through a balancing valve to a heat transfer device.

The two versions of the *two-pipe system* both use a supply main and a return main. In the *direct-return* version, water in the supply and return mains flows in opposite directions. Chilled water can pass through the heat exchanger closest to the chiller and return to the chiller without travelling through the entire piping system. As a result, an adjustable valve should be installed in the branch lines to the exchangers to balance out the load.

A more sophisticated and more common version of the two-pipe system is the *two-pipe reverse return system*, in which water flows in the same direction in both supply and return mains. The system is easier to control because the distance from the chiller to any unit and back to the chiller is essentially the same. Balancing valves are helpful for making fine adjustments in cooling supply. In return for the greater initial cost, this system offers more control and flexibility.

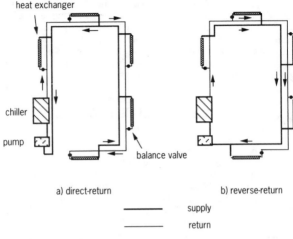

a) direct-return   b) reverse-return

———— supply

———— return

Fig. H12 Two-pipe system

Commercial Refrigeration

Commercial refrigeration systems are generally classified by evaporator temperature according to the chart on page 298. Compressors are usually designed for a general range of evaporator temperature. Running the evaporator too warm for a certain refrigerant-compressor combination may result in inadequate compressor loading that causes excessive head pressures and other troubles. The main restrictions on reducing the evaporator temperature are motor cooling and overloading. However, by changing refrigerants, it may be possible to alter the operating temperature of a certain system. To achieve temperatures below −40°F, a multistage system is normally needed. Two-stage compressors may reach as low as −80°F, and cascade systems are used for temperatures below that.

| | Evaporator temperature | |
System class	United States units	SI units
High temperature	About 0°F to 50°F	About −17.8°C to 10°C
Medium temperature	−5°F to 25°F	−20.6°C to −3.9°C
Low temperature	−40°F to 0°F	−40°C to −17.8°C
Extra low temperature	−40°F to −20°F	−40°C to −28.9°C

FIXTURES AND COOLERS

The wide variety of commercial refrigerating and freezing fixtures in use are classified as display cases, walk-in coolers, and storage freezers. There is great variation within each category, as manufacturers meet new commercial requirements.

Fixtures vary according to:

- *Condensing unit type*
- *Metering device*
- *Evaporator type*
- *Operating control*
- *Defrosting method*
- *Refrigerant*

Fixtures can also be classified by the method of transferring heat from the product or atmosphere to the evaporator:

1. Direct contact between air and cooling coil with no fan.

2. Forced air cooling using a fan to blow air across the coils and through the cooled space.

3. Indirect contact: the coil cools a brine tank which conveys heat from the product to the evaporator. The brine tank stores heat and minimizes swings in temperature.

4. Combination direct and indirect contact: part of the evaporator is in a brine tank and part contacts air in the cooled space.

Open display cases are subject to turbulence and should not be placed where they are subject to drafts from a duct or window. Display lighting can be a significant cause of warming in foods in a case, resulting in product temperatures far above case air temperature.

A regular schedule of maintenance should be adopted for meat display cases. A weekly cleaning should begin with the removal of all product and removable shelving. The machine should be shut down and cleaned with a mild soap, mild detergent, or bicarbonate of soda. Ammonia will cause discoloration of meat, so it should not be used. Use little water because it can damage electrical components.

Drains on display cases should be piped so that neither warm air nor sewer gas can enter the case. A trap in the line should be located at least 12 inches (30.5 cm) from the case outlet.

Air in a display case is usually forced by fans that are oriented to assist normal convection. The evaporator may be hung from adjustable brackets on the ceiling. Baffles may be used to direct the air flow and help maintain the temperature difference between the evaporator and the product. An adequate TD will help ensure heat transfer and minimize the size of evaporator needed. Remember that an excessive TD will lead to a great deal of dehumidifying, which can dessicate the product.

Display cases can also be cooled by plate-type evaporators. Adequate air circulation must be maintained to allow thorough cooling when using this type of evaporator.

For a list of desired storage temperature for products, see Table L6, p. 389.

MULTIPLE (COMBINED) SYSTEMS

In recent years, the industry has seen a trend toward operating several evaporators off a single condensing unit. The advent of large condensing units with more sophisticated controls accounts for the increasing use of multiple systems. Although multiple systems are undoubtedly more complex to install and service than simple systems, they have these benefits:

- *Reduced equipment and installation costs.*

- *Lower operating and maintenance costs. Fewer components are needed, and larger motors are more efficient.*

The chances of trouble increase along with the number of fixtures, and although good design can minimize trouble, it cannot eliminate it.

Display cases connected to a single condensing unit should be chosen carefully. They should produce the desired operating temperature with the same suction pressure and the same compressor running time. For proper operation, the warmest evaporator (or group of evaporators) should have no more than 40 percent of the total system load. Temperatures in the various cases can be controlled by evaporator pressure regulating valves or solenoids in the liquid lines.

The fixtures and condensing unit should be as close to each other as possible, and the suction lines must be large enough to minimize pressure drops yet still allow oil return. Installing suction line risers between display cases will help prevent oil from dripping between evaporators or from an evaporator to the compressor during the off cycle.

Defrost systems must be adapted to the conditions in the various cases, often by use of supplemental electric defrost heaters in areas most prone to frosting. A multicircuit time clock can be used to control a variety of defrost cycles on a combined system.

Combined systems may be fed by a refrigeration mechanical center serving the cooling needs of an entire supermarket. These large condensing units may save money and, by removing machinery from the display floor, allow more space for product, and offer the advantage of factory engineering and flexible location.

HEAT RECOVERY SYSTEMS

Large supermarket cooling systems may have equipment to recover condenser heat for heating the store air during the winter. A great deal of heat can be recovered and a great deal of energy cost saved. Three methods can be used:

1. *Direct air*—A housing is installed around the condenser and ducts and fans used to direct heated air to the inside during winter. The cost of equipment and operation can be high.

2. *Closed-circuit water*—Water-cooled condensers lend themselves to this conversion. A three-way valve controls the condenser

cooling water; in winter the water is routed to indoor heating devices. When heating is not wanted, the water is routed to an evaporative cooler. Because the condenser water is not particularly hot, a large radiator is needed to transfer the heat inside. The water pumps consume a great deal of electricity.

3. *Dual condenser*—In this system, a second condenser is installed in the air-handling equipment. A three-way valve routes the refrigerant outside during warm weather and inside during cold weather. Costs are low with this system, and the gas is warm enough that heat transmission to the inside air is quite rapid. While extra refrigerant tubing is needed, there is no additional pumping requirement.

PART I

OZONE AND RECYCLING

The air conditioning and refrigeration industry, long dedicated to human comfort and safe preservation of foods, is now enmeshed in a controversy over the environmental impact of halocarbon refrigerants. According to a consensus of scientists, these stable chemicals damage the ozone layer which protects Earth's surface from most ultraviolet light.

The consequences of a decrease in ozone could include an epidemic of skin cancer and cataracts and harm to major crops and many other organisms.

Ozone is an oxygen molecule which has three atoms. The more common and breatheable form of oxygen has two atoms. In 1974 two American scientists first speculated that CFCs (chlorofluorocarbons) could rise to the upper atmosphere, release chlorine, and begin destroying huge numbers of ozone molecules. The first warnings were not heeded by industry, although other scientists generally supported the theory, which said that the same stability that made CFCs such good refrigerants also allowed them to drift unharmed to the stratosphere, 8 to 30 miles high.

The initial concern centered on the use of CFCs as spray-can propellants, and this use was rapidly phased out in the United States. Then the problem faded from view until the mid-1980s, when an alarming "ozone hole" was detected above Antarctica, a discovery that suggested ozone depletion was already taking place. As other measurements showed declines in ozone above the Northern Hemisphere, strict controls became a distinct possibility.

In September, 1987, representatives of 43 nations signed the Montreal Protocol and pledged to cut CFC production in half by 1999. In March, 1988, the du Pont Corporation, maker of about 25 percent of world production, conceded the link between CFCs and ozone destruction and announced that it would discontinue making the chemicals as soon as substitutes became available. This announcement, by a firm that had long protested that the evidence was incomplete, marked a sea change in industry's attitude toward the problem.

Nature of Problem

The ozone layer is a thin but effective shield. Though if all the ozone were at atmospheric pressure, it would make a layer just ⅛ inch thick—yet it successfully blocks the majority of ultraviolet light. Although ozone is a major pollutant in the lower atmosphere (where it causes heart attacks and deteriorates materials), it is vital for intercepting ultraviolet light in the upper atmosphere.

The original theory about ozone loss has been refined but scarcely changed over the years. The stable chlorofluorocarbons rise slowly to the upper atmosphere and are split apart by intense solar radiation. This breakdown releases chlorine, which, with the solar radiation, converts ozone to a molecule of two-atom oxygen (written O_2) and a single atom of oxygen.

Unfortunately, the chlorine acts as a catalyst and emerges intact from the reaction, ready to take apart another ozone molecule. Apparently, each chlorine atom can destroy thousands of ozone molecules, and chlorine reaching to the stratosphere today is expected to remain there for as long as a century, destroying ozone the whole time.

Atmospheric concentrations of both R-11 and R-12 have increased over 100 percent between 1975 and 1985, according to a University of Chicago scientist. Within the past two decades, upper-atmosphere ozone is estimated to have fallen by two to three percent above the northern hemisphere. Each 1 percent loss in ozone is expected to increase ultraviolet light by about 2 percent at Earth's surface. This means that the existing ozone reduction above the Northern Hemisphere could cause a 4 to 6 percent increase in UV and a 10 percent increase in skin cancer.

The Ozone Trends Panel of the National Aeronautic and Space Administration (NASA) concluded in 1988 that 10 percent of stratospheric ozone would be destroyed within 70 years.

Uses of CFCs

CFCs were discovered in 1930 by a General Motors researcher who was looking for a safe, non-toxic replacement for ammonia refrigerant. Over the years, CFC's many desirable qualities—safe, non-toxic, non-flammable, good latent heat points—have made them enormously popular as vapor-compression refrigerants.

CFCs were also used to pressurize spray cans, clean electronics parts, sterilize medical equipment and expand foam for insulation and packaging. Today, residential and commercial air conditioning and refrigeration account for about 10 percent of U.S. CFC use. A related chemical found in "halon" fire extinguishers can also transport chlorine to the stratosphere.

CFC sales in the United States are running about $750 million annually. Global production in 1986 was about 2.5 billion pounds and increasing at about 3 percent annually.

TABLE I1

Uses of CFCs

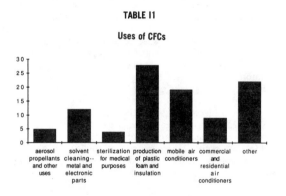

What Are the Dangers?

The concern about CFCs is that ozone depletion will cause an increase in ultraviolet light at the Earth's surface, which will damage people, plants, and animals. Ultraviolet light causes skin cancer. The rate of malignant melanoma, the most deadly form of skin cancer, increased 93 percent during the 1980s, and some form of skin cancer (most are not so deadly) will afflict one American in three. In the past decade dermatologists have repeatedly warned about the hazards of over-exposure to the sun.

Estimates of the relationship between ozone loss and skin cancer rates vary. The National Academy of Sciences estimates that a 1 percent loss in ozone will raise cancer rates by 5 to 6 percent.

Ultraviolet light also causes cataracts, a thickening of the eye's lens that clouds and blurs vision. The EPA has estimated that the increase in the number of cataracts will be reduced 92 percent by observing the Montreal Protocol.

A one-percent increase in ultraviolet radiation decreases soybean production by one percent, and soybeans are the largest single source of plant protein. One study found that one form of UV light damaged tissue in two-thirds of 200 species of plants tested. Increased ultraviolet radiation may also harm the marine microorganisms which form the foundation of the oceanic food chain.

There is also speculation that CFCs contribute to the "greenhouse effect" which is expected to increase global temperatures. The greenhouse effect occurs because certain gases in the upper atmosphere reflect heat back to Earth. If these gases, including carbon dioxide, methane and CFCs, continue increasing, the average global temperature could rise 10°F in the next century—about as much warming as has occurred since the last ice age, when parts of the northern United States were covered by one mile of ice!

The projected effects include melting of the polar ice caps, flooding of coastlines, climatic changes, shifts in agricultural zones, extinction of species, widespread storms and droughts, and enormous forest fires. Some atmospheric scientists suspect that the string of record hot summers in the 1980s signaled the beginning of greenhouse warming.

The Montreal Protocol

As evidence gathered about the dangers of ozone depletion, an international argeement was reached to limit chlorofluorocarbon production. The Montreal Protocol was signed in 1987 and ratified by the U.S. Senate the next year by a vote of 83 to 0. The agreement was hailed as the first international treaty to prevent, rather than to remedy, an environmental problem. The Protocol set increasingly strict limits on CFC production. 1990 production is frozen at the

1986 level; by 1994 it will be cut 20 percent; by 1999, cut 50 percent.

The Protocol will have wide-ranging effects on the air conditioning and refrigeration industry: CFC prices are expected to double, and common refrigerants will become scarce. Practices which release halocarbons, such as venting to the atmosphere and using refrigerant for leak testing, may be restricted and/or become more expensive.

Unfortunately, no sooner was the Protocol signed than scientists found new evidence of ozone destruction, and the ink was hardly dry when the Protocol was being called "too little, too late." Yet at this point the Protocol represents the only interational agreement governing halocarbons, although states and localities are considering stricter regulation.

Substitute Refrigerants

Substitutes for CFCs and other ozone-destroying chemicals are expected to reach the market at some point in the future. The substitutes are expected to be more expensive than present refrigerants. Some CFCs are more damaging to ozone than others. The fully-chlorinated types, particularly R-11 and R-12, carry much more chlorine to the stratosphere. Industry has had some success formulating so-called "ozone-friendly" CFCs. A version containing an additional hydrogen atom, called HCFC-22, breaks down before reaching the stratosphere. In 1988, du Pont announced a plant in Corpus Christi, Texas to make a new refrigerant. In late 1989, ICI Americas Inc. announced a $100 million plant in Louisiana to manufacture an alternative fluorocarbon called AFC 134a. This material is also expected to break down in the lower atmosphere. Many chemical manufacturers are investigating other alternatives for existing uses of CFCs, although few have reached the market. All substitutes must be thoroughly tested for toxicity and environmental effects.

Alternative chemicals may provide the long-term solution to ozone depletion, but in the near term, the solution is recovery and recycling.

Recovery and Recycling

The handling of halocarbon refrigerants is changing rapidly. While technicians once allowed great quantities to evaporate when emptying a system or testing it for leaks, this is no longer acceptable. Laws are being passed in some states to promote or require the use of recovery and recycling. In February, 1989, the Mobile Air Conditioning Society and the Environmental Protection Agency agreed to begin recycling CFCs from car and truck air conditioning and refrigeration units.

The residential and commercial sector is beginning to face similar pressure, and some manufacturers have begun making self-contained recovery and recycling units. Although these units are not cheap, one manufacturer points out that recycling may be cheaper than buying new refrigerant, especially as production cutbacks cause the price of chlorofluorocarbons to rise.

The industry distinguishes recovery—the removal of refrigerant from a system—from recycling, the cleaning of moisture and contamination from refrigerant in preparation for reuse. Recovery has been practiced for years, especially on larger systems with service valves and large charges.

With many recovery devices just reaching the market, the technology is changing rapidly. Some manufacturers sell separate recovery and recycling machines, on the theory that refrigerant collected in the field with a recovery machine can be recycled at a a central location with a recycling machine. A combination device can first recover refrigerant and then recycle it, or do both processes at once.

These types of cart-mounted machines are already on the market:

1. One recovery-recycling system (see Fig. 11) contains a miniature refrigeration system, with compressor, condenser, hoses to connect to the system being scavenged, and control valves. The unit is designed to work with proprietary refrigerant cylinders and/or standard drums and can pump either gas or liquid refrigerant, according to the size and configuration of the system. Incoming vapor refrigerant goes through an oil separator and filter before reaching the compressor. All refrigerant passes through an acid-moisture filter before entering the storage

TABLE 12

Cost-benefit of recycling

HVAC/R Cost Savings Worksheet

Typical Examples Per Service Truck	Residential Contractor	Commercial Contractor	Your Operation
1. Amount of Refrigerant Used Per Week A. Average number of systems serviced per week during A/C season	25	20	
B. Average amount of refrigerant used per system	5	25	
C. Total amount of refrigerant used per week for system recharge (A x B)	125	500	
D. Amount of refrigerant used per week for leak and pressure checking	35	100	
E. Average total used per week (C + D)	160	600	
2. Cost of Refrigerant Per Week F. Cost of refrigerant per pound	$2.00	$1.50	
G. Total cost of refrigerant used per week (E x F)	320	900	
3. Amount of Refrigerant Recoverable Per Week H. Amount recovered from systems requiring A/C service (many systems are low on refrig. when they are serviced)	80	500	
I. Amount recoverable from leak check	30	90	
J. Refrigerant recoverable (H + I)	110	590	
4. Cost Savings Per Unit Per Week (F x J)	$220	$885	

MODE 1
VAPOR RECOVERY

Description: Unit pulls refrigerant from system as a gas, cleans, liquifies and stores it in on board storage cylinder or external storage vessel.

Open red manifold valve slightly
MODE 1 WITH LIQUID LIFT

EXTERNAL STORAGE

Suction service valve

MODE 2
LIQUID RECOVERY
WHEN SYSTEM PRESSURES ARE
GREATER THAN STORAGE VESSEL PRESSURES

Description: Liquid is pulled from the receiver of the system through RecoveryII filter into on-board storage vessel. Periodically dump on-board storage into external storage vessel by opening valve A.

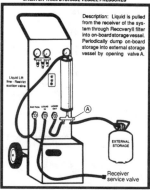

Liquid Lift line - Restrict suction valve

EXTERNAL STORAGE

Receiver service valve

MODE 3
LIQUID RECOVERY
USING LIQUID LIFT AND TWO PORT STORAGE VESSEL

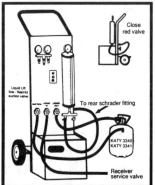

Close red valve

Liquid Lift line - Restrict suction valve

To rear schrader fitting

KATY 3340
KATY 3341

Receiver service valve

MODE 4
LIQUID RECOVERY
USING LIQUID LIFT WITH ONE PORT STORAGE VESSEL

Close red valve

Alternate OPEN - CLOSE red and blue valves (30 second intervals)

Storage vessel

To rear Schrader fitting

Receiver service valve

Courtesy of Katy Instruments, James Kamm Technologies

Fig. I1   Recovery-recycling unit

cylinder. The two ports in the storage cylinder allow vapor to be drawn from the top of the cylinder during liquid recovery from a low-pressure system. This draws down pressure and speeds recovery.

2. A second recovery and recycling machine contains a pump to transfer liquid refrigerant and a compressor to fill the storage cylinder. Instead of a condenser, this device uses a heat exchanger and oil separator to keep the refrigerant in a liquid state. To operate, the center hose of the gauge manifold (not supplied) is connected to the side of the unit and both manifold valves are opened.

The steps of recovery and recycling must be done separately. The compressor transfers refrigerant and automatically stops when the system is pumped out. Once the recovery is complete, recycling can begin. The pump circulates the liquid refrigerant through a filter-drier until the moisture indicator reads "dry." The rate of processing will vary with the amount of moisture in the refrigerant. The manufacturer indicator about two pounds per minute as a guideline rate for both recovery and recycling.

Automatic controls and indicators for refrigerant dryness, plugged lines, and full storage tank are designed to allow unattended operation. Filter-drier elements must be replaced as needed during the recovery process.

TROUBLESHOOTING

Troubleshooting is the process of tracing a symptom back to its source. Often, you must analyze several complaints and identify the source or sources of the difficulty. Good troubleshooting does not stop with replacing faulty parts—it also requires finding and correcting whatever caused the part to fail.

Although a "try this, replace that" approach is common in the trade, troubleshooting should be done logically. Each technician should develop a method that is comfortable, thorough, and effective. This part contains an overall vapor-compression system troubleshooting guide which deals with three general conditions: 1) compressor motor fails to start, 2) system cools but runs erratically, and 3) system runs but does not cool enough. Part J also contains more detailed troubleshooting guides for other components.

Consult these sections if the problem can be isolated or after consulting the system troubleshooting guide:

- *condenser*
- *expansion valve*
- *high-side float*
- *low-side float*
- *oil control system*
- *absorption system*
- *motor*
- *pump*

BASIC SYSTEM REQUIREMENTS

To function properly, a cooling system needs these capabilities:

1. Sufficient liquid refrigerant in the evaporator

312

2. Evaporator pressure low enough to allow refrigerant to boil at desired temperature

3. Sufficient contact between the cooled space and the evaporator

4. Correct temperature and pressure in the condenser

5. Properly sized condenser

6. Sufficient heat removal from the condenser

7. Liquid line large enough and not restricted

8. Little pressure drop in the suction line. Not excessive restriction in filters, driers, valves, or other line components

9. A control system capable of establishing and maintaining the desired conditions in a safe and economical manner

TROUBLESHOOTING BASICS

The first step in troubleshooting is to ask the owner or operator about the problem. Then install the gauge manifold. During troubleshooting, keep asking yourself "Why is this happening?" "What else could cause these symptoms?" "Why does this switch not stay closed?"

If a system is not running, you can take the pressure and check if the circuits are energized. But to learn more, you must get the motor running, so troubleshooting often starts with a look at electrical components.

If the system is operating but not cooling properly, concentrate on the pressure–temperature aspect, especially the operating and capacity controls. If the system is new, the problem is likely to be found in design, wiring, control setting, or proper rotation of motors. Trouble in established systems may build up for a long period before becoming apparent. Check for worn parts, plugged filters, or sagging or leaking pipes. Perhaps vibration has weakened or loosened something or a change in operating conditions has caused the problem. Has the operator recently changed a setting or procedure? Sometimes, several factors can cause the same operating deficits. These cases challenge you to sift through the possible sources of trouble and identify the true culprit.

Your ability to think through the intricacies of a cooling system is a great asset in troubleshooting. For example, a frosted crankcase does not prove that the compressor is getting enough cooling from the suction line. True, the refrigerant is cold, but it is also less dense, and thus has less ability to remove heat from the compressor. Thus subnormal suction pressure-temperature can lead, somewhat paradoxically, to overheating.

Your five senses can tell you a lot about what is going on in a balky system:

Look: for vibration, gauge readings, leaks, broken or loose parts.

Listen: for compressor knocks, valves opening or closing, switches clicking at the right time.

Feel: for temperature changes, pipes that are hot when they should be cool, or vice versa.

Smell: for burned wire insulation, hot parts, or belts slipping.

Taste: for food that has spoiled due to warm temperatures.

Vapor-Compression Systems

This part contains troubleshooting guides on the system, condenser, metering device, high- and low-side floats, and oil control systems.

If a system will not run, start troubleshooting by looking at the compressors section. Once you get the system running, you can take gauge pressures and analyze further. If you can trace the problem to a certain component, turn to the section on that component.

SYSTEM

See the following graph for a sample of a trouble shooting system.

Major symptom	Minor symptom	Problem	Test to confirm	Solution
a) Unit fails to start				
No hum	No power at motor starter or relay.	Open switch or blown fuse.	Test across line side of starter to ground with volt meter.	Find out why protector is open and close it. Replace fuse.
	Power at motor starter or relay, but contacts in starter or relay are open.	Open motor control—no signal to holding coil.	Test holding coil with voltmeter. (Relay is normally open.) If coil not powered, test through control circuit with continuity tester or voltmeter.	Isolate problem and correct.
		Open relay with energized holding coil.	Test through holding coil with continuity tester or voltmeter.	Replace holding coil.
	Contacts closed, no hum.	Burned contacts in starter.	Check load side of starter with voltmeter. Checks contacts with ohmmeter for low resistance.	Replace faulty starter if resistance is high.
		Open windings in motor.	Check motor continuity with VOM.	Replace faulty motor.

Major symptom	Minor symptom	Problem	Test to confirm	Solution
Contactor closed, motor hums.	Any motor.	Shorts or grounds in windings.	Check compressor windings with ohmmeter.	Replace motor.
	Three-phase motor.	Compressor is stuck.	Check oil level in crankcase with sight glass or dipstick. Attempt to rock compressor manually.	If good, reverse any two power wires to reverse rotation. Rebuild compressor.
	Single-phase, capacitor start and run.	Compressor is stuck or start capacitor is bad.	Check oil level in crankcase with sight glass or dipstick. Attempt to rock compressor manually. Check start and run capacitors.	Replace capacitors if needed. Try a hard start kit. Rebuild compressor.
	Single-phase, permanent split capacitor.	Compressor is stuck.	Inspect starting relay visually or test with VOM.	Replace starting relay.
		Open winding.	Test with VOM.	Replace compressor.
		Bad capacitor.	Test with capacitor checker.	Replace capacitor.
	Compressor is stuck, motor tests OK.	Refrigerant pressure not balancing in off-cycle.	Check with gauge manifold.	Low pressure cut out control set too close together. Expand differential.

				Check metering device. Replace plugged capillary tube or valve to balance pressure.
b) Unit runs erratically				
Compressor short-cycles.	Control circuit makes and breaks.	Faulty control.	Use meters to isolate problem control.	Repair or replace.
	Low-pressure control short-cycles.	Leaks, plugged filter-drier in liquid line, low air flow across evaporator, solenoid not closing, control set too close.	Use gauge manifold to isolate problem.	Repair leaks, adjust or replace components as necessary.
		Low evaporator load; low air flow.	Examine load situation; check for dirty filter plugging evaporator air flow; check for broken fan belt or motor problem.	Repair problem. Shut off unused evaporators on multi-evaporator system.
	High-pressure control short cycles.	Air-cooled condenser: plugged with debris and fan inoperative.	Compare condenser inlet to outlet-air temperatures. Inspect condenser fan and controls.	Repair or replace as indicated.

Major symptom	Minor symptom	Problem	Test to confirm	Solution
Compressor short-cycles. (cont.)		Water-cooled condenser: valve not opening, cooling tower pump not working, strainer plugged, water side of condenser fouled or scaled.	Compare inlet to outlet water temperatures in condenser. Inspect condenser pump, piping, controls, water valve. Check for plugged strainers in piping (pull out plug at bottom of strainer and check that water runs out).	Repair or replace valve; clean or replace strainer.
		Pump motor faulty.	Check relays and capacitor.	Replace part or repair motor.
	Leaving condenser water too warm.	Condenser water pump not pumping enough water.	Check holding coil of pump controller; vent condenser to check for air bind-	Repair or replace if still needed.
		Overcharge of refrigerant or noncondensables in condenser.	Check for noncondensables (see condenser procedures). If absent, check charge level.	Bleed off noncondensable or excess refrigerant.
Compressor runs continuously.	Room too cold or product temperature too low.	Thermostat not opening; contacts welded on LPCO.	Check calibration of thermostat; check action of LPCO.	Repair or replace as indicated.

c) Unit runs but does not cool sufficiently

	Room or product warm.	Lack of refrigerant.	Check for bubbles in sight glass.	Repair leak and recharge.
	High suction pressure and low head pressure.	Leaking valves or blown head gasket.	Test pressures with gauge manifold. Remove head and check gasket and valves.	Pump down, replace faulty parts, reassemble and recharge.
HPCO locks out—will not automatically reset.	Cool leaving water in condenser.	Fouled or limed condenser tubes.	Compare incoming and leaving water temperature differential—if too small, poor contact between water and refrigerant due to fouling or liming. Check pump and valve operation.	Clean tubes with brush or acid.
		Pump inoperative.		Repair or replace pump or valve.
	Hot air-cooled condenser	Noncondensables (air) in refrigerant tubing.	Check for air (see *Troubleshooting Condenser.*)	Purge air from condenser tubes.
	Evaporative condenser.	Low air movement; low water flow.	Check fan belt and motor, check water pump.	Repair or replace faulty parts; acid clean tubes.

Major symptom	Minor symptom	Problem	Test to confirm	Solution
HPCO locks out—will not automatically reset. (cont.)	Refrigerant leaving condenser is too hot.	Overcharge.	Check level of liquid refrigerant in the condenser tubes with back of your hand. Area with liquid refrigerant will be cool; area with vapor will be warm.	Remove excess refrigerant.
			A high level indicates excess refrigerant.	
Low head pressure.	Leaving condenser water is cold.	Water valve stuck open.	Check leaving condenser water temperature—should be warm.	Repair water valve.
	Bubbles in sight glass.	Low charge.	Check sight glass.	Locate leak, repair and recharge.
	Suction pressure rises fast on shut-down.	Discharge valves leaking back.	Check valves with gauge manifold. Pull head and inspect valves and gasket.	Fix problem.
	High suction pressure while running.	Internal relief open or blown; head gasket blown (high-side to low-side).	Install gauge manifold and try to pump down. If unable, pull head to inspect.	Correct problem.

High suction pressure.	Compressor runs continuously.	Large load on evaporator.	Check if load is abnormally large. System may be too small.	This may be a normal reaction to a large cooling load. If it ain't broke ... don't fix it!
	Suction line too cold.	TXV overfeeding or oversize.	Check superheat and sensing bulb placement; check valve rating.	Adjust superheat; repair or replace valve with proper size; reattach bulb securely.
	Compressor noisy.	Broken valves.	Pull head and check; check for floodback; check temperature of various heads. Cooler heads will have broken valves.	Repair or replace as indicated. Check metering device and superheat to correct floodback before restarting.
	Inadequate cooling.	Compressor will not pump because unloader stuck.	Check: oil pump discharge pressure; unloader oil pressure; electric unloader assembly solenoid; unloader valve lifter. Compare full-load amps (from nameplate) to actual amp draw.	Correct problems found.

Major symptom	Minor symptom	Problem	Test to confirm	Solution
Low suction pressure.	Bubbles in sight glass.	Lack of refrigerant.	Check sight glass.	Find leak, repair, and recharge.
		Unloaders not working due to dirty screen or wrong setting.	Check screen and setting.	Correct or consult manufacturer's information.
	Temperature drop at liquid line filter-drier.	Plugged filter-drier.	Compare temperature on each side of filter-drier.	Pump down system, clean, and recharge.
	Temperature drop at solenoid valve.	Valve not fully open.	Compare temperature on each side of valve.	Pump down system, dismantle and clean valve recharge.
	Low flow through TXV.	Power element dead; inlet screen partly plugged.	Check power element, check superheat; check screen.	Pump down, replace power element; and clean screen in TXV. (See *Troubleshooting TXV p. 326*)

d) Compressor loses oil.			
Low oil level in sight glass.	Initial oil charge was inadequate.	Check at sight glass.	Add oil.
Compressor loses oil gradually.	Oil settling out in system.	Check pitch of suction and hot gas lines for presence of traps, run compressor continuously to bring oil back to compressor.	Correct pipe pitch to remove traps and add oil if still needed.
	Dirty strainers and/or drier.	Inspect suspect parts.	Clean strainer, replace drier.
Cold crankcase.	Refrigerant flooding back and filling crankcase.	Check crankcase heater with continuity meter, check TXV superheat; check contact between suction line and TXV sensing bulb.	Correct problem.
Oil leaking outside compressor.	Loose fitting and/or gasket, other leak.	Inspect entire oil system.	Tighten fittings and/or replace gasket or leaking part.

CONDENSER

The major troubles with condensers stem from restrictions in the supply of air or water used to dispose of heat. The refrigerant temperature in an air-cooled condenser should be about 30 to 35°F (16.7 to 19.5°C) above outside ambient temperature. In a water-cooled condenser, refrigerant temperature should be about 10 to 15°F (5.6 to 8.3°C) above ambient temperature. Add this temperature to the ambient and convert to pressure to find the correct head pressure. If the system is operating at a significantly different pressure, use troubleshooting techniques to analyze the problem.

A thin film of dirt can significantly impair heat transfer to the surroundings. A dirty air-cooled condenser should be cleaned with high-pressure air or water-detergent solution. Use a pressure washer or a garden hose with a cleaning attachment.

A leaking air-cooled condenser may be repaired but a leaking water-cooled unit is usually replaced. Straighten fins with a fin comb, a plastic device that fits one or two sizes of fins. (See Part K, *Condenser procedures*, p. 345.)

TESTING CONDENSER FOR AIR

Air in the condenser can cause excess head pressure, sometimes high enough to trip limits. Air cuts efficiency because air does not condense at system pressures, and it takes up valuable condenser room.

Use the following procedure to check for noncondensible gas (mainly air) in a condenser:

1. If a purge valve is present, shut the compressor off and allow its fan or water pump to run for 15 minutes. During this time the air will reach the top of the condenser and the liquid refrigerant will gather at the bottom.

2. Compare head pressure with pressure for ambient air (or condenser water for a water-cooled condenser). The maximum difference should be about 15 psi. If it is greater than this, the difference is caused by noncondensibles.

3. Briefly open the purge valve. Again compare head pressure to

the equivalent pressure for condenser air or water. Purge again if the pressure differential is greater than 15 psi.

4. Evacuating and recharging may be necessary if a great deal of air is present.

Do not purge a water-cooled condenser so rapidly that the temperature will fall below freezing, as this could burst the condenser. Keep an eye on the pressure gauge while purging.

Scale, the buildup of minerals inside condenser water tubes, can be a major problem with water-cooled condensers. Scale must be removed with an acid solution or it can seriously impair heat transfer.

A "scale free" system has been developed to reduce the deposition of scale. An electrolyte rod is placed in the condenser water and grounded to the equipment. The system can even cause existing scale to enter solution so it can be removed from the system.

AIR-COOLED CONDENSER

Symptom	Problem	Solution
Undercooling by system.	Fan operating incorrectly.	Check motor, belts, fan speed, and operating controls. Repair as necessary. Check operation of variable or multiple-stage fans. Repair as needed.
	Fins plugged.	Clean and straighten if needed.
Head pressure excessive.	Noncondensible air robbing condenser of space.	Purge air through valve on top of condenser (see above).
	System overcharged.	Bleed off excess charge.
	Condenser cooling blocked.	Inspect and remove blockage. Check for worn fan belt; damaged fan blades; dirty, corroded, or bent fins. Repair as needed.
Head pressure too low.	System undercharged.	Add refrigerant until charge is correct.

WATER-COOLED CONDENSER

Symptom	Problem	Solution
Unit does not cool sufficiently.	Incoming condenser water too warm.	Correct problem at cooling tower or wherever heat is removed.
Condenser tubes plugged.	Scale on tubes interfering with water flow and heat transfer.	Clean with acid and begin a program to control scale if the problem is severe. Use acids carefully—they can harm you and the condenser.
Condenser pressure and temperature higher than expected, liquid line warm. Other system parameters OK.	Corrosion due to improper cleaning.	Replace condenser.
System runs erratically.	Excess oil gathering in condenser.	Install better oil control system.

METERING DEVICE

The metering device has one basic job—to control the flow of refrigerant into the evaporator under all load conditions. If the evaporator receives too little refrigerant, the superheat will be too high and the motor may overheat. If the evaporator receives too much refrigerant the superheat will be too low, and there is a danger of floodback.

The following troubleshooting guide describes the basic complaints, possible causes, and corrective actions on both automatic expansion (AXV) and thermostatic expansion (TXV) valves. The information applies to both devices unless otherwise stated. For information checking the capillary tube as a metering device, see Part D, p. 142.

See the following graph for a sample troubleshooting guide to expansion valves.

Complaint	Possible cause	Suggested solution
Low suction pressure with high superheat—inlet pressure (head pressure) too low.	Excessive vertical lift of refrigerant; inadequate head pressure; or condensing temperature too low.	Replace liquid line with correct size; increase head pressure.
	Flash gas in liquid line; insufficient charge; or noncondensible gas in system.	Depends on cause of flash gas. To ensure a solid stream of liquid at the metering device, add refrigerant; purge noncondensible gases; clean strainers and filter-driers; check size of lines; increase head pressure; add heat exchanger in liquid line.
	Orifice plugged. (If ice or wax is plugging it, suction line pressure will rapidly when the valve body is warmed.)	Moisture and dirt: install a new filter-drier. Wax: replace rise oil.
	Excess pressure drop in evaporator causes false evaporator pressure reading at TXV body.	Install external equalizer.
	Superheat adjusted too high.	Readjust according to manufacturer's instructions.
	Diaphragm or bellows ruptured.	Replace valve.
	Valve power assembly (remote sensing bulb) has lost charge.	Replace bulb or entire valve.
	Restriction elsewhere in system caused by undersizing or plugged component.	Usually marked by frost. Repair or replace problem component.

Complaint	Possible cause	Suggested solution
Low suction pressure with low superheat (usually indicates poor distribution or unequal evaporator loading).	If distribution is poor, refrigerant will take the easiest path back to the compressor.	Install a proper distributor and balance loads on the evaporators.
	Compressor oversized or running too fast.	Install capacity control on compressor; change pulleys to slow compressor.
	Inadequate air flow due to plugged filters or balky fan motor.	Clean filters; check and repair or replace fan motor.
	Evaporator too small (shows excessive icing).	Replace with the proper size evaporator.
High suction pressure with high superheat	System imbalanced; compressor too small; evaporator too large; or load too great.	Balance the system by replacing the wrong components. Test system and compare operating conditions with temperature-pressure charts.
	Compressor valves leaking.	Test compressor, repair or replace if indicated.
High suction pressure with low superheat	Compressor undersized.	Replace with proper unit.
	Superheat setting too low.	Measure suction pressure and evaporator outlet temperature to determine present superheat setting. Readjust if needed.
	Valve held open due to foreign matter.	Clean valve; repair or replace filter-drier.

Fluctuating suction pressure	External equalizer line plugged or capped.	Replace the equalizer line.
	Superheat adjustment incorrect.	Adjust superheat.
	External equalizer linked to several TXVs.	Install a separate equalizer for each TXV.
	Liquid refrigerant flooding back due to poor distributor or uneven evaporator loading.	Install proper distributor, ensure that air flow across evaporator is balanced.
	Excessive blower speed or frequent blower cycling causes large pressure differences.	Check coils, thermostat overloads, and other controls. Repair or replace as needed.
	Oversized metering device hunting.	Replace with correct size.

HIGH- AND LOW-SIDE FLOATS

The high-side float (HSF) and the low-side float (LSF) are relatively free from operating problems, and since they are rather inaccessible, this is just as well. The following conditions may arise with these controls:

LOW-SIDE FLOAT

Symptom	Problem	Solution
Lack of cooling—no refrigerant flow.	Screen ahead of seat plugged.	Pump down and clean or replace screen.
	Float stuck closed.	Tap housing with a soft hammer
	Float bound with oil (also lack of oil in crankcase)—oil return hole inside float is plugged.	Pump down and dismantle float. Clean out oil return hole.
Excess refrigerant in evaporator—possibly cold crankcase.	Float disconnected. Possible floodbacks.	Reconnect float.
Suction line frosting.	Float full of liquid or stuck open.	Pump down and disassemble. Replace float and clean float linkage.

HIGH-SIDE FLOAT

Symptom	Problem	Solution
No cooling—no refrigerant flow.	Float stuck closed.	Tap housing with a soft hammer to dislodge.
	Float full of liquid or collapsed.	Pump down system and replace float.
Suction line frosting.	Float valve open.	Tap housing with a soft hammer.
	Overcharge.	Remove some refrigerant.
	Float disconnected.	Reconnect float.

Oil Control Systems

TABLE J1
Oil Control Troubleshooting

Individual Regulator Problems

Malfunction	Probable Causes	Correction Action
An OIL REGULATOR maintains a high level. Oil feed line **COOL**.	1. OIL REGULATOR level set too high.	1. Replace OIL REGULATOR.
An OIL REGULATOR maintains a high level. Oil feed line **HOT**.	2. Leaking OIL REGULATOR valve.	2. Replace OIL REGULATOR.

An OIL REGULATOR maintains a low level or feeds slowly. Oil feed lines **COOL**.	1. Oil feed line or float valve clogged with foreign matter.
	
	2. Low reservoir pressure or gravity feed may be problem.
		1. Blow high pressure gas into feed line or inlet fitting ro remove foreign material.
		  A. Remove OIL REGULATOR from compressor and flush out.
		  B. Install OIL LINE FILTER.
		2. Increase reservoir pressure.
		3. Replace OIL REGULATOR.

System Problems

Malfunction	Probable Causes	Corrective Action
OIL REGULATORS maintain a **LOW** oil level and/or foaming observed in regulator and reservoir. Oil feed lines **HOT**. Oil failure switch may trip out.	1. Pressure differential between OIL RESERVOIR and crankcase over 5 lbs.	1. Replace RESERVOIR PRESSURE VALVE or change spring in valve to 5 lb. spring.
	2. OIL SEPARATOR float stuck open or leaking.	2. Clean or replace float assembly or replace OIL SEPARATOR.

TABLE J1 (cont)

Malfunction	Probable Causes	Corrective Action
	3a. OIL SEPARATOR not precharged with oil before installed. 3b. Not enough oil in system. 4. Worn compressor. Excessive oil being pumped. 5. Loss of oil from system. System leak.	3. Add oil until level is between sight glasses of OIL RESERVOIR. 4. Replace or repair compressor. 5. Locate and repair leak.
OIL REGULATORS maintain a **LOW** oil level. An oil level cannot be maintained in OIL RESERVOIR. Oil feed lines **COOL**. Oil failure switch may trip out.	1. OIL SEPARATOR float assembly clogged. 2. Undersized OIL SEPARATOR. Oil blowing by OIL SEPARATOR into system with discharge gas. Small amount of oil being led to OIL RESERVOIR.	1. Clean or replace float assembly or replace OIL SEPARATOR. 2. Install larger OIL SEPARATOR.
OIL REGULATORS maintain a **HIGH** oil level. Reservoir full. Oil feed lines **HOT**.	1. System Oil Logged A. OIL SEPARATOR feeding OIL RESERVOIR continuously. B. Oil entering crank-case via suction line.	1. Remove excess oil from system. See Note #1—below.
OIL REGULATORS maintain a **HIGH** oil level. An oil level is maintained in OIL RESERVOIR. Oil feed lines **COOL**.	1. Liquid refrigerant build up in crank-case of compressors (oil boils at start-up)	1. Check for over-charged system. Install SUCTION LINE ACCUMULATOR.

NOTE #1 OIL CAN BE ADDED TO OR REMOVED FROM THE OIL CONTROL SYSTEM BY USING THE VALVES ON THE OIL RESERVOIR. THE TOP VALVE FOR ADDING OIL. THE BOTTOM VALVE FOR REMOVING OIL. SEE OIL CONTROL BULLETIN FOR DETAILS. HOWEVER, FOR THE QUICK REMOVAL OF EXCESS OIL FROM AN OIL LOGGED SYSTEM, THE OIL RETURN LINE LEADING FROM THE OIL SEPARATOR TO THE OIL RESERVOIR CAN BE REMOVED. ATTACH A TESTING MANIFOLD OR SMALL VALVE TO THE LINE TO CONTROL THE FLOW OF OIL COMING FROM THE OIL SEPARATOR, DISCHARGE THE EXCESS OIL INTO A DRUM UNTIL THE OIL SEPARATOR SHUTS OFF. AT THAT

POINT MOST OF THE EXCESS OIL WILL HAVE BEEN REMOVED. THE SYSTEM AND OIL LEVEL REGULATORS SHOULD HAVE STABILIZED. REATTACH THE OIL DISCHARGE LINE BACK TO THE OIL RESERVOIR. COURTESY OF HENRY VALVE CO.

Absorption

TABLE J2
Absorption Troubleshooting

Trouble/Symptom	Probable Cause	Remedy
Low Capacity	Improper capacity control valve setting.	Reset valve to design temperature by resetting control point adjuster.
	Solution in generator below design concentration at full load.	Raise steam pressure to design. Check strainers, traps, and condensate system.
	Machine needs octyl alcohol.	Add octyl alcohol.
	Insufficient condensing water flow or temperature too high.	Check operation of tower fans. Check strainer and valves.
	Tubes are fouled (poor heat transfer).	Clean tubes. Determine if water treatment is necessary.
	High absorber loss (noncondensables in machine).	
	Malfunction of Cycle-Guard℠ (low concentration).	See Causes and Remedies under High Absorber Loss.
	Malfunction of absorber valve (solution bypass).	Check refrigerant change, thermo switch calibration and transfer valve operation.
		Contact your Carrier representative.

TABLE J2 (cont)
Absorption Troubleshooting

Trouble/Symptom	Probable Cause	Remedy
Machine shuts down on safety control	Condensing water pump or chilled water pump overloads or flow switches tripped out.	Reset. Determine reason for failure.
	Refrigerant or solution pump overloads tripped out.	Check cutout control setting. Adjust control point setting or chilled water controller to maintain design leaving chilled water temperature. Check capacity control valve adjustment and closure.
	Shutdown on low-temperature cutout.	
Crystallization at startup or during machine operation	Malfunction of Cycle-Guard® (over-concentration).	Check refrigerant charge, thermo switch calibration, and transfer valve operation.
Crystallization during shutdown	Insufficient dilution.	Check dilution float switch (SW-7). Weak solution should dilute to 56% or less during shutdown.
High absorber loss	Leakage in vacuum side of machine.	Determine noncondensable accumulation rate. Have solution analyzed for indication of air leak. Leak-test and repair if necessary.
	Purge malfunctions.	See Causes and Remedies under Failure to Keep Machine Purged.
	Inhibitor depleted.	Have solution analyzed to determine extent of depletion.
Vacuum loss at shutdown	Leakage in vacuum side of machine.	Leak-test the machine and repair if necessary.

TABLE J2 (cont)
Absorption Troubleshooting

Trouble/Symptom	Probable Cause	Remedy
Failure to keep machine purged	Noncondensable accumulation rate above pumping rate of the purge.	Determine noncondensable accumulation rate. Have solution sample analyzed for indication of leak or inhibitor depletion. Leak-test and repair or add inhibitor if necessary.
	Purge valves not positioned correctly.	Check valve positions.
	Purge crystallized.	Decrystallize.
	Lack of solution flow from solution pump to urge.	Contact your Carrier representative.

(NOTE: Table is specific to Carrier Model 16JB010-068 but gives an overview of Absorption System Troubleshooting.)
Courtesy of Carrier Corporation,
Division of United Technologies Corporation

Motors

TABLE J3
Hermetic Motor Troubleshooting

ELECTRICAL
Many motors fail as a result of a mechanical or lubrication failure. Many fail due to malfunctioning external electrical components.

GENERAL OR UNIFORM BURN
Entire winding is uniformly overheated or burned.
Correction:
Check for: (1) Low voltage.
(2) Rapid cycling of compressor.
(3) Inadequate motor cooling.
(4) Unbalanced voltage.

TABLE J3 (cont)
Hermetic Motor Troubleshooting

SINGLE PHASE BURN

Two phases of a three phase motor are overheated or burned.

A result of not having current through the unburned phase and overloading the other two phases.

Correction: (1) Replace contactor.

(2) Check terminal connections on compressor.

(3) Check for balanced voltage.

(4) Check for blown fuses.

HALF WINDING SINGLE PHASE BURN

This shows as when one half of the motor has a single phasing condition on a PART WIND MOTOR with a two contactor system.

Correction: (1) Check both contactors as one may be defective.

(2) Check timer for proper time delay.

START WINDING BURN

Only the start winding is burned in a single phase motor due to excessive current flowing through the start winding.

Correction: (1) Check C, S, and R wiring.

(2) Check starting capacitor and/or start relay.

(3) Check for compressor overloading.

RUN WINDING BURN

Only the run winding is burned in a single phase motor.

Correction: (1) Check relay.

(2) Check run capacitors.

PRIMARY SINGLE PHASE BURN

This will show as only one phase burned. Other two will be O.K. A result of losing one phase in the primary of a Δ to Y or Y to Δ transformer.

Correction: Check transformer for proper voltage incoming and outgoing.

COURTESY OF COPELAND CORPORATION

Pumps

Trouble	Probable cause
No output	Not primed. Excess suction lift. Rotation direction incorrect.
Inadequate output	Leaks or obstructions in suction line. Running too slow. Excess suction lift. Air pockets in lines. Pump damaged: impeller worn, bent shaft, packing damaged, or otherwise defective.
Intermittent output	Leaks in suction line. Pump damaged by abrasives in water. Excess suction lift. Air or grease in water.
Excess power draw	Running too fast. Lines obstructed. Mechanical problem in pump: shaft bent, parts dragging, misaligned pipe connection, misaligned flexible coupling.

STANDARD ACR PROCEDURES

All cooling system technicians should be familiar with procedures used to maintain and repair air-conditioning and refrigeration equipment. These procedures concern the compressor, condenser, drive system, pump, operating controls, refrigerants, and periodic maintenance.

Compressor Procedures

Use great care in installing and adjusting a compressor, and make sure all safety devices are working properly. The following procedures all start with the installation of the gauge manifold.

GAUGE MANIFOLD INSTALLATION

Use the following procedure to connect the gauge manifold to a system (see Fig. K1):

1. Carefully remove the pipe plugs from the suction and discharge service valves and backseat them.
2. Screw an adaptor in each valve and fasten a charging hose to it.
3. Connect the compound gauge to the port of the suction service valve. Connect the pressure gauge to the port of the discharge service valve.
4. Turn each valve one-quarter turn and you should get readings.
5. Once you have readings in both gauges, proceed with your task: troubleshooting, charging, etc.

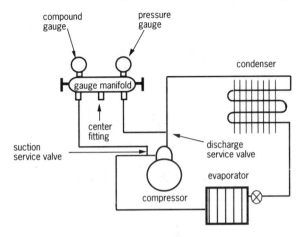

Fig. K1 Gauge manifold installation

OIL—DRAINING AND ADDING

Two methods can be used to add oil, depending on system size and design:

METHOD 1: SYSTEM WITHOUT SERVICE OR DRAIN VALVES

This method does not require a suction and discharge service valve, nor an oil drain valve. You must discharge the system before installing the Schraeder valves, so refrigerant must be added after the oil is refilled (see Fig. K2):

1. Discharge the system by opening or cutting a line.
2. Solder Schraeder valves in the suction and discharge lines to allow the gauge manifold connection.
3. Attach the gauge manifold (with both manifold valves closed) to the Schraeder valves.

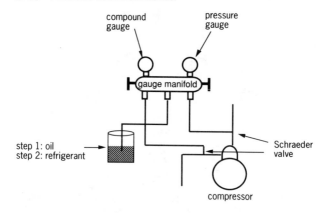

Fig. K2 Adding oil-method #1

4. Pour some refrigerant oil in a small, clean container.

5. Flare a piece of ¼-inch OD soft refrigerant tube and attach one end to the gauge manifold center fitting. Place the other end in the oil container.

6. Run the compressor for a short period to pull a vacuum (CAUTION: running without refrigerant for a long time will burn out a compressor.) Shut the compressor off.

7. Open the suction valve on the manifold and allow the system vacuum to pull in the desired amount of oil. If there is a sight glass, use it to check the oil level. In many cases a cupful is enough. Be sure the bottom of the ¼-inch tube remains immersed in the oil can or air will be sucked into the system.

8. Recharge the unit.

   a. Attach the middle manifold hose to the refrigerant drum.

   b. With the compressor running, open the low-side gauge manifold valve.

   c. Pull in the proper charge.

   d. When the proper charge is installed, close the low-side manifold valve.

   e. Disconnect the refrigerant drum from the middle manifold hose.

METHOD 2: DRAIN AND FILL SYSTEM WITH OIL DRAIN VALVE

This method is used on larger reciprocating compressors (hermetic, semi-hermetic, or open) with a sight glass welded to the side and an oil drain valve on the bottom.

1. Drain the oil (see Fig. K3a):

   a. Frontseat the suction service valve.

   b. Pump down the compressor crankcase to 1 or 2-lb. psig (117 kPa). The closer you can stay to 0 lb. (101.34 kPa), the easier this procedure will be. Make sure to maintain a positive pressure and do not run very long in this condition as the compressor can overheat.

   c. Disconnect electric power to the compressor.

   d. Disconnect any oil heaters (they must be immersed in oil to work properly).

   e. Hook a hose or piece of tube from the drain valve to a large container to hold the oil. (No matter how well you pumped down the system, the oil will foam when it reaches atmospheric pressure. A large container will prevent spills.)

   f. Open the drain valve, taking care that the crankcase is not under vacuum, which would suck in air. Drain the oil until it stops flowing, then close the drain valve. Remove the drain tube (unless you will use it to add oil).

2. Hook an intake tube to an oil pump. Place the other end of the tube in a can with new, clean oil (see Fig. K3b). Connect the pump discharge to the oil drain line.

3. Loosen the nut connecting the pump discharge tube to the drain valve and operate the pump until all air is purged from the discharge tube. Tighten the nut.

4. Open the drain valve and start the pump to transfer oil from the can to the crankcase. Make sure no air gets in. (The crankcase should still be near 0 psig (101.34 kPa). Pressure in the crankcase will make it more difficult to pump oil in.)

5. Pump in the desired amount of oil, usually to one-quarter to one-half of the sight glass.

6. Close the drain valve and remove the oil pump. Open the suction valve, reconnect the crankcase heater, switch on power to the compressor, and start the unit.

step a: draining oil

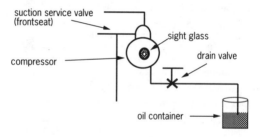

step b: adding oil

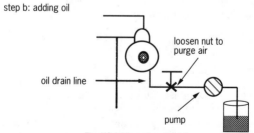

Fig. K3 Adding oil method 2

CLEANUP AFTER A HERMETIC SYSTEM BURNOUT

With the exception of total compressor failure, a motor burnout is about the worst trouble that can plague a refrigeration system. A short circuit in the motor windings will raise its temperature quickly and burn the remaining winding insulation. Although the windings must be replaced, the real problem is the carbon deposit created by the burning insulation. If this carbon is not removed before the system is returned to service, it will cause repeated burnouts. The objective of cleaning up after a burnout is to thoroughly remove contamination from all contaminated parts of the system.

A burnout in a hermetic system is more serious because the refrigerant will likely be contaminated.

When a motor refuses to respond, first check out the power supply, then look at motor, safety and operating controls, and the capacitors. Check the winding continuity. If you suspect a burnout, check the insulation of the windings with a ohmmeter or meg-ohmmeter. Then, if you are still unsure, look for carbon and acid in the refrigerant. Carbon will darken the oil, and acid can be detected with an oil test kit. (See Part F, *Motor Troubles*, p. 209.)

The cleanup procedure requires a lot of work, but shortcuts will increase the chance that the restored system will fail, necessitating a callback.

CAUTION: When you open a burned-out system, air can combine with refrigerant and carbon to form hydrochloric or hydrofluoric acid. The acidity is nothing to laugh about—it can blind you and burn your skin. Use standard precautions for working with acid, such as goggles, rubber gloves, and a rubber apron. Make sure not to spill the acid. If you get acid on your hands or eyes, wash off with a great deal of water and use baking soda to neutralize the acid. Seek medical help if appropriate.

EXTENT OF CONTAMINATION

Once you have determined that the motor has burned out, make a thorough inspection to find out how far the carbon has migrated. The extent of contamination depends on several factors. If a reciprocating compressor motor burned out before it began turning rapidly, the head valves and pistons might have protected the high side from contamination. They will not protect the low side so you are likely to find contamination some distance up the suction line. Other compressor designs have no valves to protect the system from contamination, so the extent of the problem may be greater.

If the discharge port is clean, the high side is probably clean. To check the suction line, close the service valve and cut the line a few feet away from the compressor, preferably beyond the first elbow. If the tube here is clean, replace the tube between the cut and the compressor and recharge the system. If the suction line is dirty, replace as much tube as necessary.

CLEANUP METHODS

Two methods can be used for cleaning up, with the choice depending on the size of the system. The nature of the cleanup will also depend on whether it is easy to change oil in the replacement compressor. If it is, figure on changing the oil soon after startup. If the oil is difficult to change, you must use special care to clean up the system before installing the new compressor, and use plenty of filters and driers in the system.

During the cleanup, wash any removed parts in R-11 and coat them lightly with clean refrigeration oil to prevent rust.

1. On small systems (under 25 tons), the refrigerant is usually dumped or recycled and the compressor replaced. Make sure to swab out nearby sections of piping with R-11 to remove as much carbon as possible. Install a new liquid-line drier and suction-line filter. After a few hours operation, check:

   a. The condition of the filter and drier elements. Replace if needed.

   b. Pressure drop through the suction line filter. If excessive, replace the filter element.

   c. The oil acidity (by odor, color, or test). If excessive, drain and replace the oil and change the filter-drier.

   After two days, check the oil acidity again and continue replacing drier elements until they read "no acid."

2. For larger systems, you can replace the stator (only the stator burns) and clean the rest of the compressor. Use this procedure:

a. Shut off the compressor from the system and purge it.

b. Strip the compressor as far as possible and wash the parts with R-11 or R-113.

c. Coat parts with compressor oil (never allow compressor parts to be exposed to air for longer than necessary).

d. After all parts are cleaned and oiled, slide the new stator into position and reassemble the compressor.

e. Add a new charge of oil to the crankcase.

f. Run the compressor dry (without refrigerant) for a few seconds to check that all the pieces work properly. During this period, watch the oil pressure and keep the dry run short, because the compressor is not getting any coolant.

g. Evacuate the compressor.

h. Break the vacuum with the refrigerant that will be used in the system.

i. Install a new drier in the liquid line and, if possible, a new suction-line drier.

j. Charge the system (see *Refrigerant procedures*, p. 335).

k. Operate for one hour and drain the oil. If you can, wipe out the crankcase. Then add new oil.

l. Return the system to service.

m. After one day, test the oil for acid. Change the oil and the drier elements until the oil tests clean.

Condenser Procedures

Condensers must be clean and supplied with the proper amount and quality of condensing medium. The requirements for air- and water-cooled models are similar:

- *Cooling fins must be clean and straight.*

- *The fan or pump must operate correctly under all load conditions. Fans and pumps are operated by various control devices: on smaller units the compressor control signals the fan to begin running. Check that the control on a variable-speed fan or pump operates through the whole range of speeds and load conditions. If a thermocouple is used to control the device, it will be attached to a return bend in the condenser.*

- *Belt tension and condition.*

- *Proper fan or pump rotation.*

- *Oil fan, pump, and motor shaft bearings.*

- *Damper operation (air-cooled only). Dampers usually are controlled with the help of head pressure, which is routed to a cylinder on the damper. When the compressor starts, head pressure rises and opens the damper. When the compressor stops, the spring closes the damper.*

- *Valve operation (water-cooled only). Do valve controls work as they should?*

REPAIRING A CONDENSER

Use the following procedure to repair a leaking air-cooled condenser: *Use good ventilation because heat will convert any refrigerant remaining in the condenser into toxic gas.*

1. Use a leak detector to isolate the leak. Mark the leak clearly.

2. Remove refrigerant from the system. (Do not pump down to the receiver because this will increase the amount of leaking.)

3. Remove the condenser if you must to reach the leaking area.

4. If the leak is at a brazed joint, heat it and take it apart.

5. Clean both mating surfaces and braze them back together.

6. If leak is not at a joint, clean the area thoroughly patch it with hard solder.

7. Remove flux.

8. Test the condenser by pressurizing it for a period of time.

9. Replace the condenser and restore the system to service.

REMOVING SCALE, FOULING, AND MICROBES

Water-cooled condensers can suffer from scale, microbe growth, or fouling. Any of these problems can interfere with heat transfer and water flow. (See Part E, *Water problems and treatment*, p. 163.) Scale, fouling, and microbes can removed by brushing and/or

The degree of scaling, fouling, and microbe growth varies greatly depending on the quality and hardness of the cooling water, its flow rate, the use of water-softening equipment, and other water treatments.

You can visually inspect the degree of scaling, fouling, or microbe growth in some condenser styles. In others, primarily the tube-in-a-tube and tube-and-coil models, you must make the diagnosis indirectly. Compare records of temperature difference between entering and leaving water from periods with roughly equal loads. A drop in TD will indicate problems with heat transfer. A pump failure or a partly closed cooling water valve will cause a rise in TD, while the insulating effect of scale or fouling will cause it to drop. After ruling out other problems, you can conclude that scaling or fouling is clogging the condenser.

If brushing or scraping is possible, do it first to remove as much of the offending coating as possible. Then decide what form of chemical treatment is best suited to removing the remaining material.

Acid treatment is the most effective method of removing scale, but the procedure should be undertaken with great care. Analyze the system and look for possible leaks (acid will attack metal as well as scale). Make sure the customer realizes that acid treatment may create leaks. Check for air pockets which trap fumes from the acid and escape its cleaning action. You may be able to reverse the water flow to treat all parts of the system, or you may have to install vents in the air pockets (see Fig. K4).

Problems with scale and fouling should be referred to manufacturers of cleaning chemicals. The acid treatment technique described below may be adapted for use with other treatment chemicals.

An acid pump is used to circulate the cleaning solution through the condenser. Follow the acid manufacturer's instructions regarding this procedure in every respect:

1. Add acid slowly to a plastic pail and dilute if directed by the solution manufacturer (see Acid Safety, p. 348). Leave plenty of room in the pail in case pressure in the condenser forces solution back into it.

2. Turn on the pump and monitor the pH of the system with treated paper. If the solution gets too strong, it can coat the scale and interfere with the cleaning action.

3. Monitor the pH. When the pH holds steady for one or two hours, the acid is no longer being neutralized by the scale and either the acid is spent or the scale is gone. Make a visual check. If more scale is present, add more acid and continue.

4. Neutralize the acid while it is still circulating. Add soda ash or the chemical recommended by the chemical manufacturer. When the solution measures neutral (pH 7), drain the spent solution and discard it.

Acid safety: Observe safety precautions when using acid. Dilute the acid to the proper strength by adding acid to water—not water to acid. Use a face shield and long rubber gloves. Use rubber or plastic buckets. Avoid breathing fumes and use with adequate ventilation.

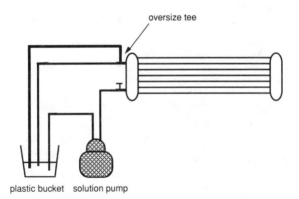

plastic bucket   solution pump

Circulate solution into lower end to move gases through the system. Use an oversize tee on the outlet to allow gas to exit one hose and liquid another.

Fig. K4 Acid washing a condenser

Drive System Service

V-belts or flexible couplings are used to transfer power from motors to compressors and fans. Procedures for dealing with each of these methods of power transfer are described here.

DETERMINING DRIVEN SPEED

It is sometimes necessary to change the size of pulleys to make a compressor run more effectively or to match a load to a motor. These quantities are mathematically related in the following formula:

$$D_r * R_r = D_n * R_n$$

D_n = diameter of driven pulley
D_r = diameter of driver pulley
R_n = speed of driven pulley
R_r = speed of driver pulley

BELT INSPECTION AND ANALYSIS

Follow this procedure to inspect a belt:

1. Shut down the power switch and tag it: "Down for maintenance. Do not turn power on." Lock the switch open.

2. Remove the guard and inspect it for wear or damage. Clean grease and debris from the guard to ensure good ventilation.

3. Notice the temperature. A belt that is too hot to touch just after the drive is shut down has problems. Find and correct the source of overheating before returning the drive to service.

4. Inspect the belt. Mark a starting point and work your way around, looking for cracks, nicks, frays, cuts, or unusual or uneven wear. Replace belts with excessive wear, cuts, or missing teeth.

5. Check alignment by removing the belt and laying a straight edge along the outside edges of both pulleys (see below). Misalignment will increase the chances for premature wear, instability, and turnover.

6. Inspect other parts of the drive: motor and pulley mounting, and housing.

ALIGNING A BELT

To prevent premature wear and failure, belt drives must be in proper alignment, with the shafts parallel and the pulleys in the same plane. If your inspection reveals a misalignment, corrective action is indicated. A belt can have either angular misalignment and/or parallel misalignment. (Misalignment can also result from a pulley that is damaged or improperly mounted.)

1. Angular misalignment can be detected by a long straight edge; a tape measure, string, or straight board can be substituted on a long drive (see Fig. K5b). In general, pulley alignment should be within 1/10 inch per foot (8.4 mm per meter) of the span between the pulleys. Correct a misalignment by loosening the mounting bolts and rotating one piece of equipment until both shafts are aligned. Then tighten the mounting bolts and check for parallel misalignment.

2. To check for parallel misalignment, use a square to show that each shaft is at 90° to the straightedge (see Fig. K5c). Correct by loosening pulley mounting screws and sliding the pulley until both edges of both pulleys line up to the straightedge.

INSTALLING AND TENSIONING A BELT

Belts must be properly installed and tensioned for good performance. Overtight belts will cause compressor seals to leak, and bearings and belts to wear prematurely. Loose belts will slip, heat up, and fail. New belts will stretch slightly, so manufacturers recommend

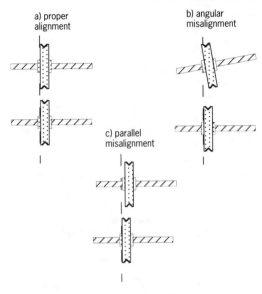

a) proper
alignment

b) angular
misalignment

c) parallel
misalignment

Fig. K5 Belt alignment

they be installed somewhat tighter than normal. Always check and retension a new belt after 4 to 24 hours of operation.

After performing the inspections suggested above, use this procedure to replace and tension a belt:

1. Check the number on the belt to order a replacement. If the number is illegible, measure the length (along the outside) before removing it from the drive. (Check the belt section later or use a gauge on the sheave to find the section.)

2. Loosen the motor mount and slide the motor toward the compressor to slack off the belt.

3. Remove the old belts without prying them.

4. Install the proper size belt. All belts should be replaced on a multiple drive to ensure that they pull equally.

5. Slide the motor back into position to tighten the belt.

6. Check and adjust alignment using the above procedure. Check tension by deflecting the belt at the midpoint between the pulleys. (Rotate multiple-belt drives by hand to seat them in the grooves and even out the tension before checking tension.) Although belt tension gauges are available, most mechanics deflect the belt manually and check that the belt moves a little without having excess slack. Use this rule of thumb: a force of 10 pounds (4.5 kg) should deflect a belt about ½ inch (1.3 cm).

7. Tighten motor mounting bolts to the proper torque.

8. After 4 to 24 hours of operation, recheck and readjust the tension.

FLEXIBLE COUPLING SERVICE

Flexible couplings are the second major method of connecting a motor to a compressor. Actually, flexible couplings cannot correct for poor alignment, which will cause leaking seals and other problems. Therefore, you must use care to align the coupling to the manufacturer's tolerances (see Fig. K6). Because the compressor is usually fixed by its piping, it is best to move the motor into alignment instead of the compressor. The motor is moved by adding or subtracting shims from its mounting. If you do this often, you can buy a calculator to help you figure what shim to use.

Jack screws must be used to move a large motor into alignment. If the jack screws must be fabricated, find a piece of plate steel. Cut a hole large enough to slip a bolt through and weld a nut to the edge of the hole. (An alternative is to drill and tap the hole). If jack screws are not available, use a pry bar or jack to move the motor and tighten the mounting screws while taking readings.

Use this procedure (and some patience because it takes time):

1. Assemble your tools: wrenches, shims, dial indicator, and jack screws.

2. Mount two jack screws to each motor foot. One jack screw will push the motor sideways, the other forward and back.

3. Disassemble the coupling, leaving one flange on the motor shaft and the other on the compressor shaft.

4. Check the existing alignment:

   a. Mount the dial indicator to the motor flange with the feeler button riding on the circumference of the compressor flange. This will check the parallel alignment.

   b. With the motor mounting bolts still tight, spin the compressor flange and take a series of readings at each 90° rotation.

   c. If all the readings are equal, move the indicator to the inside face of the coupling and check the angular alignment. If not, proceed to step 5.

   d. If this also shows equal readings, the coupling is also angular aligned. This is the desired condition when this procedure is finished. If parallel alignment is good but angular alignment is not, proceed to step 8.

5. Keep a record of alignment and adjustments. Loosen the mounting bolts, then begin correcting the problems just found by moving the jack screws.

6. Retighten the mounting bolts and take another reading on the circumference.

7. When the dial gauge reads equal (or zero) all the way around, the shafts are parallel aligned.

8. Place the feeler button inside the face of the compressor flange to check the angular alignment. Spin the flange and take readings. If the indicator does not read "0" all the way around, you have an angular misalignment. Loosen the motor mount screws and add or remove shims to level the motor. Do not allow dirt under the shims because it can throw off the adjustment.

9. When the motor is level, then go back and recheck the parallel alignment, with the jack screws holding the motor in position. When both readings are correct, tighten the mounting and remove the jack screws.

10. Reassemble the coupling and run the compressor for a while. After the coupling warms up, disassemble and recheck both readings. Make further corrections if necessary.

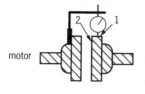

a) proper alignment
—check with needle
on circumference
(1) and face (2)

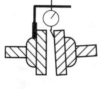

b) angular
misalignment—needle
on face of coupling

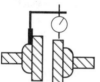

c) parallel misalignment
—needle on
circumference of
coupling

Fig. K6 Aligning flexible coupling

Pump Procedures

The following inspections and checks will help ensure proper operation of centrifugal and reciprocating water or brine pumps.

Pump part	Inspect and check
Motor and pump shaft	Alignment
Impeller	Abnormal wear
Foot valve	Opening should be at least as large as the suction pipe

Pump part	Inspect and check
Units	Must have level and sturdy base
Pump speed	Same as on pump nameplate?
Pressure gauge on discharge	Meets specifications?
Suction line	Slopes gradually to prevent formation of air pockets
Suction lift	Generally should not exceed 15 feet or 4.6 meters (including losses to friction)

Refrigerant Procedures

REMOVING REFRIGERANT

In systems without a receiver, you must generally remove refrigerant from the system to work on a component between the high-side service valve and the king valve (on the condenser outlet). Four methods may be used to remove refrigerant: discharging to the atmosphere, using a recovery apparatus, pumping down to a drum, or pumping down to the receiver. For information on recovery of refrigerants, see Part I, *Recovery and recycling*, p. 307.

DISCHARGING TO THE ATMOSPHERE

This method is prohibited in some places because chlorofluorocarbons are damaging ozone in the upper atmosphere. The practice should also be discouraged due to the increasing cost of refrigerants.

Make sure the sudden drop in pressure and temperature will not damage the system. A water-cooled condenser is especially prone to damage from freezing. Halocarbon refrigerants are heavier than air and will displace the oxygen in a room. If an open flame is present (for example in a furnace) halocarbons may be converted into toxic gases. Vent to the outside or use an air pack when venting to the atmosphere in the presence of a flame. Another problem is that some oil will leave the system along with the refrigerant, and you will have to guess how much oil to replace.

PUMPING DOWN TO A DRUM

This method converts the drum into an auxiliary condenser. It can be used on a large system with a discharge service valve, and a charging valve in the liquid line. This method is being replaced by the use of recovery apparatus.

STEP A

1. Install the gauge manifold as shown in Fig. K7 with both valves closed.

2. Invert a 125-lb. empty refrigerant drum (inverting the drum prevents most of the refrigerant from flashing to gas, which would quickly equalize pressure).

3. Connect the largest possible hose or copper tube to the liquid line charging valve.

4. Purge the hose of air by bleeding some refrigerant from the system. Secure the hose to the drum valve.

5. Open the liquid line charging valve and draw off as much refrigerant as possible.

6. When the pressures in the system and tank equalize, begin step B.

STEP B

7. Close the liquid line charging valve and disconnect the drum.

8. Connect the drum to the center fitting of the gauge manifold.

9. Arrange to spray the storage tank with water (or better, surround it with dry ice) to help condense the refrigerant.

10. Open the high-side valve on the gauge manifold.

11. Start the unit and slowly front-seat the discharge valve to increase the flow into the drum (closing the valve too quickly would overload the line into the drum). NEVER frontseat the discharge valve completely. Prevent head pressure from becoming excessive. If pressure gets too high, stop the compressor immediately.

12. Measure the superheat on the suction line. When you reach

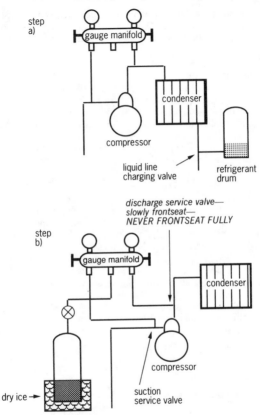

Fig. K7 Pumping down to a drum

the superheat limit set by the manufacturer, stop the motor to prevent overheating. Use auxilliary equipment to finish the evacuation or blow the rest of the charge to the atmosphere.

CAUTIONS:

Do not fill the drum more than 80 percent full, to allow for expansion. In semi-hermetic and hermetic systems, watch for motor overheating, as the amount of refrigerant available to cool the motor will be steadily reduced. The head pressure reading on the gauge manifold will always be slightly below actual head pressure. The internal relief valve will bypass discharge gas to the suction side of the compressor. These valves do not always reseat automatically, and this can lead to overheating the compressor.

PUMPING DOWN TO A RECEIVER

A complete pumpdown to the receiver is needed when servicing the liquid line, evaporator, or suction line in a reciprocating compressor. This is different from the partial pumpdown used in some normal operating cycles. For a complete pumpdown, the receiver and condenser combined must be large enough to hold the complete system charge, and there must be a shutoff valve in the liquid line (the compressor discharge valves shut off the other end in a reciprocating compressor). Some condensers are large enough to hold the charge by themselves, but as a rule, tube-within-a-tube models are not.

Use the following procedure to pump down to a receiver:

1. Install the gauge manifold.

2. Temporarily disable the low-pressure cutout. Either

   a. connect a jumper cable with a toggle switch across the cutout terminals; or

   b. hold the switch in the "made" position. (If the cutout is in an electronic control circuit, consult the manufacturer's recommendations, as these methods may cause damage.)

3. Close the king valve and let the compressor run until the suction pressure falls to about 10-inch Hg vacuum (66.6 kPa). Remember that the suction gas is becoming less dense, so hermetic motors are in danger of overheating at this point. Do not run the compressor indefinitely in this condition.

4. Stop the compressor and let the low-side pressure build up. If it reaches 20 psig (241 kPa), repeat until the pressure settles at about 2 to 3 psig (117 to 124 kPa). (Never open a system if it has a vacuum, because air and moisture will be sucked in. The only exception to this rule is an ammonia system, which should have a slight vacuum when it is opened to prevent escape of ammonia.)

5. Now that the system is pumped down, try to lock the main disconnect switch open. If this is impossible, place a tag on the switch explaining that the compressor is down for service.

6. Frontseat the discharge service valve. Do not depend on compressor head valves to hold the pressure during a service pumpdown.

DRYING (EVACUATING) A SYSTEM

Drying, also called evacuating, is used to eliminate moisture and air before charging a new or repaired system. Moisture: 1) can freeze and plug a line or the metering device, and 2) in the presence of steel and halocarbons can form powerful acids that reduce oil's ability to lubricate and attack motor windings.

Possible sources of moisture in cooling systems include: 1) mistakes in factory or field, 2) wet oil or refrigerant, 3) low-side leaks, or 4) a burst water-cooled condenser. When working on a system, make every effort to avoid these trouble sources. (Evacuating and charging are not necessary for factory-sealed and charged systems.)

The goal of evacuating is to remove air and create a vacuum high enough to boil water in the system. This forces the water to evaporate, allowing it to be removed with the vacuum pump. As the water vaporizes, it will raise the system pressure and require further evacuation.

Observe these guidelines before starting the evacuation:

- *If a liquid line drier is present, be sure to remove its element.*

- *If a great deal of refrigerant has mixed with the oil, the evacuation will take a long time because the vacuum pump must boil the refrigerant out of the oil.*

- *On systems with a great deal of water, blow out the lines with refrigerant or nitrogen before pulling the vacuum. This will save a lot of pump wear and shorten the evacuation time. Place a moisture trap (available from vacuum pump manufacturers) in the line linking the pump to the system to prevent most of the water from reaching the pump. After evacuating, reinstall the drier.*

- *In relatively dry systems, you can omit the vacuum pump stage and use a liquid line dryer instead. You may need to replace several drier elements before all the moisture is removed.*

SINGLE-EVACUATION

This method can be used to dry a system if the ambient temperature is at least 70°F (21°C). At this temperature, water will boil out when system pressure is 2000 microns or below. If ambient temperature is below about 70°, use the triple-evacuation method. The single-evacuation method requires a high vacuum pump and a method of reading a deep vacuum. It can only be used in a system capable of sustaining a high vacuum. An open system cannot withstand a high vacuum and must be evacuated with the triple method. Even though the compound gauge on a gauge manifold will read 30 inches of vacuum (near 0 Pa), it is not accurate enough for single-evacuation. Instead, read the pressure with a wet-bulb thermometer, an electronic high-vacuum gauge, or a mercury manometer.

Make sure the system is empty of refrigerant before starting this evacuation. Use special vacuum pump hoses or copper tubing instead of gauge manifold hoses for these connections. Run a recovery apparatus before starting (see Fig. K8):

1. Hook the vacuum pump line to a tee to allow you to connect it to a device to measure system vacuum. Hook a wet-bulb thermometer, a mercury manometer, a micron gauge, or an electronic vacuum gauge to the tee.

2. Connect this tee to a second tee linked to the discharge and suction service valves as shown. This will connect the vacuum pump to both sides of the metering device.

   (If you cannot attach the vacuum lines to the compressor through service valves, you must plan how you will remove the lines because they will be under vacuum or pressure when you finish. This is generally done by installing valves—where the tubes connect to the system.)

3. Check that all valves are open. Open solenoids in the system either manually or by applying electric power.

4. Shut off power to the compressor motor and crankcase heaters. *Keep the power off while the vacuum pump operates* or the windings can be damaged.

5. Start the vacuum pump and run it until you get and maintain a deep enough vacuum to vaporize the water in the system. Most vacuum gauges read direct. When a wet-bulb thermometer measures and holds 15°F (−9.5°C), you have a vacuum of 29.84″ Hg; 2,500-microns Hg (electronic gauge); or 2.5-mm Hg (mercury manometer).

6. Close both service valves and shut off the pump.

7. Watch the vacuum gauge for 30 to 45 minutes. A rise indicates either a leak or that water is boiling inside the system. The warmer the ambient temperature, the faster water will vaporize

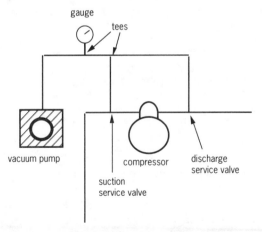

Fig. K8 System evacuation

at any given vacuum. A rise in pressure caused by a leak will increase the pressure all the way to atmospheric pressure. A rise caused by water boiling will level off at a certain pressure. If you feel abnormally cold spots in the system, assume that moisture is evaporating here. You can hasten the drying process by warming these spots with a heat lamp.

8. If the resulting pressure in the system exceeds the manufacturer's specifications, continue evacuating. When you can hold a deep vacuum for the period specified by the manufacturer, the procedure is finished.

TRIPLE-EVACUATION

During cool conditions (below about 70°F or 21.1°C) the best means of ensuring complete drying is a procedure called "triple evacuation," in which refrigerant is used as a blotter to absorb moisture. This procedure will likely be restricted for environmental reasons. Note that the exact procedure can vary from that listed below. Some manufacturers suggest that the first two evacuations reach 1500 microns, that the final evacuation reach 500 microns, and that the vacuum be broken with 2 psig (117.2 kPa) of system refrigerant.

1. Install the apparatus as shown in Fig. K8 and pull a vacuum of about 25-inch Hg (16.7 kPa) with a vacuum pump.

2. Charge the system with refrigerant or nitrogen to about 5 psig, measured at the compressor. (This charge breaks the surface tension so moisture can evaporate during the next evacuation.)

3. Remove the refrigerant with the vacuum pump and discharge it to the atmosphere. Better, use a recovery apparatus to withdraw the refrigerant.

4. Repeat the procedure twice more and then pull the required vacuum before making the final charge. In some cases, more or fewer operations will be needed to reach the desired vacuum conditions.

EVACUATING AN OPEN COMPRESSOR

When evacuating an open system, you must take care not to pull air into the system through the crankshaft seal. This will not cause permanent damage but will prevent you from sustaining a vacuum.

You can get around the problem of a leaking seal by evacuating the piping before the compressor. Look the system over to find the best way of isolating the piping system from the compressor. Connect the vacuum pump and shut off the proper valves. Evacuate the piping to a high vacuum, then evacuate the compressor to a slightly lower vacuum, just enough to vaporize the water inside it. (See Fig. K9a.)

If the piping cannot be isolated from the compressor, use this procedure (see Fig. K9b):

1. Connect a vacuum pump to the discharge service valve and a compound gauge to the suction service valve.

2. Move both service valves two turns off the backseat.

3. Run the vacuum pump down to the vacuum pressure specified by the compressor manufacturer. Use the triple-evacuation method (see previous page) to remove air.

4. Backseat the discharge service valve and shut off the vacuum pump.

5. Remove the vacuum pump.

6. Recharge the system or install a holding charge (enough refrigerant to raise the pressure to about 2 psig).

7. Backseat the suction service valve and remove the gauge.

8. Replace and tighten plugs in the valve ports.

CHECKING THE CHARGE

A cooling system relies on a proper refrigerant charge. Some systems, particularly those with a receiver, are less sensitive to charge level than "critical-charge" systems. Critical charge systems, which typically use a flooded evaporator or a capillary tube as the metering device, require close control of refrigerant level.

If you find a low charge, it is probably due to a leak which must be repaired before recharging. However, systems that were recently serviced and have performed poorly since then may have been charged incorrectly.

1. Assuming all components of the system are in good condition

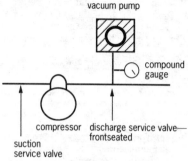

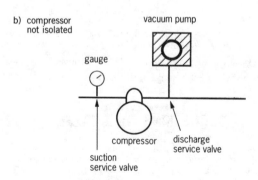

Fig. K9 Evacuating an open compressor

and operating properly, you can check the charge by examining head pressure:

a. Find the design condenser temperature from the specifications.

    b. Convert that temperature to pressure.

    c. Charge to that head pressure while the compressor is running.

2. If a sight glass is installed in the liquid line, use it to check for bubbles, which indicate, but do not prove, a low charge. A clamp-on sight glass may be installed to "listen" electronically for bubbles. A restriction in the line ahead of the sight glass may cause foaming and falsely indicate a low charge. Lack of bubbles does not prove a full charge, however, and another method, such as measuring superheat, may be chosen to complement the sight glass method.

3. A receiver may be fitted with two petcocks, one above the other. When the charge is correct, the upper petcock will emit vapor, and the lower petcock will emit liquid.

4. In systems with a water-cooled condenser, the hot vapor will be above the cool liquid. Use your hand to feel the liquid level.

5. In cap tube systems, measure the superheat. Superheat decreases as the charge increases, because the evaporator becomes increasingly full of refrigerant. Select a safe superheat, perhaps 12°F to 20°F (6.7°C to 11.4°C), and adjust to that figure by adding or subtracting refrigerant. Other methods sometimes used to check the charge in cap tube systems, such as measuring full-load motor current draw or looking at the frost line or sweat line, have proven inaccurate.

CHARGING A SYSTEM

Six methods can be used to charge refrigerant to a system: by sight glass, by charging table, by weight, by frost line, by liquid charging a flooded evaporator, and by using the charging cylinder. The chosen method should be selected based on system size, component configuration, and the presence or absence of service valves and sight glasses. Refrigerant can be added as either a gas (for small systems) or a liquid (for large systems). Gas charging is more accurate but liquid charging is faster. *Never put liquid into the suction line—this can destroy a compressor.*

    The first step in all these methods is to purge the gauge manifold hoses of air with refrigerant from a tank and to install the gauges.

1. BY SIGHT GLASS

Ideally, the sight glass should be installed just ahead of the metering device, because this is where a solid stream of liquid should be found. However, the sight glass is more often found nearer the condenser.

GAS

Gas charges are added into the suction line near the compressor. You can speed up the transfer by putting the charging cylinder in a pail of warm water. Never use a flame to speed the transfer (see Fig. K10):

1. Install the gauge manifold and run the unit until it stabilizes.

2. Attach the refrigerant cylinder to the center hose of the gauge manifold.

3. Frontseat the suction service valve almost all the way so the compressor pulls crankcase pressure below the cylinder pressure.

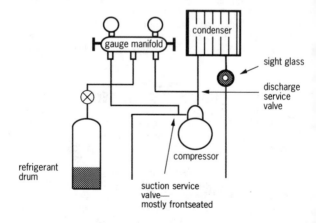

Fig. K10 Gas sight glass charging

4. When the pressure has fallen, open the suction valve on the manifold and pull gas from the cylinder into the crankcase.

5. After a period of transfer, based on your judgement, backseat the suction service valve. Run the unit normally and see if the foaming in the sight glass clears up. When a full charge is reached, no bubbles will be visible in the sight glass.

6. Backseat both service valves and remove the gauge manifold.

LIQUID

This method is used on large units with a charging valve located on a tee in the liquid line. A valve at the condenser outlet (a king valve) is also required. Use caution as a charge can be transferred rather quickly. Experience will help you transfer the proper charge without overcharging (see Fig. K11):

1. Install the gauge manifold as shown. Connect the refrigerant drum to the liquid line charging valve. Make sure the drum outlet is flooded by liquid.

2. Start the compressor and close the king valve to stop the flow of refrigerant.

3. Run the unit until the suction pressure is below refrigerant drum pressure (if the drum is at room temperature, use a pressure-temperature chart to find the drum pressure).

4. With the compressor still running, open the charging valve to draw liquid into the system.

5. After a period of time, shut the charging valve and open the king valve.

6. Operate the system and check the charge in the sight glass. Repeat if needed.

2. BY A CHARGING CHART

This method requires a charging chart provided by the compressor manufacturer. This chart shows the relationship between ambient air temperature, suction line pressure, and suction line temperature. The chart may be affixed to the inside of the control panel door. Note that charts are made for specific machines using a specific refrigerant. Sometimes these figures are given in a table instead of a chart.

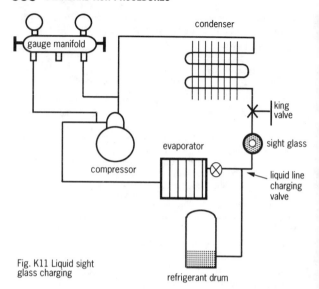

Fig. K11 Liquid sight glass charging

1. Install the gauge manifold and run the unit until it stabilizes. Note the pressure and temperature of the suction line.

2. Measure the entering air temperature (ambient temperature) at the condenser.

3. Find the curved line on the chart listing the suction pressure you found. Find the ambient temperature on the left-hand scale and read across to the intersection with the suction pressure line.

4. Read down from the intersection to find the proper suction line temperature. For example, (refer to Fig. K12) if the actual suction line pressure is 60 lb. and entering air temperature is 80°, the suction line temperature should be about 53°F.

5. If your measurements do not agree with the chart, the charge is probably wrong.

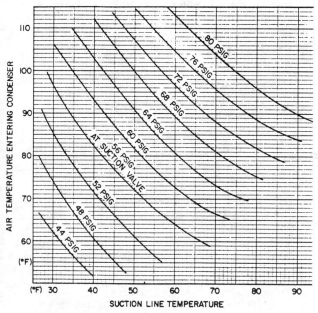

Fig. K12 Charging chart

6. In this example, you would add refrigerant if the suction line were much warmer than 53°F and bleed refrigerant if it were much below 53°F.

3. BY WEIGHT

This method can only be used to install a full charge, using either the gas or the liquid charging method:

1. Find the proper charge from manufacturer's literature.
2. Install the gauge manifold.
3. Put the refrigerant drum on a scale.
4. Subtract the desired charge from the drum weight to find the target weight.
5. Start the unit and begin charging until the scale reaches the target weight.
6. Disconnect the charging hose.

4. BY FROST LINE

This method can install a full or partial charge, but only in small systems which use a capillary tube metering device. Charge with gas only. Use special care to ensure the charge is accurate, especially if the suction line is short:

1. Install the gauge manifold and run the unit.
2. Add refrigerant to the system until you notice frost on the suction line.
3. Stop when the frost is visible just outside the evaporator. The frost shows that the evaporator is being fully used but no liquid is flooding back.
4. Check the superheat to ensure the accuracy of the charge.

5. LIQUID CHARGING A FLOODED EVAPORATOR

Never let the evaporator pressure drop below the freezing point of water because liquid refrigerant added in these conditions may freeze the water pipes. Use one of these techniques to prevent freezing and rupturing the evaporator:

    a. Keep the chilled water circulating by manually controlling the chilled water pump.

    b. Drain the chilled water circuit.

    c. Charge the refrigerant as a gas until the pressure exceeds the freezing point of water. Then liquid charge the remaining refrigerant, always keeping the pressure above the freezing point.

To liquid charge a flooded evaporator:

1. Connect the refrigerant drum to the liquid charging valve. Keep the drum outlet flooded by liquid.

2. Start the compressor and open the liquid charging valve to start the flow of refrigerant into the system.

3. After a period of time, shut the charging valve.

4. Operate the system and check the liquid level in the sight glass. Repeat if needed.

6. USING THE CHARGING CYLINDER

A charging cylinder can conveniently measure a full charge. The columns on the cylinder safety shroud are graduated in pounds and ounces for the various refrigerants. Rotate the shroud to line up the sight tube with the column for the refrigerant you are charging. Read the level of refrigerant before starting. If the charging cylinder has a digital readout, follow the manufacturer's directions (see Fig. K13).

First fill the charging cylinder with the amount of refrigerant you will add to the system with this procedure:

1. Depress the Schraeder valve on the top of the charging cylinder to bleed out excess pressure. Close the valve.

2. Connect the charging cylinder to the storage tank on your truck, using a charging hose.

3. Open the liquid refrigerant valve on the storage tank (you will have to invert a small storage tank to make sure the outlet is flooded).

4. Open the valve on the bottom of the charging cylinder to start the flow of refrigerant. (Never fill a refrigerant cylinder to the top—this may lead to an explosion.)

5. When the cylinder has the correct charge, close the valves on the storage tank and the charging cylinder and disconnect.

Use the following procedure to transfer refrigerant from the charging cylinder to the system:

1. Install the gauge manifold to Schraeder fittings or service valves on the suction and discharge lines. Crack the service valves (Schraeder valves will open automatically).

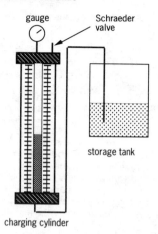

Fig. K13 Charging with a charging cylinder

2. Connect the hose from the gauge manifold center fitting to the charging cylinder. For a liquid charge, connect to the lower fitting on the cylinder (the one that was used to fill the cylinder). For a gas charge, attach to the upper cylinder fitting. (If you are using an electric heater in the cylinder, be sure it has a thermostat shutoff and that the charging cylinder has a pressure relief.)

3. Turn on the compressor and open the gauge manifold suction valve. Use the compressor to pull refrigerant from the cylinder into the system. Open the suction valve very carefully to install a liquid charge to avoid slugging the compressor. You may place a device to allow the liquid refrigerant to flash to a gas in the line leading to the suction service valve.

4. Monitor the amount of refrigerant being transferred from the column on the cylinder or the digital readout. Shut down the compressor when the correct amount is transferred.

5. Close the valve on the cylinder. Close the manifold suction valve and backseat service valves. Remove the cylinder and the gauge manifold from the system.

Maintenance Procedures

It's a good idea to establish a periodic maintenance schedule for cooling system equipment.

WEEKLY

1. Check oil level in the compressor. Low readings may occur because oil is trapped in the system. Run the compressor at full load for a few hours and check again. Add oil if the level is still low.

2. Check oil pressure differential. Oil pressure should be 20 to 35 psi (138 to 241.5kPa) above crankcase pressure.

3. Inspect any air filters and air-handling equipment.

4. Check all important operating conditions, especially sight glasses,

system pressures, and temperatures. List operating conditions on the maintenance log. Investigate significant departures from past conditions.

5. Inspect crankshaft seal (open systems only) for leaks.

MONTHLY

Perform weekly maintenance plus:

1. Lube motor and fan bearings (follow manufacturer's directions— do not overlube).
2. Check tension and alignment of V-belts. If sheaves are loose, realign before tightening.
3. Condensers: check fan, control, dampers, and cleanliness of air-cooled models. Check water condition of water-cooled condensers and treat if microbes, fouling, or scale are present.

ANNUAL PROCEDURES

If the system will be run year-round, perform these procedures at least once a year. See below for system shutdown and startup techniques. The system must be shut down to carry out these procedures.

1. Perform monthly maintenance above.
2. Flush all pipes of water-cooled condenser. Inspect condenser tubes and clean if needed. Clean air-cooled condenser.
3. Flush pumps and sump tank of cooling tower or evaporative condenser. Check for corrosion and paint as needed.
4. Replace worn V-belts.
5. Inspect all bearings for wear and proper end-play.
6. Clean all water strainers and inspect or replace filter-driers.
7. Inspect contacts in motor starters and repair or replace as indicated.

SEASONAL SHUTDOWN

Traditionally, all systems were pumped down into the condenser or receiver in the winter to prevent loss of refrigerant through the crankshaft seal and low side. The procedure is not used as often because hermetic systems have no crankshaft seal.

HERMETIC SYSTEM

Follow this procedure if a pumpdown is desired:

1. Close the liquid line shutoff and start the compressor. The compressor will run until the low-pressure cutout shuts it down and most refrigerant will be in the high side.

2. Open the compressor disconnect and frontseat the discharge and suction service valves. Close liquid line service (king) valve. See additional procedures for all systems below.

OPEN SYSTEM

Pump down the system with these steps:

1. Install the gauge manifold.

2. Close the king valve and manually open any liquid line solenoid valves. If the solenoid cannot be manually opened, adjust its control setting so it will stay open during the pumpdown.

3. Place a jumper across the LPCO, as you will run the suction pressure below its normal cutout setting.

4. Run the compressor until the suction gauge reads 2 psig (117.2kPa). Open the compressor disconnect. (A deeper vacuum could draw contaminants into the system through the crankshaft seal.)

5. Backseat both service valves. Remove the gauge manifold and replace the plugs.

6. Frontseat both service valves. Replace valve caps.

7. Remove the jumper on the LPCO. See additional procedures below.

ALL SYSTEMS

Do the following additional work:

1. Check the condenser and receiver for leaks with an electronic detector.

2. Check that the condenser is full of water and close all water valves leading to it. (A full condenser will rust less than an empty one.) Replace water with antifreeze if the condenser will be subject to freezing conditions.

3. Drain the cooling tower or evaporative condenser, if used. Inspect the condition of metal and paint it if needed.

4. Lock the master disconnect in the open position.

5. Leave a warning near the safety switch, explaining which valves must be moved before the compressor is started up. Do not assume that the person performing the startup will know much about air conditioning and refrigeration systems.

SEASONAL STARTUP

Use the following schedule to place a system into service at the beginning of the year:

1. Drain the antifreeze if it was used in a water-cooled condenser.

2. Perform annual maintenance specified by manufacturers of motors, fans, drives, compressor, air-handling equipment, and pumps.

3. Fill the water sump on a cooling tower or an evaporative condenser to the correct level and add water treatments if needed to control scaling, fouling, or microbes.

4. Open shutoff valves to water-cooled condenser.

5. Check all pumps and fans for proper rotation and action. Check the water spray in a cooling tower or evaporative condenser.

6. Check that all solenoid valves are set on automatic control.

7. Open the liquid line shutoff valve and backseat the compressor suction and discharge valves.

8. Install the gauge manifold.

9. Unlock the master disconnect and close it.

10. Check the compressor safety controls using the procedures in Part D.

11. Start the system.

12. Adjust the bleed-off valve to the proper position as recommended by the supplier of the water treatment used in the evaporative condenser or cooling tower.

13. After about 15 minutes of running, check oil level, oil pressure, and refrigerant level. Monitor system pressures and temperatures and write them down on the operating log. Adjust the thermostat to desired setting.

PART L
APPENDICES

APPRENTICESHIP PROGRAM

Apprenticeship is a system to train new workers for technical occupations, such as air-conditioning and refrigeration installation and repair, which require a broad range of knowledge and skills. The training combines planned, supervised work experience with classroom study about topics relevant to the trade.

An apprenticeship program is based on a written agreement between an employee and an employer describing the terms and conditions for the apprentice's training and employment. The National Apprenticeship Act has given the Bureau of Apprenticeship Training (B.A.T.) in the U.S. Department of Labor responsibility for servicing and assisting apprenticeship programs. States that operate under federal law are known as B.A.T. states. States with their own standards are known as S.A.C. states, for the State Apprenticeship Committee. S.A.C. states use federal law as a minimum and have standards that generally exceed federal law.

Committees are established to oversee the various areas of instruction in S.A.C. states. Each committee has an equal number of labor and management representatives. All apprenticeship programs are required to meet U.S. Department of Labor standards for equal employment opportunity. Information on apprenticeship programs is available from Bureau of Apprenticeship Training, state apprenticeship agencies and employment service offices, labor unions, employers, and school guidance counselors.

Estimating Jobs

Estimating is one of the toughest challenges facing a contractor. Estimate too low, and you can lose money. Estimate too high, and your bid can be rejected.

Estimates must be made for both materials and labor. Formulas given in books on construction estimating can help you estimate labor and material requirements for certain tasks, but they can never be 100 percent accurate. Estimating books are only helpful if workers meet standard rates of production and local costs are similar to those used by the organization preparing the book.

Contractors also use their own records for estimating jobs, which is a good reason to keep records up to date.

Follow these hints for accurate estimating:

- *Keep a record of time requirements and cost for past jobs.*

- *Watch out for special situations that will change costs.*

- *Explain to the customer the tradeoffs between low first cost and high operating costs. For example, omitting service valves will reduce installation costs but raise service costs in the long run.*

Measurements and Mathematics

Mathematics plays an important role in several areas of cooling system work: for planning system capacity and choosing components, for installing piping and components, and for troubleshooting. Measuring is needed to translate figures on blueprints into structures that faithfully mirror the blueprints. The mathematical skills required to work with feet and inches, fractions, decimals, angles, area, perimeter and volume of shapes, and the various systems of measurement are described below.

The United States is the only major country still using feet and inches, properly called the English system. Scientists and the rest of the world use the International (metric) system. Many of the measurements needed in air conditioning and refrigeration work are commonly given in both measuring systems. Some, such as high vacuum pressures, are more convenient in microns, one-millionth of a meter, than in fractions of inches.

Although the United States system predominates in the industry, in the long run, the SI, formerly called the metric, system will probably grow in importance. One of the major advantages is the exclusive use of decimals instead of fractions. Another advantage is the simplicity of converting among the different units. Furthermore, all calculations can be made easily with a hand calculator. And the international acceptance of metric units will make the system more important as imported equipment becomes more common.

The basic unit of length in the metric system is the meter (39.37 inches). The basic unit of weight is the kilogram (2.2 lb). While some parts of the SI system are baffling to people trained in feet and inches, SI units are already used for such important measures as sound (decibel, or dB), acidity (pH), and electricity (all units).

The metric system uses prefixes to indicate multiples and decimals of the basic units. The important prefixes are:

$$\begin{aligned}
\text{micro} &= .000,001 \\
\text{milli} &= .001 \\
\text{centi} &= .01 \\
\text{kilo} &= 1000 \\
\text{mega} &= 1 \text{ million}
\end{aligned}$$

Thus one centimeter equals 0.01 meter, and one kilometer equals 1,000 meters. To convert from one measurement to another, just shift the decimal place. Thus 2.566 meters can be expressed as two meters 566 millimeters, 256.6 centimeters, or 2566 millimeters.

The SI system uses the Celsius degree of heat (formerly called centigrade). Each degree Celsius equals 1.8°F. Boiling is 100°C and freezing is 0°C. The Kelvin scale uses the Celsius unit, but starts at absolute zero, −273°C.

TABLE L1

Measurement Conversions

American	SI System
1 inch	2.54 centimeter
1 foot	30.4 centimeter
1 yard	91.4 centimeter
0.032 foot	1 centimeter
3.28 feet	1 meter
1.093 yard	1 meter
1 square foot	0.092 square meter (m^2)
1 square yard	0.836 square meter
0.155 square inches	1 square centimeter (cm^2)
10.763 square feet	1 square meter
1.195 square yards	1 square meter

American	SI System
1 cubic inch	16.387 cubic centimeter
1 cubic foot	0.028 cubic meter (m³)
1 cubic yard	0.764 cubic meter
0.061 cubic inch	1 cubic centimeter (cm³)
35.314 cubic foot	1 cubic meter
1.307 cubic yard	1 cubic meter

Area and Volume Conversions

1 sq. in. =	1/144 sq. ft.
1 sq. ft. =	144 sq. in.
1 sq. yard =	1296 sq. in.
1 sq. ft. =	1/9 sq. yard
1728 cu. in. =	1 cu. ft.
1 cu. in. =	1/1728 (0.00057) cu. ft.
1 cu. ft. =	1/27 (0.037) cu. yd.
1 cu. yd. =	27 cu. ft.

Energy

Equivalents in the U.S. System

Heat to mechanical	1 Btu/hr = 0.000393 hp
Heat to electrical	1 Btu/hr = 0.293 watts (W)
Mechanical to heat	1 hp = 2546 Btu/hr
	778 ft. lb. = 1 Btu
Mechanical to electrical	1 hp = 746 W
Electrical to mechanical	746 watt = 1 hp
Electrical to heat	1 watt = 3.412 Btu/hr
	1 kilowatt (kW) = 3412 Btu/hr

Energy conversions

Tons of refrigeration to Btus	tons × 12,000 = Btus
Tons to hp	tons × 4.716 = hp
hp to Btu/min	hp × 42.44 = Btu/min
hp to kilocalories/min	hp × 10.7 = kilocalories/min

Equivalents Between U.S. and SI Systems

The unit for all three forms of energy in the S.I. system is the joule (J). For measuring electrical power, the kilowatt hour is also used.

1 J = 0.7376 ft. lb.	1 ft. lb. = 1.3558 J = 1.356 Nm
1 J = 1 N*m = 0.737 ft. lb.	1 ft. lb./s = 1.3558 W
1 kW = 1.34 hp = 3412 Btu/hr	1 hp = 0.746 kW
1 W = 0.7376 ft. lb./s	

Pressure Conversions		
atmospheres X	1.013 =	bars
	29.92	inches of mercury
	1.033	kilograms/sq. centimeter
	14.7	pounds per square inch
	104.4	kilopascals
pounds per square inch ×	.068	atmospheres
	2.036	inches of mercury pressure
inches of mercury vacuum	=	29.9 − inches of mercury absolute pressure
inches of mercury absolute pressure + inches of mercury vacuum	=	29.2

TABLE L2
Fraction / Decimal / Millimeter
Conversion Table For One Inch

Fraction	Decimal	Millimeters (Approx.)	Fraction	Decimal	Millimeters (Approx.)
1/32	.03125	0.794	17/32	.53125	13.494
1/16	.0625	1.588	9/16	.5625	14.288
3/32	.09375	2.381	19/32	.59375	15.081
1/8	.125	3.175	5/8	.625	15.875
5/32	.15625	3.969	21/32	.65625	16.669
3/16	.1875	4.763	11/16	.6875	17.463
7/32	.21875	5.556	23/32	.71875	18.256
1/4	.250	6.350	3/4	.750	19.050
9/32	.28125	7.144	25/32	.78125	19.844
5/16	.3125	7.938	13/16	.8125	20.638
11/32	.34375	8.731	27/32	.84375	21.431
3/8	.375	9.525	7/8	.875	22.225
13/32	.40625	10.319	29/32	.90625	23.019
7/16	.4375	11.113	15/16	.9375	23.813
15/32	.46875	11.906	31/32	.96875	24.606
1/2	.500	12.700	1	1.000	25.400

TABLE L3
Abbreviations

1φ	single-phase current	CSIR	Capacitor start, induction run
3φ	3-phase current	cu. ft.	cubic foot = ft^3
ΔD	difference	cu. in.	cubic inch = in^3
A	ampere, or amp	D	diameter
A	area	DA	direct acting
A.N.S.I.	American National Standards Institute	DBV	discharge bypass valve
A.S.M.E.	American Society of Mechanical Engineers	dc	direct current
		deci	one-tenth (SI system)
ac	alternating current	deka	10 (SI system)
AEV or AXV	automatic expansion valve	dm	decimeter
		dp	double-pole (switch)
ASC	auxiliary side connection	DR	discharge regulating
		dt	double-throw (switch)
ASHRAE	American Society of Heating, Refrigeration, and Air Conditioning Engineers	EER	energy efficiency ratio
		emf	electromotive force
		EPR	evaporator pressure regulator
ASTM	American Society for Testing and Materials	F	farad
		fd	farad
Btu	British thermal unit	FPT	female pipe thread
Btu/h	British thermal unit per hour	FS	flow switch
		ft	foot, feet
C	capacitance	ft. lb.	foot pound
cal	calorie	g	gram
CDA	close on decrease of ambient	gpm	gallons per minute
		gr	grain
centi	one-hundredth (SI system)	h	enthalpy per unit mass
		h	hours
CFC	chlorofluorocarbon	hecto	100 (SI system)
cfm	cubic feet per minute	hp	horsepower
cm	centimeter	HPCO	high-pressure cutout
Cp	specific heat (sp. h.t)	HSF	high-side float
CPR	crankcase pressure regulator	hz	hertz (cycle per second)
CRO	close on rise of outlet (pressure)	I	impedance (in ohms)
		ID	inside diameter
CROT	close on rise of outlet temperature	in. Hg	inch of mercury vacuum = inch Hg
CSR	Capacitor start, induction run motor	J	joule
		Kcal	kilocalorie

TABLE L3

Abbreviations (cont)

kcal	kilocalorie	ORD	open on rise of differential
kg	kilogram		
kilo	1,000 (SI system)	ORI	open on rise inlet (pressure)
kJ	kilojoule		
kPa	kilopascal	OROA	open on rise of outlet
kV	kilovolt	OTC	oi-temperature control
kVA	kilovolt-ampere	P	pressure
kW	kilowatt	Pa	pascal
kwh	kilowatt hour	pcb	polychlorinated biphenyl
L	liter		
lb	pound	PE	pneumatic-electric (switch)
lb./cu. ft.	pound per cubic foot		
LPCO	low-pressure cutout	ppm	parts per million
LSF	low-side float	PSC	Permanent split capacitor motor
M	mass		
m	meter		
mA	milliamp	psi	pound per square inch = lb/sq. in.
mega	one million (SI system)		
mfd	microfarad	psia	pounds per square inch atmospheric
micro	one-millionth (SI system)	psig	pounds per square inch gauge
milli	one-thousandth (SI system)	qt	quart
		R	gas constant
mm	millimeter	r	radius of circle
MOPD	maximum operating pressure differential	RA	reverse acting
		RH%	relative humidity
MPT	male pipe thread	RMS	root-mean-squared (the effective voltage of an ac current)
MTC	motor temperature control		
mV	millivolt	SAE	Society of Automotive Engineers
MW	megawatt		
N	newton	sec	seconds
NC	normally closed	SORIT	solenoid open on rise in temperature
NO	normally open		
OD	outside diameter	sp	single-pole (switch)
OA	outdoor air	sq. ft.	square foot = ft²
ODF	outside diameter female	sq. in.	square inch = in²
		st	single-throw (switch)
ODM	outside diameter male	TD	temperature difference
Ω	ohm	TDR	time-delay relay
OPCO	oil pressure cutout	TDS	time delay switch
		ton	ton of refrigeration effect

TABLE L3

Abbreviations (cont)

T_r	reference temperature	VA	volt-ampere
TXV or	thermostatic expansion	W	watt
TEV	valve	°C	degree Celsius
UV	ultraviolet light	°F	degree Farenheit
V Max	maximum voltage in	°K	degree Kelvin
	ac cycle	°R	degree Rankine
V	volt	π	pi (3.1416)
v	volume		
MOP	maximum operating		
	pressure		

DECIMALS

Decimal systems use a system based on 10, in which digits represent groups of 1, 10, 100, etc. For example, 324 equals 3 hundreds, 2 tens, and 4 ones. The same relationship is true on the right of the decimal point. 3.24 equals 3 ones, 2 tenths, and 4 hundredths. This number can be pronounced either three point twenty four, three point two four, or three and twenty four hundredths.

United States money uses the decimal system, with each dollar divided into 10 dimes or 100 cents. Thus $1.25 equals one dollar 25 cents. Decimal calculations are much simpler than fraction calculations, especially with an electronic calculator. Decimals are exclusively used in the SI system.

To multiply by 10, just move the decimal place to the right.

■ **EXAMPLE:** $1.25 \times 10 = 12.5$

To divide by 10, move the decimal place to the left.

■ **EXAMPLE:** $1.25 \div 10 = .125$

This is usually expressed as 0.125 to make the decimal point obvious.

ROUNDING OFF

Calculations may produce an answer with more decimals than necessary, and these numbers can be rounded off for simplicity. In working with pipes and setting up equipment, you will rarely need to deal with measurements more exact than tenths of an inch or hundredths of a foot. Some calculators can round off automatically.

Round digits 5 and up to the next higher number. For example, 3.45 would round to 3.5.

Round digits below 5 to the next lower number. For example, 3.44 rounds to 3.4.

When rounding, ignore all decimals except the one to the right of the final digit you want to find. Thus, 3.47 rounds to 3.5 (look at the 7 hundredths) if you want to retain tenths. But it rounds to 3 (look at the 4 tenths) if you want an integer as the result.

MEASURING ANGLES

Angles are measured with a system of degrees. 360 degrees (written 360°) equals one full circle. 90° is a right angle and 180° is a straight angle. Degrees are broken into 60 minutes (written 60′). Each minute is broken into 60 seconds (written 60″).

Angles less than 90° are called acute angles. Angles between 90° and 180° are called obtuse angles.

AREA, PERIMETER, AND VOLUME

Perimeter is the length of the outside of a two-dimensional shape. Perimeter is useful for calculating material needs of entire structures. Area is the amount of space occupied by a two-dimensional shape. Area calculations may be needed when estimating cooling loads.

Volume is the three-dimensional space occupied by a structure and is often equal to area times height. Cooling system techicians must know how to figure volume of shapes.

Shape	Area	Perimeter	Volume
Triangle	B × H ÷ 2	AB + CB + AC	
Rectangle	L × W	2 × (L + W)	
Circle	$\pi \times R^2$	$\pi \times D$	
Sphere	$4 \times \pi \times R^2$		$4/3 \times \pi \times R^3$
Cylinder	$(2\pi \times R^2) + (\pi \times D \times H)$		$\pi \times R^2 \times H$

NOTES: Circumference is the term used for the perimeter of a circle. R^2 means "radius squared." To square a number, multiply it by itself. π, or pi, pronounced "pie," is the ratio of circumference to diameter. 3.14 is close enough to the value of π for most work. The exact value is close to 3.1416.

$$\text{Diameter} = \text{Radius} \times 2$$
$$\text{Radius} = \text{Diameter} \div 2$$

Charts and Tables

Additional tabular material follows on pages 388 through 398.

TABLE L4

Pressure Settings for Fixtures

Vacuum—Inches of Mercury • ( )   Pressure • Pounds Per Square Inch Gauge • Bold Figures

APPLICATION	REFRIGERANT							
	12		22		502		717	
	Out	In	Out	In	Out	In	Out	In
Ice Cube Maker—Dry Type Coil	4	17	16	37	22	45	—	—
Sweet Water Bath—Soda Fountain	21	29	43	56	52	66	33	45
Beer, Water, Milk Cooler, Wet Type	19	29	40	56	48	66	5	24
Ice Cream Trucks, Hardening Rooms	2	15	13	34	18	41	4	8
Electric Plates, Ice Cream Truck	1	4	11	16	16	22	—	—
Walk In, Defrost Cycle	14	34	32	64	40	75	23	55
Reach In, Defrost Cycle	19	36	40	68	48	78	30	57
Vegetable Display, Defrost Cycle	13	35	30	66	38	77	—	—
Vegetable Display Case—Open Type	16	42	35	77	44	89	—	—
Beverage Cooler, Blower Dry Type	15	34	34	64	42	75	24	55
Retail Florist—Blower Coil	28	42	55	77	65	89	44	67
Meat Display Case, Defrost Cycle	17	35	37	66	45	77	—	—
Meat Display Case—Open Type	11	27	27	53	35	63	—	—
Dairy Case—Open Type	10	35	26	66	33	77	—	—
Frozen Food—Open Type	(7)	5	4	17	8	24	—	—
Frozen Food—Open Type—Thermostat	2°F	10°F	—	—	—	—	—	—
Frozen Food—Closed Type	1	8	11	22	16	29	—	—

TABLE L5

Storage Data For Perishables

Recommended temperature, relative humidity, and approximate length of storage period for the commercial storage of fresh, dried, and frozen fruits; nuts; fresh, dried, and frozen vegetables; vegetable seeds; and the average freezing points of these commodities

Commodity	Temperature	Relative humidity	Approximate length of storage period	Average freezing point[1]
Fresh fruits:	° F.	Percent		° F.
Apples	(²)	85 to 90	(³)	28.4
Apricots	31 to 32	85 to 90	1 to 2 weeks	28.1
Avocados	(²)	85 to 90	(²)	27.2
Bananas	(²)	(²)	(²)	(⁴)
Blackberries . . .	31 to 32	85 to 90	5 to 7 days²	28.9
Cherries	31 to 32	85 to 90	10 to 14 days . . .	(⁵)
Coconuts	32 to 35	80 to 85	1 to 2 months . . .	25.5
Cranberries . . .	36 to 40	85 to 90	1 to 3 months . . .	27.2
Dates	(²)	(²)	(²)	−4.1
Dewberries . . .	31 to 32	85 to 90	5 to 7 days²	
Figs, fresh	31 to 32	85 to 90	10 days	27.1
Grapefruit	(²)	85 to 90	(²)	28.4
Grapes:				
Vinifera . . .	30 to 31	85 to 90	3 to 6 months . . .	24.9
American . . .	31 to 32	85 to 90	3 to 4 weeks² . . .	27.5
Lemons	(²)	85 to 90	1 to 4 months . . .	28.1
Limes	48 to 50	85 to 90	6 to 8 weeks	29.3
Logan blackberries	31 to 32	85 to 90	5 to 7 days²	29.5
Mangoes	50	85 to 90	15 to 20 days . . .	29.8
Olives, fresh . . .	45 to 50	85 to 90	4 to 6 weeks	28.5
Oranges	(²)	85 to 90	(²)	(⁶)
Paypayas, firm-ripe	45	85 to 90	7 to 21 days	30.1
Peaches and nectarines	31 to 32	85 to 90	2 to 4 weeks	29.4
Pears:				
Bartlett	30 to 31	90 to 95	(²)	28.5
Fall and winter varieties	30 to 31	90 to 95	(²)	(⁷)
Persimmons, Japanese	30	85 to 90	2 months	28.3

TABLE L5 (cont)

Recommended temperature, relative humidity, and approximate length of storage period for the commercial storage of fresh, dried, and frozen fruits; nuts; fresh, dried, and frozen vegetables; vegetable seeds; and the average freezing points of these commodities

Commodity	Tempera-ture	Relative humidity	Approximate length of storage period	Average freezing point[1]
Fresh fruits—Continued	° F	*Percent*		° F
Pineapples:				
Mature-green	50 to 60	85 to 90	2 to 3 weeks	29.1
Ripe	40 to 45	85 to 90	2 to 4 weeks	29.9
Plums, including prunes	31 to 32	85 to 90	3 to 4 weeks[2] . . .	28.0
Pomegranates	34 to 35	85 to 90	2 to 4 months	
Quinces . . .	31 to 32	85 to 90	2 to 3 months . . .	28.1
Raspberries . . .	31 to 32	85 to 90	5 to 7 days[2].	29.9
Strawberries . . .	31 to 32	85 to 90	7 to 10 days[2] . . .	29.9
Tangerines	31 to 38	90 to 95	2 to 4 weeks	28
Dried fruits	[2]	[2]	[2]	
Frozen fruits	[2]	[2]	[2]	
Nuts	[2]	65 to 75	8 to 12 months	[8]
Fresh vegetables:				
Artichokes:				
Globe	32	90 to 95	30 days	29.1
Jerusalem . . .	31 to 32	90 to 95	2 to 5 months . . .	27.5
Asparagus	32	85 to 90	3 to 4 weeks	29.8
Beans:				
Green, or snap	45 to 50	85 to 90	8 to 10 days	29.7
Lima:				
Shelled . . .	32	85 to 90	15 days	
	40	85 to 90	4 days	30.1
Unshelled	32	85 to 90	14 to 20 days . . .	
	40	85 to 90	10 to 14 days . . .	
Beets:				
Topped	32	90 to 95	1 to 3 months . . .	26.9
Bunched . . .	32	90 to 95	10 to 14 days . . .	
Broccoli (Italian, or sprouting) . .	32	90 to 95	7 to 10 days	29.2
Brussels sprouts	32	90 to 95	3 to 4 weeks	

TABLE L5 (cont)

Recommended temperature, relative humidity, and approximate length of storage period for the commercial storage of fresh, dried, and frozen fruits; nuts; fresh, dried, and frozen vegetables; vegetable seeds; and the average freezing points of these commodities

Commodity	Temperature	Relative humidity	Approximate length of storage period	Average freezing point[1]
Cabbage:				
Early	32	90 to 95	3 to 6 weeks	31.2
Late	32	90 to 95	3 to 4 months . . .	
Carrots:				
Topped	32	90 to 95	4 to 5 months . . .	
Bunched . . .	32	90 to 95	10 to 14 days . . .	29.6
Cauliflower . . .	32	85 to 90	2 to 3 weeks	30.1
Celeriac	32	90 to 95	3 to 4 months	
Celery	31 to 32	90 to 95	2 to 4 months . . .	29.7
Corn, sweet . . .	31 to 32	85 to 90	([2])	28.9
Cucumbers . . .	45 to 50	85 to 90	2 to 3 weeks	30.5
Eggplants	45 to 50	85 to 90	10 days	30.4
Endive, or escarole	32	90 to 95	2 to 3 weeks	30.9
Garlic, dry	32	70 to 75	6 to 8 months . . .	25.4
Horseradish . . .	30 to 32	90 to 95	10 to 12 months . .	26.4
Kohlrabi	32	90 to 95	2 to 4 weeks	30.0
Leeks, green . . .	32	90 to 95	1 to 3 months . . .	29.2
Lettuce	32	90 to 95	2 to 3 weeks	31.2
Melons:				
Watermelons	36 to 40	85 to 90	. . . . .do	[9]29.2 [10]28.8
Cantaloups (muskmelons):				
Full-slip . .	40 to 45	85 to 90	4 to 8 days	29.0
Half-slip . .	45 to 50	85 to 90	1 to 2 weeks	[10]28.4
Honey Dew	45 to 50	85 to 90	2 to 3 weeks	[9]29.0 [10]28.8
Casaba	45 to 50	85 to 90	3 to 6 weeks	
Crenshaw and Persian	45 to 50	85 to 90	1 to 2 weeks	
Mushrooms, cultivated . . .	[2]32	85 to 90	3 to 5 days	30.2
Okra	50	85 to 95	2 weeks	30.1

TABLE L5 (cont)

Recommended temperature, relative humidity, and approximate length of storage period for the commercial storage of fresh, dried, and frozen fruits; nuts; fresh, dried, and frozen vegetables; vegetable seeds; and the average freezing points of these commodities

Commodity	Temperature	Relative humidity	Approximate length of storage period	Average freezing point[1]
Fresh vegetables— Continued				
Onions	32	70 to 75	6 to 8 months . . .	30.1
Onion sets	32	70 to 75	. . . . .do	29.5
Parsnips	32	90 to 95	2 to 4 months . . .	30.0
Peas, green . . .	32	85 to 90	1 to 2 weeks	30.0
Peppers:				
Chili, dry . . .	(2)	65 to 70	6 to 9 months . . .	
Sweet	45 to 50	85 to 90	8 to 10 days	30.1
Potatoes:				
Early-crop . .	(2)	85 to 90	(2)	
Late-crop . . .	(2)	85 to 90	(2)	28.9
Pumpkins	50 to 55	70 to 75	2 to 6 months[2] . .	30.1
Radishes:				
Spring, bunched	32	90 to 95	10 to 14 days . . .	29.5
Winter	32	90 to 95	2 to 4 months . . .	
Rhubarb	32	90 to 95	2 to 3 weeks	28.4
Rutabagas	32	90 to 95	2 to 4 months . . .	29.5
Salsify	32	90 to 95	. . . . .do	28.4
Spinach	32	90 to 95	10 to 14 days . . .	30.3
Squashes:				
Summer	32 to 40	85 to 95	. . . . .do	29.0
Winter	50 to 55	70 to 75	4 to 6 months . . .	29.3
Sweetpotatoes	55 to 60	85 to 90	. . . . .do	28.5
Tomatoes:				
Ripe	50	85 to 90	8 to 12 days	30.4
Mature-green .	55 to 70	85 to 90	2 to 6 weeks[2] . . .	30.4
Turnips	32	90 to 95	4 to 5 months . . .	30.5
Vegetable seeds	32 to 50	50 to 65	(2)	
Dried vegetables	(2)	70	1 year	
Frozen vegetables	(2)		(2)	

[1] THESE FIGURES, EXCEPT FOR SUMMER SQUASH, REPRESENT ACTUAL COMMODITY TEMPERATURES RECORDED WHEN FREEZING OCCURRED IN TESTS.

2 SEE DEPARTMENT OF AGRICULTURE HANDBOOK 66.
3 SEE DEPARTMENT OF AGRICULTURE HANDBOOK 66, TABLE 4.
4 GREEN: FLESH, 30.2°; PEEL, 29.8°. RIPE; FLESH, 26.0°; PEEL, 29.4°.
5 EASTERN SOUR, 28.0°; EASTERN SWEET, 24.7°; CALIFORNIA SWEET, 24.2°.
6 FLESH, 28.0°; PEEL 27.4°.
7 WINTER NELIS, 27.2°; ANJOU, 26.9°.
8 PERSIAN (ENGLISH) WALNUTS, 20.0°; PECANS, 19.6°; CHESTNUTS (ITALIAN) 23.8°;
PEANUTS, 13.4°; FILBERTS, 14.1°.
9 FLESH.
10 RIND.

TABLE L5 (cont.)

Food Storage Temperatures For Meat And Dairy

Commodity	Storage temp °F	Relative humidity %	Approximate length of storage period
Dairy			
Butter	32–40	80	2 months
Butter, frozen	−10 to 0	80	1 year
Cheese	30–40	65	varies
Eggs, fresh	29–31	80	6–9 months
Eggs, frozen	0 or below		1 year or more
Milk, fluid	33		7 days
Milk, sweetened, condensed	40		few months
Fish and meat			
Bacon, frozen	−10 to 0	90	4 months
Bacon, packer style	34–40	85	2–4 weeks
Beef, fresh	33	88–90	1–5 weeks
Beef, frozen	−10 to 0	90	9–10 months
Fish, fresh	33–35	90	5–15 days
Fish, frozen	−10 to 0	90	8 months
Fish, smoked	45	55	6 months
Lamb, fresh	33	85	6–12 days
Lamb, frozen	−10 to 0	90	8 months
Livers, frozen	−10 to 0	90	3 months
Shellfish, fresh	33	90	3–7 days
Shellfish, frozen	−20 to 0	90	3–8 months
Veal	33	90	5–8 days
Flowers			
Most flowers	31	80–85	varies
Calla lily, camellia, orchid	40–45	80–85	up to 1 week

TABLE L6 Pressure-Temperature Chart for Common Refrigerants

Temperature, °F

PSIG	FREON 114	FREON 12	FREON 500	FREON 22	FREON 502
10*	20	-38	-44	-57	-65
9*	23	-36	-42	-55	-63
8*	25	-34	-41	-53	-61
7*	27	-33	-39	-52	-60
6*	28	-31	-37	-50	-58
5*	30	-29	-36	-48	-57
4*	32	-28	-34	-47	-55
3*	34	-26	-33	-46	-54
2*	36	-25	-31	-44	-52
1*	37	-23	-30	-43	-51
0	39	-22	-28	-41	-50
1	42	-19	-26	-39	-47
2	45	-16	-23	-36	-45
3	48	-14	-21	-34	-42
4	50	-11	-18	-32	-40
5	52	-9	-16	-30	-38
6	56	-7	-14	-28	-36
7	58	-4	-12	-26	-34
8	60	-2	-10	-24	-32
9	63	0	-8	-22	-30
10	65	2	-6	-20	-29
11	67	4	-4	-19	-27
12	69	5	-2	-17	-25
13	71	7	0	-15	-24
14	73	9	1	-14	-22
15	75	11	3	-12	-20
16	77	12	4	-11	-19
17	78	14	6	-9	-17
18	80	15	8	-8	-16
19	82	17	9	-6	-15
20	83	18	10	-5	-13
21	85	20	12	-4	-11
22	87	21	13	-2	—

PSIG	FREON 114	FREON 12	FREON 500	FREON 22	FREON 502
145	190	114	102	81	73
150	193	117	104	83	75
155	196	119	106	85	77
160	198	121	108	87	80
165	201	123	110	89	82
170	203	125	112	91	83
175	205	128	114	92	85
180	208	130	116	94	87
185	210	132	118	96	89
190	212	134	120	98	91
195	214	136	122	100	93
200	217	138	124	101	95
210	221	141	128	105	98
220	225	145	131	108	101
230	229	148	134	111	104
240	233	152	138	114	108
250	236	155	140	117	111
260	240	158	144	120	114
270	243	162	147	123	116
280	247	165	150	126	119
290	250	168	153	128	122
300	253	170	156	131	125
310	256	173	158	133	127
320	259	176	160	136	130
330	262	179	163	138	132
340	265	182	166	141	135
350	268	184	168	143	137
360	271	187	171	145	139
370	273	189	173	148	142
380	276	192	175	150	144
390	278	194	178	152	146
400	281	196	180	154	148

Chemical Names and Formulae for "Freon" Refrigerants

Registered Trademark	Chemical Name	Formula	Boiling Point °F
"Freon" 11	Trichlorofluoromethane	CCl_3F	74.9
"Freon" 12	Dichlorodifluoromethane	CCl_2F_2	-21.6
"Freon" 13	Chlorotrifluoromethane	$CClF$	-114.6
"Freon" 13B1	Bromotrifluoromethane	CF_3BR	-72.0
"Freon" 22	Chlorodifluoromethane	$CHClF_2$	-41.4
"Freon" 113	Trichlorotrifluoroethane	$CCl_2F—CClF_2$	117.6
"Freon" 114	Dichlorotetrafluoroethane	$CClF_2—CClF_2$	38.8
"Freon" 500	Azeotrope of "Freon" 12 and 1,1-difluoroethane		-28.3
"Freon" 502	Azeotrope of "Freon" 22 and "Freon" 115		-49.8
"Freon" 503	Azeotrope of "Freon" 13 and "Freon" 23		-126.1

E. I. DU PONT DE NEMOURS & CO. (INC.)
"FREON" PRODUCTS DIVISION
WILMINGTON, DELAWARE 19898

25	91	26	17	1	-7
26	93	27	18	2	-6
27	94	28	20	4	-5
28	96	29	21	5	-3
29	97	31	22	6	-2
30	98	32	23	7	-1
32	101	34	26	9	1
34	104	37	28	11	3
36	106	39	30	13	5
38	109	41	32	15	7
40	111	43	34	17	9
42	113	45	36	19	11
44	116	47	38	21	13
46	118	49	40	23	15
48	120	51	42	24	16
50	122	53	44	26	18
52	124	55	45	28	20
54	126	57	47	29	21
56	128	59	49	31	23
58	130	60	50	32	24
60	132	62	52	34	26
62	134	64	54	35	28
64	136	65	55	37	29
66	137	67	57	38	30
68	139	68	58	40	32
70	141	70	60	41	33
75	145	74	63	44	36
80	149	77	66	47	40
85	153	81	70	51	43
90	156	84	73	53	46
95	160	87	76	56	49
100	163	90	79	59	51
105	167	93	82	62	54
110	170	96	84	64	57
115	173	99	87	67	59
120	176	102	90	69	62
125	179	104	92	72	64
130	182	107	95	74	67
135	185	109	97	76	69
140	188	112	99	78	71

TABLE L6   Pressure-Temperature Chart for Common Refrigerants

Temperature, °F

PSIG	FREON 11	FREON 113	FREON 13B1	FREON 13	FREON 503
27*	-20	18	-142	-177	-190
26.5*	-15	23	-138	-173	-186
26*	-10	28	-135	-170	-183
25.5*	-6	32	-132	-168	-180
25*	-2	36	-129	-165	-178
24.5*	1	40	-126	-163	-176
24*	5	44	-124	-160	-173
23*	10	50	-120	-157	-170
22*	15	55	-116	-154	-166
21*	20	60	-112	-150	-163
20*	25	65	-109	-148	-160
19*	29	68	-106	-145	-158
18*	32	72	-104	-143	-155
17*	36	76	-101	-141	-153
16*	39	80	-99	-138	-151
15*	42	83	-96	-136	-149
14*	45	86	-94	-134	-147
13*	47	88	-92	-133	-146
12*	50	91	-90	-131	-144
11*	53	94	-88	-129	-142
10*	55	96	-87	-128	-140
9*	57	99	-85	-126	-139
8*	60	101	-83 σ	-124	-138
7*	62	104	-82	-123	-136
6*	64	106	-80	-122	-135
5*	66	108	-79	-121	-134
4*	68	110	-77	-119	-133
3*	70	112	-76	-118	-132
2*	71	114	-75	-117	-131
1*	73	116	-73	-116	-129
0	75	118	-72	-115	-128
1	78	121	-69	-112	-126
2	81	125	-67	-110	-124
3	85	128	-65	-108	-122
4	87	131	-63	-106	-120

PSIG	FREON 11	FREON 113	FREON 13B1	FREON 13	FREON 503
95	206	257	25	-28	-45
100	209	261	28	-26	-43
105	213	265	31	-23	-40
110	216	269	33	-21	-38
115	220	272	36	-19	-36
120	223	276	38	-17	-34
125	226	279	41	-15	-32
130	229	282	43	-12	-30
135	232	286	45	-10	-29
140	235	289	47	-8	-27
145	238	292	49	-7	-25
150	241	295	52	-5	-23
155	243	298	54	-3	-22
160	246	301	56	-1	-20
165	249	304	58	-1	-18
170	251	306	60	3	-17
175	254	309	62	4	-15
180	256	312	63	6	-14
185	259	314	65	7	-12
190	261	317	67	9	-11
195	263	319	69	11	-9
200	266	322	70	12	-8
210	270	327	74	15	-5
220	275	331	77	18	-2
240	283	340	83	24	3
250	287	344	86	26	5
260	291	348	89	29	8
270	294	352	92	31	10
280	298	356	95	34	12
290	302	360	97	37	14
300	305	364	100	39	17

Courtesy of E.I. du Pont de Nemours and Company

TABLE L6B

Temp. F	Pressure psig	Temp. F	Pressure psig
27.9*	-105	21.3*	-68
27.8*	-104	21.0*	-67
27.7*	-103	20.7*	-66
27.6*	-102	20.4*	-65
27.5*	-101	20.0*	-64
		19.7*	-63
27.4*	-100	19.4*	-62
27.3*	-99	19.0*	-61
27.2*	-98		
27.1*	-97		
26.9*	-96	18.6*	-60
26.8*	-95	18.2*	-59
26.7*	-94	17.8*	-58
26.6*	-93	17.4*	-57
26.4*	-92	17.0*	-56
26.3*	-91	16.6*	-55
		16.2*	-54
26.1*	-90	15.7*	-53
26.0*	-89	15.3*	-52
25.8*	-88	14.8*	-51
25.6*	-87		
25.5*	-86	14.3*	-50
25.3*	-85	13.8*	-49
25.1*	-84	13.3*	-48
24.9*	-83	12.8*	-47
24.7*	-82	12.2*	-46
24.5*	-81	11.7*	-45
		11.1*	-44
24.3*	-80	10.6*	-43
24.1*	-79	10.0*	-42
23.9*	-78	9.3*	-41
23.7*	-77		
23.4*	-76	8.7*	-40
23.2*	-75	8.1*	-39
23.0*	-74	7.4*	-38
22.7*	-73	6.8*	-37
22.4*	-72	6.1*	-36
22.2*	-71	5.4*	-35
		4.7*	-34
21.9*	-70	3.9*	-33
21.6*	-69	3.2*	-32
		2.4*	-31

TABLE L6

Temp					
5	90	134	-61	-104	-118
6	93	137	-59	-103	-116
7	96	139	-57	-101	-114
8	98	142	-55	-99	-112
9	101	145	-53	-98	-111
10	103	147	-51	-96	-110
11	105	152	-49	-95	-108
12	107	154	-48	-93	-107
13	110	154	-46	-92	-105
14	112	157	-45	-90	-104
15	114	159	-43	-89	-103
16	116	160	-42	-88	-102
17	118	162	-40	-86	-100
18	120	164	-39	-84	-99
19	121	166	-37	-83	-98
20	123	169	-36	-82	-97
21	125	171	-35	-81	-96
22	127	173	-34	-80	-95
23	128	175	-32	-79	-93
24	130	176	-31	-78	-92
25	132	178	-30	-77	-91
26	133	180	-29	-76	-90
27	135	181	-27	-75	-89
28	136	183	-26	-74	-88
29	138	185	-25	-73	-87
30	139	186	-24	-72	-86
32	142	189	-22	-70	-85
34	145	192	-20	-68	-83
36	148	195	-18	-66	-81
38	150	198	-16	-65	-80
40	153	201	-14	-63	-78
42	155	203	-12	-61	-76
44	158	206	-10	-60	-75
46	160	209	-9	-58	-74
48	163	211	-7	-57	-72
50	165	213	-5	-55	-71
52	167	216	-3	-54	-69
54	169	218	-2	-52	-68
56	171	220	0	-51	-66
58	173	223	1	-50	-65
60	175	225	3	-48	-64
62	177	227	4	-47	-62
64	179	229	6	-46	-61
66	181	231	7	-44	-60
68	183	233	8	-43	-59
70	185	235	10	-42	-58
75	189	240	13	-39	-55
80	194	244	16	-36	-53
85	198	249	19	-35	-52
90	202	253	22	-31	-48

Pressure-Temperature Chart —Ammonia R717

TABLE L6B

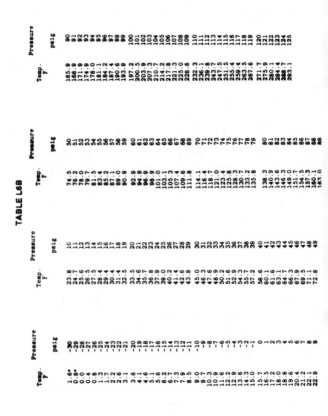

Temp. °F	Pressure psig	Temp. °F	Pressure psig	Temp. °F	Pressure psig	Temp. °F	Pressure psig
1.6*	-30*	23.8	10	74.5	50	165.9	90
0.8*	-29*	24.7	11	76.2	51	168.9	91
0.0	-28	25.6	12	78.0	52	171.9	92
0.4	-27	26.5	13	79.7	53	174.9	93
1.3	-26	27.5	14	81.4	54	178.0	94
1.7	-25	28.4	15	83.4	55	181.1	95
2.1	-24	29.4	16	85.2	56	184.2	96
2.6	-23	30.4	17	87.1	57	187.4	97
3.1	-22	31.5	18	89.0	58	190.6	98
3.6	-21	32.5	19	90.9	59	193.9	99
4.1	-20	33.5	20	92.9	60	197.2	100
4.6	-19	34.6	21	94.9	61	200.5	101
5.1	-18	35.6	22	96.9	62	203.9	102
5.6	-17	36.8	23	98.9	63	207.3	103
6.2	-16	37.8	24	101.0	64	210.7	104
6.7	-15	39.0	25	103.1	65	214.2	105
7.3	-14	40.2	26	105.3	66	217.8	106
7.9	-13	41.4	27	107.4	67	221.3	107
8.5	-12	42.6	28	109.6	68		108
9.0	-11	43.8	29	111.8	69	228.6	109
9.7	-10	45.0	30	114.1	70	232.3	110
10.3	-9	46.3	31	116.4	71	236.1	111
10.9	-8	47.6	32	118.7	72	239.8	112
11.6	-7	48.9	33	121.0	73	243.7	113
12.2	-6	50.2	34	123.4	74	247.5	114
12.9	-5	51.6	35	125.8	75	251.5	115
13.6	-4	52.9	36	128.2	76	255.4	116
14.3	-3	54.3	37	130.7	77	259.4	117
15.0	-2	55.7	38	133.2	78	263.5	118
15.7	-1	57.2	39	135.8	79	267.6	119
16.5	0	58.6	40	138.3	80	271.7	120
17.2	1	60.1	41	140.7	81	275.9	121
18.0	2	61.6	42	143.6	82	280.1	122
18.8	3	63.1	43	146.3	83	284.4	123
19.6	4	64.7	44	149.0	84	288.7	124
20.4	5	66.3	45	151.7	85	293.1	125
21.2	6	67.9	46	154.5	86		
22.1	7	69.5	47	157.3	87		
22.9	8	71.1	48	160.1	88		
	9	72.8	49	163.0	89		

Formulae

FIGURING BTU/HOUR AND WATER FLOW

The amount of cooling in a water-cooled condenser can be calculated. The relationship between the volume of cooling water through the condenser, the temperature rise in that water, and the compressor's output in Btu/hour is:

Btu/h   = 500 * gpm * TD * SG
gpm   = gallons per minute
TD   = temperature difference between entering and leaving water (500 converts gpm to lb./hour: 8.3 lb./gallon * 60 min/hour)
SG   = specific gravity of cooling water (should equal 1 unless additives are used.)

To find TD when the other factors are known, use this formula:

$$TD = (Btu/hour)/ (500 * gpm * SG)$$

PRESSURE DROP IN CHILLER

If you know specification gpm, actual pressure drop, and rated pressure drop, you can find the actual gpm for a condenser.

$$gpm_{actual} = gpm_{specs} * \sqrt{\frac{P_s}{P_a}}$$

P_s = specification pressure drop
P_a = pressure drop measured at outlet

According to this formula, a condenser with a pressure drop above specifications will have a slower flow than specified, and one with a lower pressure drop will have a faster flow.

TONS AND BTU/DAY

One ton of refrigeration effect is the cooling power that would be realized by melting one ton of ice per day:

1 ton = 12,000 Btu/hour = 288,000 Btu/day.

Rules of Thumb

CONDENSER

Heat rejected by condenser in Btu/hour = 1.25 × 12,000 × tonnage rating (motor not cooled by condenser).

Air-cooled: Entering air + 30 to 35°F (16.7 to 19.4°C) = pressure inside coil (head pressure)

To test for noncondensables: Run condenser fan for 10 minutes (with compressor off) and measure head pressure. Add 10°F (5.6°C) to ambient air temperature and convert this temperature to pressure. This should equal head pressure. If head pressure is greater than this, there is probably a noncondensable gas in the system.

Water-cooled: Entering water + 15 to 20°F (8.3 to 11.1°C) = pressure inside coil

Cooling tower: Entering water should be 7 to 11°F (3.9 to 6.1°C) cooler than leaving water.

OTHER COMPONENTS

Liquid line should be just warm to touch at 105°F (40.6°C) condenser temperature.

Length of ⅛-inch solder in a joint = 1.5 × diameter of pipe.

Use an equalizer on a TXV if a refrigerant distributor is used.

TXV operation depends on good temperature feedback from the sensing bulb.

Subcooling is the number of degrees difference between the temperature of a liquid refrigerant and its saturation temperature-pressure. To figure the amount of subcooling, measure head pressure and convert to temperature. Measure temperature at condenser outlet and subtract from head pressure. The difference is the amount of subcooling.

Example for a system using R-12:

Head pressure =	123 psig =	165°F	73.9°C
Liquid line temperature =		− 105°F	− 40.6°C
Subcooling =		60°F	33.3°C

Addresses of Associations, Unions, and OSHA

Many groups have been established to serve the industry by providing education, certification, promotion, research, and information:

Air Conditioning Contractors of America
1535 16 St.
Washington, D.C. 20036

Air Conditioning and Refrigeration Institute
1501 Wilson Blvd.
Arlington, VA 22209   703-524-8800

American National Standards Institute, Inc. (ANSI)
1430 Broadway
New York, N.Y. 10018

The American Society of Heating, Refrigeration and Air Conditioning Engineers (ASHRAE)
345 W. 47 St.
New York, N.Y. 10017

American Society for Mechanical Engineers (ASME)
345 W. 47 St.
New York, N.Y. 10017

American Society for Testing and Materials (ASTM)
1916 Race St.
Philadelphia, PA 19103-1187

Canadian Standards Association
178 Rexdale Boulevard
Rexdale, Ontario, Canada M9W 1R3

Copper Development Association, Inc.
PO 1840
Greenwich CT 06836

Mechanical Contractors Association of American (MCCA)
5530 Wisconsin Ave., Suite 750
Washington, D.C. 20015

National Fire Protection Association
470 Atlantic Ave.
Boston, MA 02110

National Safety Council
444 Michigan Av.
Chicago, IL 60611

Occupational Safety and Health Administration (OSHA)
U.S. Department of Labor
200 Constitution Ave. N.W.
Washington, D.C. 20210

Refrigeration Engineers and Technicians Association
111 E. Wacker Drive
Chicago, IL 60601

Refrigeration Service Engineers Society
1666 North Rand Rd.
Des Plaines, IL 60016

United Association of Journeymen and Apprentices of the Plumbing
and Pipe Fitting Industry of the United States and Canada
901 Massachusetts Ave.
P.O. Box 378000
Washington, D.C. 20013

Safety

Any form of construction can be dangerous, and workers and management are obliged to cooperate to ensure a safe workplace. The following material is intended as minimum requirements and should not be considered a comprehensive guide to job safety.

Some conditions greatly increase the chance for accidents in any working environment. These conditions include crowded work areas, blocked passageways, overloaded platforms and hoists, inadequate support for scaffolds, elevators without proper guards, damaged tools or power cords, poor ventilation or lighting, defective or worn protective equipment and clothing, improper storage or use of chemicals, and unsafe use of flammable materials.

Some types of behavior also boost the odds of accident and injury. These behaviors include inattention, creating sparks or flames near flammable materials, creating toxic fumes in unventilated areas, riding equipment not designed for personnel, removing guards from machinery, stacking materials poorly, and neglecting to wear protective clothing. Playing around and working when tired are also common causes of accidents.

Further information on tool safety is listed in Part A, beginning on page 1.

The American Society of Heating, Refrigeration and Air Conditioning Engineers (ASHRAE) sponsors a safety code. Copies are available from the organization.

The Occupational Safety and Health Administration is responsible for establishing and enforcing workplace health and safety standards. Although the detailed regulations are complex, OSHA booklets summarize standards that are frequently overlooked and would prevent the most hazardous situations.

OSHA booklet number and name

2201 General Industry Digest
2202 Construction Industry
3097 Electrical Standards for Construction

The following are some OSHA standards and other safety practices applicable to air conditioning and refrigeration work:

ACCIDENT REPORTING

The employer must maintain a log and summary (OSHA Form no. 200 or equivalent) of all reportable injuries and illnesses for each work site. Reportable events are those which result in fatality, hospitalization, lost workdays, medical treatment, job transfer or termination, or loss of consciousness. Incidents must be entered in the log within six days of the date the employer learns of them. An annual summary of this log must be compiled each year and posted at the work site from February 1 until March 1.

ASBESTOS

The mineral fiber called asbestos was used as insulation for decades, and is found in numerous public and private buildings. Asbestos is known to cause cancer and lung disease when its fibers are inhaled or swallowed, so you must use great care when working around it. State hygiene laboratories and asbestos removal companies should be able to test a sample of material for asbestos.

The hazard is greatest when the asbestos is damaged, flaking, or powdered. Undamaged asbestos is sometimes coated and left alone since the hazard of removal is greater. The use of a respirator is a minimum precaution if you are exposed to this dangerous mineral.

ELECTRICITY

OSHA requires compliance with the 1971 National Electric Code in most cases. Circuits of 15- and 20-amp, single-phase, 120-volt current at construction sites must use ground fault interrupters or an assured equipment grounding program if they are not part of permanent structural wiring. One or more employees at the job site should make daily inspections of temporary wiring and electrical equipment.

Other guidelines for electrical safety:

1. Check electrical equipment before using. Equipment must be grounded. Don't use equipment with frayed cords or damaged insulation.

2. Never operate electrical equipment when standing in wet or damp areas.

3. Electric cords must be the three-wire type. Do not hang cords from nails or wires. Splices must be soldered and adequately insulated.

4. Keep electrical wires off the ground. Never run over wires with equipment.

5. Plug receptacles must be the approved, concealed contact type.

6. Exposed metal parts of electrical tools that do not carry current must be grounded.

7. Shut off power in case of a problem or accident.

8. Do not touch anyone who is in contact with live electrical current. Instead, first shut off the power. Then move the person by pushing him or her with a dry piece of lumber. Give mouth to mouth resuscitation if the victim is not breathing. Call an ambulance.

FIRE

On larger jobs, a fire fighting program must be followed throughout the construction work. The job site must have an alarm system to alert employees and the fire department of a fire. Each floor of a building must have two separate fire exits to allow quick exit if one is blocked for any reason.

Worksites must follow these fire prevention measures: Store oily or greasy rags in a tight-closing metal container. Remove all flammable waste daily. Maintain adequate clearance between heat sources and flammable materials (see below for rules on flammable liquids).

BURNING MATERIAL AND THE PROPER EXTINGUISHING TECHNIQUE

Wood, paper and rags	Water or any fire extinguisher
Flammable liquid	Smother with dry chemical, foam, carbon dioxide, sand, vaporizing liquid, or other approved fire extinguisher.
Electrical fires	Dry chemicals, carbon dioxide, vaporizing liquid, or compressed gas.

FLAMMABLE LIQUIDS

Flammable liquids pose a fire and explosion danger. Pour gasoline with an approved gooseneck filler. Keep the spout in contact with the metal opening to the tank to prevent sparks from static electricity. Do not smoke while filling. Never fill a machine while it is running. Store gasoline in approved cans away from any possible fire, sparks, or mechanical hazard.

HAND TOOLS

Wear safety glasses or goggles when using any striking tools. Check that the handle is securely attached before using a hammer. Never pound one hammer with another. Use the correct size hammer for the job. Throw out a hammer or chisel with dents, cracks, chips, or mushrooming.

Electric hand tools must have double insulation, proper grounding, or a ground fault circuit interrupter. Dead-man switches, which require constant pressure on the trigger to operate, are required for electric tools at construction sites.

HOUSEKEEPING

Good housekeeping reduces hazards and increases efficiency by allowing work to flow smoothly and reducing searches for tools or materials. OSHA requires that job sites be orderly and clear of debris and recognized hazards:

- *Material storage and waste disposal yards should be convenient but out of the way.*
- *Traffic lanes should permit efficient movement.*
- *Store hazardous materials in proper containers and away from the work area.*
- *Obstacles and uneven ground are significant causes of accidents. Clear away trash, piles of fill, and other obstacles.*
- *Remove ropes, electric cords, and tools from the working area and keep it as clear as possible during construction.*

LIFTING AND CARRYING

Proper lifting and carrying procedures can prevent falls, back injuries, and hernias. Before carrying something heavy, make sure the route is clear of obstructions and has good footing. Wipe off oil or grease. Wear gloves if necessary. Get a firm grip on the object, being wary of splinters, nails, and other hazards. Then lift it with your knees, keeping your back straight and vertical. Set the object down as you lifted it, with your knees and not your back. Make sure your fingers and toes are clear before setting the object down.

When carrying a long object on your shoulder, lower the front end to give a clear view of the path. Use special care when turning. Ask for help when you need it.

PERSONAL PROTECTION

Employees must wear and use OSHA-approved safety equipment. Wear steel toes to prevent foot injury. Do not use lifelines or lanyards for any purpose except employee safeguarding. (See Part A, *Safety equipment*, p. 25.)

HEAD

Protective helmets must be worn in areas where head injuries are possible due to flying or falling objects, impact, or electrical shock or burns. Helmets for impact protection must meet the requirements of ANSI Z89.1—1969.

HEARING

OSHA sets standards for maximum noise at job sites. If exposure levels surpass these levels, engineering and administrative efforts must be taken to reduce the noise. If these efforts fail, workers must wear hearing protection. Plain ear cotton is not acceptable for such protection.

Duration per day in hours	Maximum sound level (dBA slow response)
8	90
6	92
4	95
3	97
2	100
1½	102
1	105
½	110
¼ or less	115

Exposure to impact noise must not exceed 140 dB peak sound pressure level.

EYE AND FACE

Eye and face protection is required whenever there is a danger of injury. This equipment must meet the requirements of ANSI Z87.1—1968 "Practice for Occupational and Educational Eye and Face Protection." Employees working with torches must wear appropriate filters and safety goggles.

RESPIRATORY PROTECTION

Employers must provide respiratory protection in cases where other efforts to control toxic dusts and vapors are ineffective. Employees must be trained to use this protective equipment. Protective devices must be appropriate to the danger and the nature of the work requirements and inspected daily before use.

PROTECTIVE RAILINGS AND FLOOR OPENINGS

Railings are required on all platforms that are 10 feet or more above adjacent surfaces. Railings are also required on exposed edges of platforms that are narrower than 45 inches (114.3 cm) and 4 feet (122 cm) or more above the ground. Standard railings have a top rail 42 inches to 48 inches (107 to 122 cm) above the floor and an intermediate rail centered between the top rail and the floor. Any point along the rail must be capable of withstanding

200 pounds (91 kg) of pressure in any direction. A toe board at least 4 inches (10.2 cm) high is required at floor level.

Openings in floors may have standard railings or be covered with planks or steel plate. Do not cover floor openings with plastic as this will hide the danger. Ladderway openings require standard railings except at the entrance. Passage through the entrance must be guarded by a swinging gate or the path can be offset so a worker cannot walk directly into the opening.

REFRIGERANTS

Halocarbon refrigerants were designed to be nontoxic, nonflammable, and stable. However, they are subject to two hazards: 1) In the presence of flame, they will form toxic gas. Do not allow any flames in an atmosphere containing halocarbon refrigerants. Shut off furnaces and pilot lights before allowing gas to escape. 2) Halocarbon refrigerants will displace air and can cause asphyxiation. The hazard is especially acute in low areas, because the gas is heavier than air.

Make sure an emergency medical crew does not administer adrenalin to someone who is overcome by inhalation of halocarbons, as this can cause ventricular fibrillation (spasm of the heart muscles). Administer oxygen to counteract the effects of such inhalation.

Ammonia will cause shortness of breath, irritation of eyes, and damage to skin, eyes, and breathing passages. The symptoms depend on the concentration and length of exposure. At 3 to 5 parts per million (ppm), you can detect the gas. By 30 ppm, you need a respirator. OSHA sets the 30-minute exposure limit at 50 ppm. A concentration of 5000 ppm can be lethal. Concentrations ranging between 15 percent and 27 percent are flammable.

Do not drill or saw into an ammonia system. Prevent excess pressure in the system. A high-pressure ammonia stream can blind you. When opening a valve, stand to the side and crack it first, as the packing could leak, sending a stream of ammonia at you. Use an air pack when you suspect problems with an ammonia system.

TORCH

Because acetylene burns fiercely, and oxygen accelerates the combustion of other materials, soldering and brazing torches can be dangerous. OSHA's extensive standards for safety when using a torch are merely summarized here.

Tanks must be shipped with the caps screwed over the valve for protection. Secure tanks in an upright position during use. Leave protective caps in place when tanks are moved (unless they are on a special cart or device) or is removed from service. Check that the tanks, hoses, and fittings have no leaks. Do not damage the gauges. Move tanks by rolling on bottom edges. Protect tanks from damage, heat, improper filling, and abuse. Do not oil the regulator. Never mix oxygen and oil, as the oil may spontaneously combust.

Always wear the proper eye protection and gloves while using a torch. Never use flux or brazing material containing cadmium, which creates poisonous fumes. Never solder or braze piping that is under pressure. Work with adequate ventilation on tubing or components that have contained halocarbon refrigerants because these refrigerants break down to form toxic gases when they are heated. Never use oxygen to pressure-test piping, because oxygen and oil form an explosive mixture.

Glossary

Accumulator. Storage tank at the evaporator exit or suction line used to prevent floodbacks to the compressor.

ACR tube (air-conditioning and refrigeration) tube. Copper tube (usually hard-drawn) sold to the trade cleaned and sealed with nitrogen inside to prevent oxidation. Identified by actual OD.

AEV. Automatic expansion valve, used to control flow of refrigerant into the evaporator depending only on evaporator pressure.

Ambient temperature. Temperature of the fluid (usually air) which surrounds the object under discussion.

Ampere (amp). Unit of electric current, equal to one coulomb of electrons flowing past a point each second.

Anneal. Process of heating a metal to reduce work hardening and allow further manipulation.

Anode. Positive terminal in an electric cell.

Azeotropic mixture. Mix of refrigerants which has constant maximum and minimum boiling points.

Back pressure. Pressure on system low side; also called suction, evaporator, or low-side pressure.

Bellows. Accordion-like container used to detect changes in pressure.

Bimetal strip (Bimetallic strip). Strip made of two metals which have different rates of expansion. Used to measure temperature.

Bleed. To reduce pressure by slightly opening a valve; to remove unwanted fluids such as air from a system.

Booster. The compressor that forms the first stage of a cascade system.

Bourdon tube. Tube of elastic metal bent into circular shape that is found inside a pressure gauge.

British thermal unit (Btu). The amount of heat needed to warm one pound of water by 1°F.

Calorie. Unit of heat in SI system. One small calorie will warm 1 cubic centimeter of water 1°C. One large calorie will warm 1 kilogram of water 1°C.

Capacitance. The ability of a material to hold electric energy on oppositely charged plates. Measured in Farads.

Capacitor. Device which has the ability to store electricity as capacitance; used to start motors, among other purposes.

Cascade system. A refrigeration system with multiple compressors and evaporators. The evaporator of the first compressor cools the condenser of the second compressor. Capable of very cold temperatures.

Cathode. Negative terminal, the source of electrons in an electric cell.

Celsius scale (°C). Temperature scale in SI system. Water freezes at 0°C and boils at 100°C.

Change of state (change of phase). A change of the condition of a substance from one phase and another, accompanied by a gain or loss of latent heat.

Charles' law. The volume of a given mass of gas is proportional to its temperature.

Chiller. An air-conditioning system which circulates cooled water to the conditioned space; an evaporator which cools the water used in a chiller system.

Clearance space. The volume left in a reciprocating compressor cylinder when the piston is at top dead center $= \pi \cdot r^2 \cdot h$.

Coil, holding. Electromagnetic coil in a motor starter used to hold the contacts closed.

Compound system. A system in which the first compressor feeds refrigerant to the second compressor. Capable of high suction and low temperatures.

Compression ratio. Total cylinder volume divided by clearance space. See pumping ratio.

Compressor displacement. Compressor volume in cubic inches found by multiplying piston area by stroke by number of cylinders. Displacement in cubic feet per minute: $= \dfrac{\pi \cdot r^2 \cdot L \cdot \text{rpm} \cdot n}{1728}$

Condense. To change from gas to liquid by removing the latent heat of condensation.

Condenser limiter. See condenser pressure regulator.

Condenser pressure regulator. A valve that maintains high-side pressure so an adequate pressure drop will take place at the metering device.

Conditioned space. The room, cabinet, or other area being cooled or heated by a system.

Constant-temperature valve. See evaporator pressure regulator.

Convection. Movement of heat in a fluid propelled by a difference in density.

Cooling load. Amount of heat that must be removed from a conditioned space in twenty-four hours to maintain design conditions.

Critical charge. An exact charge of refrigerant; commonly found in a system using a flooded evaporator or a capillary tube.

Cross-charged. A fluid used in a TXV sensing bulb that contains a different refrigerant than that used in the system.

Cut-in. The temperature or pressure at which a control device signals a piece of equipment to operate.

Cut-out. The temperature or pressure at which a control device signals a piece of equipment to stop operating.

Dalton's law. The total pressure in a vessel equals the sum of the vapor pressures of the individual gases.

Dehumidification. The process of removing water vapor from air.

Design pressure. The highest or lowest expected pressure in a system.

Dessication. Removal of moisture from a product or substance.

Desuperheater, liquid. Valve that allows a small amount of liquid refrigerant to enter the low side to cool the suction gas.

Dew point. The temperature at which water vapor in a mass of air will begin to condense; the temperature at which relative humidity would reach 100 percent. Equal to saturation temperature.

Differential, control. The difference between the cut-in and cut-out settings.

Differential. A valve which opens at one pressure and closes at another. Allows a system to adjust itself with a minimum of over-correction.

Direct expansion evaporator. An evaporator in which an automatic or a thermostatic expansion valve serves as the metering device.

Discharge gas. Hot, high-pressure vapor refrigerant which has just left the compressor.

Discharge line. The line from the compressor to the condenser; contains discharge gas.

Dry-bulb temperature. The actual temperature of air as measured on an ordinary thermometer. Compare to wet-bulb temperature.

Electromechanical. A device in which electricity creates a motion, or a motion affects the electrical properties of the device.

Energy efficiency ratio (EER). The ratio found by dividing rated cooling capacity in Btu/hour by watts of electricity consumed.

Enthalpy. The total heat content of a substance, compared to a standard value (32°F (0°C) for water vapor, −40°F (−40°C) for refrigerant).

Evaporation (boiling). Process of taking up latent heat and changing from liquid to a gas.

Evaporator pressure regulator. A valve to maintain a high pressure in warmer evaporators in systems with several evaporators.

Evaporator temperature. The temperature of the refrigerant boiling in the evaporator.

External equalizer. Tube from the body of a thermostatic expansion valve to the suction line; used to register an accurate suction line pressure at the valve.

Farad (F). The unit of electrical capacitance. One farad can store one coulomb of electrons across a potential of one volt.

Flash gas. An undesirable phenomenon in which some refrigerant vaporizes (flashes) just ahead of the metering device. Interferes with the metering device and reduces capacity.

Floodback (slugging). A return of liquid refrigerant to the compressor via the suction line. Likely to cause compressor damage.

Flooded system. System in which the evaporator is nearly filled with liquid refrigerant.

Frost back. Frosting of suction line due to entry of liquid refrigerant.

Fusible plug. Safety device designed to release pressure from a vessel in a fire or malfunction. Made of metal that melts at a low temperature.

Galvanic action. Corrosion of two metals that touch each other, caused by electric currents created between them.

Gas, non-condensable. A gas (usually air) that is unable to condense at temperature and pressures found in the condenser. Robs the system of capacity.

Ground wire. Safety wire used to conduct electricity from a component to the ground in case of malfunction.

Halogen. An element from the halogen group: chlorine, flourine, bromine, and iodine. Two halogens may be present in chloroflourocarbon refrigerants.

Head pressure (high-side pressure). Pressure in the condenser.

Head pressure control. See condenser pressure regulator.

Heat of compression. Heat added to a system by the work of the compressor.

Heat of condensation. See latent heat of condensation.

Heat of fusion. See latent heat of fusion.

Heat of vaporization. See latent heat of vaporization.

Heat, latent. The amount of heat required to change the state of a substance without changing temperature.

Heat, sensible. Heat that can be detected with a thermometer.

Heat. Form of energy that increases the motion of molecules and may raise the temperature of a substance.

Hermetic compressor or system. A sealed unit containing a motor and a compressor.

Hertz (hz). Correct expression for cycles per second.

Hg (mercury). Metal that is liquid at room temperature; used to measure pressure in some manometers and to make contact in a mercury switch or relay.

High side. Segment of a system between the compressor and the metering device; under high-side pressure.

Holdback valve. See condenser pressure regulator.

Hot gas bypass. System allowing refrigerant to bypass the condenser; used to control cooling capacity.

Hot gas defrost. System that pumps discharge gas directly to the evaporator for defrosting.

Humidification. The process of adding water vapor to air.

Humidity, absolute. The mass of water vapor in a given quantity of air. Expressed as grains per pound (7000 grain = 1 lb.)

Humidity, relative. Proportion of actual moisture in a volume of air compared to the maximum the air could hold at that temperature.

Hunt (cycle). To cycle erratically because the control cannot establish the desired conditions.

Hygrometer. Instrument used to measure moisture in the air.

Impedance. Opposition to flow of current in an AC circuit; similar to resistance in a DC circuit. Measured in ohms.

Joule. One newton operating through one meter. An SI unit of heat and energy.

Kelvin scale. Absolute SI temperature scale; 0°K is absolute zero. Ice thaws at 273°K.

King valve. A valve at the condenser outlet used for service procedures.

Latent heat of condensation. Amount of latent heat that must be removed so a substance will condense without changing temperature.

Latent heat of fusion (freezing). Amount of heat that must be removed to freeze or crystallize a substance with no change in temperature.

Latent heat of vaporization (boiling). Amount of heat that must be added to boil a substance without change in temperature.

Limit. A safety device to prevent system conditions from becoming unsafe; may measure pressure or temperature.

Limitizer. See condenser pressure regulator.

Low pressure cut-out (LPCO). Control that shuts down the compressor if suction pressure drops below a safe level.

Low side. Portion of system between metering device and compressor. Entire area is at evaporating, or low-side, pressure.

Low-side, pressure. Pressure in the low side.

Manifold, gauge. Device with three outlets and two gauges used for diagnostic and service procedures.

Manifold. A chamber connecting several ducts, tubes, or components, usually all having the same pressure.

Manometer. Device for reading pressure by measuring its effect on a fluid, usually water or mercury.

Megohm. Million ohms.

Megohmmeter. Instrument capable of reading resistances in the million-ohm range; used to test motor insulation.

Micron gauge. Meter capable of measuring vacuums close to absolute; reads in microns of mercury.

Modulating system. A refrigeration system which can match capacity to demand. In a compound system, the number of compressors operating at any time depends on the demand. A single compressor may modulate capacity with the use of unloading devices.

Motor, induction. A motor in which electromagnetism is induced in the rotor by the field magnets. No electrical connection to the rotor is needed.

Multiple system. System with several evaporators connected to a single condensing unit.

Newton. The unit of force in the SI system; sufficient to accelerate one kilogram by 1 m/sec^2.

Nominal size tubing. Plumbing tube with actual OD about ⅛-inch larger than the nominal size; includes water tube and drainage tube, not ACR tube.

Oil binding. A layer of oil on top of refrigerant which prevents normal evaporation in the evaporator; also jamming of a mechanism by presence of excess oil.

Oil pressure cutout. Limit switch that shuts down the compressor if oil pressure drops near crankcase pressure.

Overload protector. Device to shut down compressor motor during overload. May detect overload by measuring current, pressure, or temperature.

Ozone. The form of oxygen with three atoms (O_3). A pollutant in the lower atmosphere but an essential barrier to ultraviolet light in the upper atmosphere. Ozone in the upper atmosphere is destroyed by released halocarbon refrigerants.

Package unit. Complete system, including compressor, condenser, and evaporator in one spot.

Partial pressure. The pressure of a single gas in a mixture of gases.

pH. Scale for measuring acidity and alkalinity. 7 is neutral; lower numbers are acidic and higher numbers are alkaline (basic).

Phase. State of matter (solid, liquid, gas, or plasma). Also the number of waves of AC flowing in a single circuit.

Pipe. Steel or other cylindrical material used to convey fluids; connected by threads or welding (for ammonia systems). See tube.

Plenum chamber. An equalizing or mixing chamber to which several supply ducts are connected.

Pound of air. Generally taken to indicate a pound of dry air.

Power factor. Ratio to describe actual capacity for work of an AC circuit. Measures the degree to which the current and voltage waves coincide.

Power. The rate at which work is done; measured in horsepower or watts.

Pressure drop. Difference is pressure between two points in a system.

Pressure motor control. Control that operates a motor by measuring low side pressure.

Pressure regulator, evaporator. Device to keep evaporator pressure above a setting. Used to prevent abnormally low temperature.

Pressure, absolute. Total pressure in pounds per square inch absolute (psia) or kilopascals. The sum of gauge pressure and atmospheric pressure.

Pressure, gauge. Pressure in pounds per square inch gauge (psig). 0 gauge pressure equals atmospheric pressure at sea level. Not used in the SI system.

Pressure-reducer valve. See evaporator pressure regulator.

psi. Pressure in pounds per square inch.

Psychrometer (wet-bulb hygrometer). Device for measuring the relative humidity of air.

Psychrometric chart. A chart listing the following aspects of air: absolute humidity, temperature (dry bulb and wet bulb), dew point, vapor pressure, total heat (enthalpy), and relative humidity.

Pump down. To use the system compressor to pump most refrigerant into the condenser or receiver for storage or service.

Pump, fixed displacement. A pump which moves a given amount of fluid with each stroke.

Pumping ratio. The ratio of absolute discharge pressure to absolute suction pressure. See also compression ratio.

Quick-connect. A connector used to join pre-charged systems without the need for evacuation.

Recover. To remove refrigerant from a system and store it in a tank.

Recycle. To remove moisture and other contaminants from recovered refrigerant prior to reuse.

Reed valve. Flat metal element used in compressor head for intake and discharge valves.

Refrigerant, primary. A refrigerant containing a pure chemical. See azeotropic mixture.

Relative humidity. See humidity, relative.

Relay, current. Relay which measures current of a circuit.

Relay, potential. Relay which measures voltage of a circuit.

Relay, thermal (hot wire relay). Control device that uses a hot wire to convert electricity to heat. When the current rises above the setting, it creates too much heat, forcing a contact to bend and break the circuit.

Relay. Electromagnetic switch operated by control circuit voltage that is capable of switching line voltage.

Remote system. Cooling system in which the evaporator is far from the condensing unit.

Resistance. The opposition to flow. In electricity, measured in ohms.

Riser valve. Valve in vertical piping used to control flow.

Riser, suction. Vertical length of suction line.

Rotor. Part of motor or other device which rotates. Also called armature.

Running time. Number of hours a machine operates in each twenty-four-hour day.

Safety control. Control (also called a limit) designed to prevent unsafe operating conditions.

Saturated air. Air holding the maximum water vapor possible (100 percent relative humidity) at its temperature and pressure.

Saturated gas. A gas which exists in equilibrium with its liquid phase; the amount of evaporation equals the amount of condensation.

Saturation pressure-temperature. Condition in which both liquid and vapor phases are present and the temperature is constant. Found inside an evaporator. The rate of boiling does not necessarily equal the rate of condensation.

Schraeder valve. Valve which permits flow in one direction if pressure exceeds a setting and in the other if the pin is depressed.

Sensible heat. Heat that can be measured by a thermometer. Compare to latent heat.

Sensor. Device that detects a change in conditions and creates a signal that can be interpreted by another device.

Short cycling. Changing rapidly between on and off; harmful to equipment.

SI system. International system of measurement, commonly called the metric system.

Sine wave. Type of wave characteristic of AC. Current and voltage occur both above and below zero once during each cycle.

Slugging. See floodback.

Solenoid. Electromagnetic device used to move a valve or switch.

Specific gravity. Density of fluid compared to water, which has a specific gravity of 1.0.

Specific heat capacity. The amount of sensible heat needed to change the temperature of a substance 1°F in the English system and 1°C in the SI system. Measured in Btu/lb. per °F and joules per kilogram kelvin (J/kg*K).

Split phase motor. Motor with two stators; one for starting only, the other for starting and running.

Static pressure. Pressure exerted by a gas against all the walls of its container. See velocity pressure.

Stator. Part of motor which is stationary; contains field windings. Also called field.

Sublimate. Change directly from solid to gas, as with dry ice.

Suction pressure regulator. See evaporator pressure regulator.

Superheat. Increase in temperature above boiling point for a given pressure; increase in temperature of suction line gas over the evaporator.

Sweat. 1) Water that condenses on a surface; 2) to join with soldering or brazing.

Temperature, absolute. Temperature measured using absolute zero as the starting point. Uses either the Rankine or Celsius scale.

Therm. Amount of heat equal to 100,000 Btus.

Thermistor. An electronic sensor in which resistance is proportional to temperature sensed.

Thermocouple. A temperature-sensing device having two metals in contact each other; creates a current proportional to temperature.

Thermostatic expansion valve (TXV or TEV). Valve used to control entry of refrigerant into an evaporator based on suction line temperature and evaporator pressure.

Three-phase power. Electric supply with three phases flowing simultaneously. Each current is 120° out of phase with the other two.

Throttle (modulate). To close or open gradually, in response to a manual or automatic adjustment.

Ton of refrigeration. Cooling capacity equal to melting one ton of ice in 24 hours. Equals 12,000 Btu/hour or 288,000 Btu/day.

Torque, starting. Amount of turning force developed by a resting motor when current first enters it.

Two-temperature valve. See evaporator pressure regulator.

Universal motor. Motor capable of operating on AC or DC.

Unloader. 1) A device to reduce compressor capacity or starting load; 2) a valve that temporarily prevents a compressor cylinder from pulling in and compressing refrigerant.

Valve, backseating. Valve which in normal position does not allow the fluid to pressurize the packing. Used in suction and discharge service valves.

Vapor, saturated. Vapor held in pressure and temperature such that any cooling will cause condensation.

Vapor. The gaseous phase of a material.

Vaporization. Change from liquid to vapor state with the addition of the latent heat of vaporization.

Velocity pressure. Pressure due to movement of fluid. Compare to static pressure.

Viscosity. The resistance to flow of a fluid (commonly oil).

Volumetric efficiency. Ratio of actual pumping of a compressor or vacuum pump to its theoretical maximum.

Watt (W). Unit of electric power equal to 1 J/sec. One kilowatt/ hour is the equivalent to 1000 W operating for one hour.

Wet-bulb depression. The difference between wet-bulb temperature and dry-bulb temperature; used to find relative humidity with a psychrometric chart.

Wet-bulb temperature. The temperature of air as indicated on a thermometer subject to evaporation. Cooling due to evaporation reduces the temperature below dry-bulb temperature.

INDEX